African American Combat Units in World War II

by
Alexander M. Bielakowski

Number 6 in the American Military Studies Series

University of North Texas Press
Denton, Texas

10 9 8 7 6 5 4 3 2 1

Permissions:
University of North Texas Press
1155 Union Circle #311336
Denton, TX 76203-5017

The paper used in this book meets the minimum requirements of the
American National Standard for Permanence of Paper for Printed Library
Materials, z39.48.1984. Binding materials have been chosen for durability.

Library of Congress Cataloging-in-Publication Data

Bielakowski, Alexander M., author.
 Proud warriors : African American combat units in World War II /
Alexander M. Bielakowski.
     pages cm
 Includes bibliographical references and index.
 ISBN-13 978-1-57441-839-2 (cloth)
 ISBN-13 978-1-57441-849-1 (ebook)
 1. LCSH: World War, 1939–1945—Participation, African American.
2. Discrimination in the military—United States. 3. United States—
Armed Forces—African American troops. 4. United States—Armed
Forces—African American officers. 5. BISAC: HISTORY / Military / World
War II 6. HISTORY / African American & Black.

 D810.N4 B386 2021
 355.0089/96073--dc23
                    2021028044
     Number 6 in the American Military Studies Series

The electronic edition of this book was made possible by the support of the
Vick Family Foundation. Typeset by vPrompt eServices.

This book is dedicated to my best friend in the world—my wife, Dr. Rae Sikula Bielakowski—without whose help it would have been impossible for me to write this book.

Contents

Section VI: Officers, Pilots, and Skilled Experts

Section VII: Conclusions

Preface

I hope that this book will appeal to both the more serious scholarly audience as well as a popular audience who is interested in African American history and/or World War II history. For more serious scholars, I believe this book will be a one-stop-shop to find out everything you need to know about African American combat units during World War II. If you want to know more about a specific unit, the extensive bibliography will direct you to the book or books on that topic. As regards the general reading public, I think the book is lively enough and broad enough to find an audience.

I do not believe there are truly any competing titles to this book. There are certainly other books about African Americans in World War II, but none of them focuses exclusively on combat units. Likewise, some books discuss in detail the combat experiences of specific African American combat units in World War II. However, these books focus on a single or small group of African American combat units while this book covers all African American combat units.

I believe that there will be two principal critiques of this book. First, some historians will argue that this book leaves too much out because it does not deal with noncombat units—which is not the point of the book. Second, other historians will argue that the book does not cover specific units in enough detail—which is also not the point of this book.

I want to include several comments about language and terminology in this book. First, I have only used the so-called n-word four times in this book. In each case, I believe that it was appropriate as it was a period quote. Second, as a former Army Reserve officer, I am aware of the difference between service and support units, but I have chosen for simplicity and readability to refer to all noncombat arms units as support units. Likewise, I realize that there is a difference between deactivating and disbanding a military unit, but I have chosen to always use the term "disbanded" for simplicity and readability. I have omitted the postscript "(Colored)" which was used to label every African American unit in the Army during this period because it seemed utterly redundant in a work exclusively about African Americans. Lastly, I have chosen to reject the military's current trend to capitalize anything and everything they can—most particularly, the terms soldier, sailor, airman, marine, or coast guardsman.

Finally, for those curious as to why I did not include a chapter about African American Army engineers, the answer is simply that the overwhelming majority of them were used as nothing more than physical laborers—usually stevedores. From my research, I know of precisely three legitimate African American combat engineer battalions in the Army during World War II—the 162nd Engineer Combat Squadron of the 2nd Cavalry Division, the 317th Engineer Combat Battalion of the 92nd Infantry Division, and 318th Engineer Combat Battalion of the 93rd Infantry Division. The 162nd Engineers were disbanded on 22 March 1944 before ever seeing combat. The 318th Engineers also never saw combat and the experience of the 317th Engineers was insufficient to support an entire chapter. If there is an omission in this book, this is the only one that I am aware of. This previous sentence is one which I will, no doubt, later regret!

Acknowledgments

It would have been impossible to complete this project without the hard work done by other scholars of African American history. For the purposes of this project, no single person provided more useful research and information than Dr. Daniel Haulman at the U.S. Air Force Historical Research Agency, Maxwell Air Force Base, Alabama. Dr. Haulman's work is an example of the tireless primary research done by government scholars who unfortunately receive far too little credit for their work. I would also like to thank Dr. Gene Preuss of the University of Houston-Downtown who encouraged me to send my manuscript to the University of North Texas Press. Finally, I would like to recognize the efforts of Ronald Chrisman, the Director of the University of North Texas Press, who turned my manuscript around in what must have been record time!

Introduction

Though World War II was arguably the defining event of the 20th century, the role of African Americans in that conflict has not received the attention it deserves. This lack of attention was undoubtedly due to racism and/or sheer ignorance on the part of the white majority in America. During the past twenty years or so, however, there has been a move to fill a gap in the existing historical literature and draw due attention to the unexamined accomplishments of African American soldiers, sailors, airmen, marines, and coast guardsmen. This process has been part of the larger effort by historians to capture the history of previously underrepresented people in American history. Despite these recent efforts by historians, an important portion of the historical picture remains missing—namely, African American combat units who not only honorable served their country under oppressive conditions but also did so in direct combat with the enemy.

During World War II, the racist policies of the U.S. government usually, but not always, relegated African Americans to tasks that were both more physically demanding and often more demeaning than those assigned to whites. As a result, the existing historical literature has focused more on African Americans in support units, because African Americans disproportionately manned these units. Unfortunately, in an odd twist of fate, historians have often forgotten that African Americans did serve their country in combat roles.

During World War II, tens of thousands of African Americans served in segregated combat units in U.S. armed forces. The majority of these units were found in the U.S. Army, and African Americans served in every one of the combat arms. In the Army's combat arms, African Americans found opportunities for leadership unparalleled in the rest of American society at the time. Several African Americans reached the field grade officer ranks, and one officer reached the rank of brigadier general. While the U.S. Navy's senior leadership initially resisted extending the role of African American sailors beyond ships' kitchens, eventually the crew of two ships was composed exclusively of African Americans. Unfortunately, fewer than fifty African Americans served as officers in the Navy during World War II. The outbreak of World War II found the U.S. Marine Corps without a single African American and was the last branch of the military to admit African Americans when it did so in June 1942. The first African American Marine Corps officer was not commissioned until after World War II, but two African American combat units were formed and did see service during the war. The U.S. Coast Guard, while not technically a military service, operated as part of the U.S. Navy and saw combat during World War II. Like the Navy, the Coast Guard, with a few small exceptions, stopped recruiting African Americans to serve in capacities other than stewards after World War I. However, the Coast Guard became the first service to integrate African Americans—first with two shipboard experiments and then with the integration of most of their fleet.

The valor and achievements of these African Americans have received far too little attention in the existing historical literature. Not only have many of these African American combat units received no significant historical recognition, but no single monograph has ever synthesized the African American combat experience throughout U.S. armed forces. This book is an attempt to redress these omissions by documenting and discussing the accomplishments of African American combat units in World War II. Rather than merely a celebratory history, this work attempts to make the case that without the efforts of these World War II African American combat, desegregation of the U.S. armed forces might have taken decades longer and the progress of the Civil Rights Movement might also have been hampered.

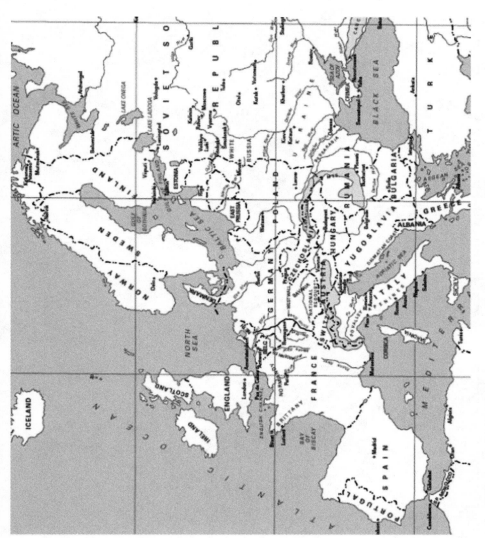

Map of Europe. (USMA)

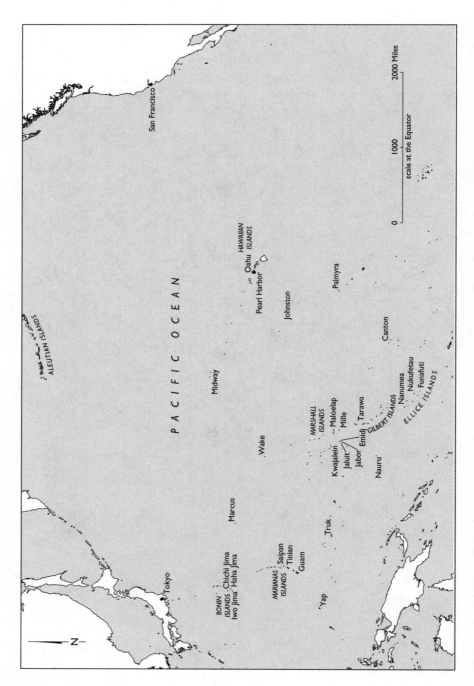

Map of the Pacific. (USMA)

Section I

Before World War II

Chapter 1

African Americans in the U.S. Armed Forces, 1775–1941

African Americans, whether officially or unofficially, volunteers or draftees, free or enslaved, have honorably served the United States in every major conflict (and most minor) throughout the nation's history. Despite this fact, the majority of Americans, irrespective of their race, are probably unaware of the extent of African American military service. Before the Civil Rights movement, most whites probably held the incorrect opinion that African Americans were, by nature, cowardly and intentionally avoided military service. These opinions were most often the result of either historical ignorance or a concerted effort on the part of some whites to propagate racist ideology. A summary of African American military service before World War II is useful for establishing a baseline regarding the extent of and circumstances under which this service was performed.

On 19 April 1775, African American militiamen participated in the first battles of the American Revolution at Lexington and Concord. However, since slavery was still legal in Massachusetts, the service of African Americans in the militia was still somewhat sensitive. In May 1775, the issue of African Americans in the Massachusetts militia was clarified by the Committee for Safety from the Massachusetts legislature. The Committee presented a resolution that read:

> Resolved that it is the opinion of this Committee, as the contest now between Great Britain and the Colonies respects the liberties and privileges of the latter, which the Colonies are determined to maintain, that the admission of any persons, as soldiers, into the army, now raising, but only such as are freemen, will be inconsistent with the principles that are to be supported and reflect dishonor on the colony, and that no slaves be admitted into this army, upon any consideration whatever.[1]

The British were keenly aware of the irony that the American colonists fighting against tyranny still owned slaves, and they sought to exploit that irony wherever possible. The British authorities encouraged slaves to run away from their plantations and join the British forces whenever they could. The British went so far as to offer freedom to those slaves in exchange for service with the British forces. John Murray, Earl of Dunmore and Royal Governor of Virginia, issued a proclamation on 7 November 1775 declaring the slaves of rebel colonists free and encouraging them to enlist in the British forces.

> I do require every Person capable of bearing Arms, to resort to His MAJESTY'S STANDARD, or be looked upon as Traitors to His MAJESTY'S Crown and Government, and thereby become liable to the Penalty the Law inflicts upon such Offences; such as forfeiture of Life, confiscation of Lands, &c. &c. And I do hereby further declare all indented Servants, Negroes, or others, (appertaining to Rebels,) free that are able and willing to bear Arms, they joining His MAJESTY'S Troops as soon as may be, for the more speedily reducing this Colony to a proper Sense of their Duty, to His MAJESTY'S Crown and Dignity.[2]

Murray even raised a regiment of African Americans known as the "Ethiopian Regiment," which though it only lasted a year, saw combat against American forces. The regiment never amounted to more than about three hundred men and was disbanded in 1776 after a smallpox outbreak decimated their ranks.[3]

In addition to Murray's regiment, several other African American units were recruited by British forces. The two most prominent of these were the "Black Company of Pioneers" and the "Black Brigade." The Black Company of Pioneers was recruited largely from the survivors of the Ethiopian Regiment. Their duties consisted largely of typical military engineer tasks, such as road construction, building fortifications, and general maintenance. The company retained the same motto as Murray's regiment, "Liberty to Slaves," which they frequently embroidered on their uniforms. The Black Brigade was not truly a brigade-sized formation, rather it was a guerrilla band of only about two dozen men led by a runaway slave known as Titus Cornelius or as he was sometimes also called "Colonel Tye."[4] "Colonel Tye" had served in Murray's Ethiopian Regiment, but when the unit dissolved, he continued to serve the Loyalist cause. "Colonel Tye" was supported in his mission of destabilization by the Royal Governor of New Jersey, William Franklin, the son of American patriot Benjamin Franklin. The Black Brigade often worked in concert with the Queen's Rangers, a regiment of loyalists who fought alongside British forces during the American Revolution.

Murray's success in recruiting African Americans caused the colonists some consternation. In December 1775, George Washington, Commander-in-Chief of the Continental Army, who had previously rejected the idea of allowing African Americans to enlist on the colonists' side, now requested permission from the Continental Congress to allow free African Americans to serve.[5] While this was certainly an incentive to free African Americans to remain loyal to the American cause, it did nothing to entice the loyalty of the tens of thousands of enslaved African Americans. Slave participation in the American Revolution was still the exclusive purview of the British forces. It was not until 1779 that desperation caused the colonists to allow the enlistment of slaves in the American forces. However, though slaves were allowed to enlist in the American forces with the permission of their masters, they were not given any guarantee that this service eventually led to freedom. Those who did serve more often than not were simply returned to their masters upon the end of the conflict.[6]

Perhaps the boldest proposal for the use of African Americans during the American Revolution came in the spring of 1779. At that time John Laurens, one of Washington's aides and the son of the former President of the Continental Congress, proposed raising a regiment of African Americans to fight in South Carolina. He proposed to pay slaveholders $1,000 for each slave enlisted in the purpose and then to grant freedom to the slaves at the end of the conflict. Alexander Hamilton, who was a friend of Laurens, supported the idea but argued that most slaveholders would probably rather lose the Revolution and give up their slaves. Indeed, the idea was rejected by the South Carolina Assembly by an overwhelming vote.[7] Unlike the Continental Army, the Continental Navy had no restrictions on African American service. While none of the African Americans were ships' officers, significant numbers of African Americans served among crews, including ships' pilots, a position analogous to a modern-day commissioned officer.[8]

The single most successful effort to utilize African American manpower during the American Revolution was the 1st Rhode Island Regiment. Rhode Island, which was the smallest colony both in terms of territory and population, struggled to recruit sufficient numbers for their militia. In 1778, the colony's main seaport, Newport, was occupied by the British which completely strangling their economy. Brigadier General (BG) James M. Varnum, a Rhode Island native, suggested allowing African Americans to serve the colony regardless of whether they were free or slave. The Rhode Island legislature promised to pay slave owners for any slaves that enlisted and to grant freedom to the slaves at the end of the conflict. While the unit never actually reached regimental size, it never numbered more than 226 people, it was significant as the first American unit of African American soldiers. The unit first saw combat in August 1778 at the Battle of Rhode Island. Though still relatively green, the small unit fought well during the losing battle. At one point, the 1st Rhode Island withstood three assaults by British-paid German mercenaries without breaking. The men of the 1st Rhode Island served a total of five years until the very end of the American Revolution. To boost the size of the regiment, enlistment was ultimately opened to anyone regardless of race. By the end of the war, the 1st Rhode Island was arguably the first fully integrated unit in American history.[9]

By the end of the American Revolution, of the roughly three hundred thousand soldiers who served in the Continental Army, approximately three thousand or 1 percent were African Americans. While only a tiny minority of those who served in the Continental Army, this number was still significant because these individuals had chosen to support the Revolution when the British and Loyalists were arguably making them a better offer. While their service was widely recognized within their communities, the participation of African Americans in the American Revolution was almost completely written out of the historical record following the conflict. The African American Loyalists who had supported the British cause found themselves in dire straits at the end of the conflict. They could not return to their former homes for fear of re-enslavement and they were, therefore, forced to emigrate. More than three thousand African Americans were evacuated by the British and they largely settled in one of two places: Nova Scotia, Canada, or in African where the present-day country of Sierra Leone is located.[10] A large concentration of their descendants still resides in Nova Scotia in the 21st century. More than thirty thousand white Loyalists were also evacuated at the same time though they were also given the option to settle in the United Kingdom.

The status of African Americans in the U.S. armed forces was largely codified for the next seventy years by the Second Militia Act of 1792. The act explicitly mandated the service of every "free able-bodied white male citizen" between the ages of 18 and 45 in the militia.[11] This situation was not officially altered until 1862. While the Continental Navy was more open-minded to African American service during the American Revolution, most people do not realize that the Continental Navy and Continental Marine Corps ceased to exist after the Revolution. The U.S. Navy and U.S. Marine Corps were not established until 1798. The U.S. Navy, like its predecessor, was open-minded regarding African American service. The U.S. Marine Corps, on the other hand, took a very different attitude. When it was established in 1798,

Marine Corps rules explicitly stated that "no Negro, Mulatto or Indian" was permitted to enlist.[12] As it regarded African Americans, that rule remained unchanged until June 1942.

The next major military conflict for the United States was the War of 1812. African Americans were largely excluded from serving in the Army and most state militias, though a handful of African Americans served in local militia units at the behest of friends and neighbors who thought highly of them. The Navy, on the other hand, again freely enlisted African Americans. An estimated 10 to 15 percent of all American sailors in the War of 1812 were African Americans.[13] Not surprisingly the British again took advantage of the presence of slaves whenever they could. Just as during the American Revolution, slaves were offered their freedom in exchange for service with British forces. When the British invaded the Chesapeake Bay in 1814, as many as five thousand slaves flocked to the British forces. Vice Admiral Sir Alexander Cochran, the commander of British forces in the Chesapeake, offered the slaves either the opportunity of serving in the British forces or to immigrate to Canada. While the exact number who served is unknown, more than one hundred former slaves served with British forces as members of the Corps of Colonial Marines and participated in the sacking of Washington, DC, which culminated in the burning of the White House on 24 August 1814.[14]

On the other hand, African American soldiers were among those who defended New Orleans from the British in 1815. In their desire to serve the United States, these African Americans found an unlikely ally in the person of Andrew Jackson. Jackson, a slave owner who was not known for his tolerance of African Americans or North American Indians, was forced to use both groups in his desperation to defend the city of New Orleans. The diverse group which Jackson assembled for the defense of the city included not only North American Indians and free African Americans but also French privateers (most people would have used the term "pirates")— the Lafitte brothers. The free African Americans who participated in the defense of the city were mostly of Creole background and many had partic- ipated in militia formations when New Orleans was previously under the control of the French or Spanish empires. Of the roughly six thousand

Americans who fought at the Battle of New Orleans approximately five hundred or 8.5 percent were African Americans.[15]

Since African Americans were prohibited from enlisting in the Army their participation in frontier combat from the end of the War of 1812 until the Civil War was almost nonexistent. The only major conflict during this period was the Mexican-American War. This war was a very divisive conflict in the United States. This division of opinion regarded the reason for the war itself. While the annexation of the Republic of Texas was the spark that ignited the conflict, the underlying issue was the expansion of slavery into new territories. Southerners, in general, and slave owners, in particular, desired the annexation of Texas so that more land was available for slavery. Northerners, in general, and abolitionists, in particular, opposed the war for the very same reason. As a result, even if permitted to serve, doubtless few African Americans would have wanted to fight a war that increased the amount of territory opened to slavery.[16]

Despite the debate to the contrary, the American Civil War was fought over one issue—slavery. Without the issue of slavery, the biggest division within America was not between the North and the South but rather rural versus urban and/or agricultural versus industrial. As this was still an era in which the majority of Americans lived on farms, the issue that separated Northern farmers from Southern farmers was slavery. Were it not for slavery, a farmer from Illinois would have had more in common with a farmer from Alabama than either would have had with someone living in New York City or Boston or any other major urban center. In his first inaugural address, President Abraham Lincoln was unequivocal in stating that his only goal was the preservation of the Union. Lincoln promised to not even discuss the institution of slavery if only the states that had already seceded from the Union would peacefully return. Preservation of the Union was also the motivation of the overwhelming majority of Northerners when the Civil War began.

Acknowledging that the central issue behind the Civil War was slavery does not mean that the average soldier personally fought for or against slavery. The average Union soldier was not an abolitionist and did not take up arms to free the slaves. Most Northerners had no contact with slaves and quite possibly had never even met an African American. Likewise, the average Confederate soldier did not consciously fight to support slavery, because the average Confederate soldier did not own slaves, nor did he ever have the hope of accumulating enough wealth to own slaves. Nevertheless, by fighting to defend the Confederate States of America, the average Confederate soldier did ultimately fight for the institution of slavery. Likewise, following the Emancipation Proclamation in January 1863, the average Union soldier did ultimately fight against the institution of slavery.

Ironically, the first African Americans to offer their services during the Civil War volunteered in the Confederate States of America.[17] These volunteers came from the city of New Orleans where a large population of free African Americans lived, and many were the sons or grandsons of the men who served under Andrew Jackson during the War of 1812. According to the 1860 census, approximately ten thousand free African Americans lived in the city of New Orleans. While free African Americans volunteering to serve the Confederacy seems perplexing to the modern mindset, these men, mostly from multiracial Creole backgrounds, were volunteering to defend their city and their state, and, perhaps astonishingly, a few of them were also slave owners.

On 22 April 1861, the free African Americans of New Orleans began to organize a militia unit, which eventually took the name the 1st Louisiana Native Guard. On 29 May 1861, the 1st Louisiana Native Guard was formally accepted as part of the Louisiana militia. The three field grade officers of the regiment (one colonel, one lieutenant colonel, and one major) were white while all of the company-grade officers, noncommissioned officers (NCOs), and enlisted men were African Americans. The men of the regiment were not supplied with weapons or uniforms and were forced to arm and equip themselves out of their own pockets. The regiment never saw combat and was forced to disband on 15 February 1862 following the decision of the Louisiana state legislature to allow only free white males to serve in the militia.[18]

After the fall of New Orleans to the Union on 1 May 1862, Major General (MG) Benjamin Butler had less than ten thousand men to occupy the city and the surrounding countryside. According to the 1860 census, New Orleans was the most populous city in the Confederacy with almost 170,000 people. Butler made a reputation for himself early in the war by declaring runaway slaves as "contraband of war" which soon became Union policy. A lawyer and prewar politician, he reasoned that since the Confederates refused to recognize the humanity of their slaves, then the slaves were "contraband of war" just as cattle, grain, or other items. When Butler was approached by former members of the 1st Louisiana Native Guard to reorganize the regiment as a Union unit, he readily accepted their assistance. The new regiment, also confusingly called the 1st Louisiana Native Guard,[19] was organized on 27 September 1862. Less than 10 percent of the members of the new regiment served with its previous Confederate incarnation and the majority of the new enlistees were still legally slaves even though the official U.S. policy was to enlist only freedmen. Recruiting officers (then as now) were less concerned with exact policy and more concerned with meeting quotas. Recruitment efforts were so successful that in November 1862 a second regiment was organized, followed in December by a third regiment. As with its previous incarnation, the field-grade officers of all three regiments were white while the company-grade officers, NCOs, and enlisted men were all African Americans.

By November 1862, Butler was removed by the Lincoln Administration as a result of his unpopularity among the white residents of New Orleans. Butler's replacement was MG Nathaniel Banks, who took a very different view of African American soldiers. Most importantly, Banks wanted to get rid of all African American commissioned officers. Through browbeating and threats, he managed to secure the resignations of all African American officers in the 2nd Louisiana Native Guard, but the African American officers of the 1st and 3rd regiments refused to resign.[20] From their organization until May 1863, the regiments engaged largely in fatigue duties and guarded railroad depots while individual companies were assigned to the various forts around New Orleans. The 1st and 3rd Louisiana Native Guard Regiments were first used in combat during the siege of Fort Hudson where they participated in assaults on 27 May and 14 June 1863. In June 1863, the regiments were redesignated as the 1st, 2nd, and 3rd Regiments of the *Corps d'Afrique* along with all other African American units organized in the state of Louisiana.[21] In April 1864, the *Corps d'Afrique* was disbanded and absorbed into the United States Colored Troops (USCT). The soldiers of the 1st, 2nd, and 3rd Louisiana Native Guard were used to form the 73rd and 74th U.S. Colored Infantry Regiments of the USCT.

The next major change for African Americans during the Civil War came with the Militia Act of 1862. The Militia Act of 1862 revised the Second Militia Act of 1792 and allowed African Americans to serve in the militia, which meant that they were also eligible to serve in the U.S. Army.[22] The decision to allow African Americans to serve was driven by several factors. With the war already a year old, the enthusiasm for volunteering among many white Northerners was beginning to wane. Lincoln also sensed that the involvement of African Americans would change the tone of the war. It is important to remember that originally the Civil War, from the Northern point of view, was all about the restoration of the Union, not about freeing the slaves. However, with Northern support for the war softening, Lincoln, a longtime abolitionist, saw an opportunity to change the national motivation for the war. In August 1862, Secretary of War Edwin Stanton officially approved the recruiting of African Americans. The next month President Lincoln issued the Emancipation Proclamation which, though it did not take effect until 1 January 1863, granted freedom to, "… all persons held as slaves within any State or designated part of a State, the people whereof shall then be in rebellion against the United States."[23]

After the 1st Louisiana Native Guard, the next African American unit to see combat was the 1st Kansas Colored Volunteers. The 1st Kansas was already in the process of organizing before the official approval came from the War Department. The African American soldiers of the regiment were a mix of runaway slaves from Missouri and Arkansas and freedmen from Kansas and Nebraska. As a result of the 1st Kansas' early recruitment, the regiment saw combat only a month after the Emancipation Proclamation was issued. On 28 October 1862 at Island Mound, Missouri, the 1st Kansas repulsed a Confederate attack. On 17 July 1863, the 1st Kansas participated in the Battle of Honey Springs in Oklahoma. On that day, the Confederate forces mistook the repositioning of a Union regiment as a retreat. When the Confederate line swept forward, they encountered the 1st Kansas in a defensive position, and, after enduring three volleys from the regiment, the Confederate line broke. This battle represented the first use of an entire African American regiment in combat during the Civil War. The Union commander on the battlefield, MG James Blunt, wrote that the 1st Kansas had "… particularly distinguished itself; they fought like veterans, and preserved their line unbroken throughout the engagement."[24] On 13 December 1864, the 1st Kansas was redesignated the 79th U.S. Colored Infantry Regiment and became part of the USCT. Throughout its wartime service, the regiment lost 344 officers and men to disease, wounds, and combat, which was a higher casualty total than that sustained by any other regiment from Kansas during the Civil War.

Another early African American regiment was the 1st South Carolina Volunteer Infantry Regiment. This regiment was recruited almost exclusively from escaped slaves from South Carolina and Florida. The 1st South Carolina did not participate in any major battles but did fight in a few skirmishes. It is probably most remembered today for the inaccurate portrayal it received in the motion picture *Glory* where it was depicted as an ill-disciplined and poorly led unit. The incident portrayed in the movie did happen but was the result of decisions made by white Union officers and in no way the fault of the men of the 1st South Carolina. The 1st South Carolina was redesignated the 33rd U.S. Colored Infantry Regiment and became part of the USCT on 8 February 1864.[25]

The second African American infantry regiment to see major combat was also undoubtedly the most famous—the 54th Massachusetts Infantry Regiment. The 54th Massachusetts was organized under the command of Colonel (COL) Robert Gould Shaw, a member of a prominent abolitionist family from Boston. Shaw had already seen combat as a captain in the 2nd Massachusetts Infantry Regiment at several battles, most notably the Battle of Antietam. Many prominent members of the African American community in New England supported the organization of the 54th Massachusetts, most notably Frederick Douglass whose own sons, Charles and Lewis, served in the regiment. Unlike the 1st Kansas or the 1st South Carolina, the 54th Massachusetts was composed almost exclusively of freedmen.[26] Recruiting efforts were so successful that eventually a second African American regiment, the 55th Massachusetts, was recruited.

After the regiment was mustered into federal service in May 1863, it faced many hardships before it ever entered combat. Uniforms, shoes, rifles, and other items were in short supply and the 54th Massachusetts was frequently the last unit to receive them. Also, the men of the 54th Massachusetts were paid less than white soldiers. A white private was paid $13 per month, but the soldiers of the 54th Massachusetts were only paid $10 a month and had $3 of that amount subtracted from their pay for uniforms, something not done to white soldiers. Shaw, as well as all of the officers and men of the 54th Massachusetts, refused to accept their wages on principle as a result of this ill-treatment. It took 18 months and an act of the U.S. Congress to finally solve the pay problem.

The 54th Massachusetts was sent to South Carolina and initially used mostly in fatigue duties such as road construction and other forms of heavy labor. Shaw begged for the opportunity to have his men prove themselves in combat. Except for a few skirmishes, this opportunity did not present itself until July 1863. Shaw volunteered his regiment to lead an assault on Fort Wagner, a Confederate-controlled fort that defended the harbor of Charleston, South Carolina. On 18 July 1863, the 54th Massachusetts assaulted Fort Wagner, and, despite great heroism on the part of the men, the attack was a failure. Of the regiment's 600 men present for the battle, 270 were killed or wounded during the assault—a 45 percent casualty rate.[27] Shaw was among those killed in the assault and his body was buried by the Confederates in a mass grave along with the African American soldiers, which they did as an insult. When the fort was later captured by Union forces, the Union commander offered to find and disinter Shaw's body and return it to his family in Massachusetts. Shaw's father, also an ardent abolitionist, stated that he considered his son's burial site as an honor and refused the offer. The regiment continued to serve for the remainder of the war and was one of only a small handful of African American units not merged into the USCT.

The actions of one African American soldier during the assault on Fort Wagner received greater recognition than most of his comrades. Sergeant (SGT) Henry Carney retrieved the 54th Massachusetts' regimental colors when the color guard were all killed or wounded. Despite multiple wounds, Carney carried the flag both forward in the battle and then safely returned it to the Union lines after the battle. In 1900, thirty-seven years after the battle, Carney received the Medal of Honor for his actions that day. Oddly, the delay in Carney receiving his Medal was not an example of prejudice but rather was a common occurrence for Civil War Medals of Honor. Almost half of all Civil War Medals of Honor were not issued until decades after the battlefield incidents for which they were received. While Carney's actions represented the first for which an African American received the Medal of Honor, the first African American to physically receive the Medal of Honor was Sergeant Major Christian Fleetwood. Fleetwood served in the 4th U.S. Colored Infantry Regiment and was cited for his actions at the Battle of Chaffin's Farm on 29 September 1864. The official citation for his Medal of Honor stated that he "Seized the colors, after two color bearers had been shot down, and bore them nobly through the fight."[28] Ultimately, twenty-five African Americans received the Medal of Honor for their actions during the Civil War, eighteen from the Union Army, and seven from the Union Navy.

After initial recruiting efforts by the states, in May 1863, the War Department decided to centralize the recruiting of African American soldiers with the creation of the USCT. Unfortunately, the USCT barred African Americans from serving as commissioned officers and the only African American commissioned officers served in state-recruited regiments. While an exact number is unknown it is believed that fewer than one hundred African Americans served as officers in the Union Army during the Civil War. Nevertheless, all told almost 180,000 African Americans served in the Union Army during the war. The USCT ultimately consisted of 135 regiments of infantry, 14 regiments of artillery, and 6 regiments of cavalry. It is important to note that the USCT represented roughly 10 percent of the entire Union Army strength during the war.[29] Also, several hundred thousand other African Americans worked as civilian contractors for the Army and Navy or other parts of the federal government.

Although just a minor tactical action in the greater scheme of the war, the attack on Fort Pillow became a major event as regards the treatment of African American soldiers by the Confederacy.[30] In March 1864, the Union occupied Fort Pillow on the Mississippi River with detachments from the 13th Tennessee Cavalry Regiment and the 6th U.S. Colored Artillery Regiment totaling 557 men under the command of Major (MAJ) Lionel F. Booth. The Union second-in-command was MAJ William F. Bradford, who commanded the white pro-Union Tennessee cavalrymen. On 12 April 1864, almost fifteen hundred Confederates under the command of MG Nathan Bedford Forrest converged on Fort Pillow. The Union gunboat, USS *New Era*, on the Mississippi River began firing to prevent Confederate forces from enveloping the fort from the north. Around 1:00 p.m., the *New Era* pulled away to allow her guns to cool. Despite almost three hundred shells fired by the gunboat at the Confederates, they had virtually no effect. Booth was killed early on and, when Forrest sent a demand for surrender in the afternoon, Bradford refused. The Confederates not only outnumbered the defenders almost three-to-one but were also each armed with one or more pistols—a close-range advantage over the defenders armed with single-shot, muzzle-loading Springfield rifles.[31]

Confusion reigned as the Confederate and Union troops intermingled and Bradford then shouted for a retreat, which panicked his troops. As the Union forces fled to the riverbank, Union Navy Lieutenant James Marshall, captain of the USS *New Era*, planned to engage the Confederates with canister rounds but was thwarted since the soldiers were mixed up. The Confederates killed many Union soldiers on the riverbank while others drowned while trying to escape by swimming the Mississippi River. Though the Union subsequently claimed it was a massacre, Bradford had not formally surrendered. Approximately 230 Union soldiers died, while Confederate casualties were only 14 killed in action (KIA) and 80 wounded in action (WIA). The disparity between casualties based on race was striking—only 58 African Americans (~20 percent) were taken prisoner, while 168 (~60 percent) white Union soldiers were captured.[32] Though doubtless many African Americans refused to surrender because they feared enslavement, most likely Confederates shot indiscriminately at the Union soldiers, some of whom were indeed attempting to surrender.

Despite the many positive contributions of African American soldiers and sailors to the Union cause during the Civil War, not all Union commanders were convinced that African Americans should be allowed to fight. Perhaps the most notable example of a Union commander missing an opportunity for victory as a result of his prejudice against African American troops was during the Battle of the Crater. The Battle of the Crater was an effort by the Union to get through the defenses around the Confederate capital of Richmond, Virginia. A 75-foot long chamber was dug underneath the Confederate lines and filled with approximately 8,000 pounds of gunpowder. MG Ambrose Burnside then trained a division of USCT troops (4th Division, IX Corps, Army of the Potomac) to lead the assault after the gunpowder was exploded. The USCT troops were to assault around the crater at the exposed Confederate flanks and await support from white troops. Unfortunately, the day before the attack MG George Meade, the commander of the Army the Potomac, ordered Burnside to use white troops in the assault rather than the USCT. Though Burnside protested to Union General-in-Chief Ulysses Grant, he was forced to comply. The white division (1st Division, IX Corps) selected to lead the assault was commanded by BG James Ledlie, who failed to brief his men on how they were to conduct the assault and during the battle was both drunk and behind the lines in a bomb shelter providing no leadership. Meade later dismissed Ledlie from the Union Army after a Court of Inquiry formally criticized his actions during the battle.[33]

On 30 July 1864, the gunpowder under the Confederate line was detonated. The ensuing crater was 200 feet long, 50 feet wide, and 25–30 feet deep. The explosion completely disoriented the Confederates and killed at least three hundred soldiers instantly. Unfortunately, the untrained white division was as disoriented as the Confederates and waited for almost ten minutes before they began their attack. When they reached the crater itself, instead of attacking around as per the training of African American troops, they charged into the crater itself and found themselves largely unable to get up the other side. By this time the Confederates began to regroup and counterattacked, firing rifles and artillery at the now trapped men inside the crater. Burnside then ordered the African American division to support their trapped white comrades. Unfortunately, they also charged into the crater and were likewise slaughtered. By the end of the day, almost four thousand Union soldiers were casualties with five hundred KIA and another fourteen hundred missing or captured.[34] Grant later stated that "... [the Battle of the Crater was] the saddest affair I have witnessed in this war."[35]

The Union Navy began the Civil War with much the same attitude toward African American service as the Union Army. By the summer of 1861, however, the Union Navy was forced to formulate policy independent of specific orders from the Lincoln Administration. This situation was caused by the number of runaway slaves who attempted to flee aboard Union ships whenever they landed along the Southern coastline. Secretary of the Navy Gideon Wells even issued an order in July 1861 allowing the Union Navy to employ runaway slaves. After the Emancipation Proclamation, the majority of occupational specialties in the Navy were opened to African Americans. By the end of the war, approximately 15 percent of the Union Navy's sailors were African American. Also, African American sailors did not suffer from pay discrimination and had more career opportunities than in the Union Army. However, no African Americans were commissioned in the Navy until 1944.[36]

By the time the war ended in 1865, more than thirty-seven thousand African American soldiers and sailors had died while in the service of the country, which represented almost 21 percent of all African Americans who served. With the war over, white Union regiments were quickly mustered out of service and the USCT regiments were used to occupy portions of the former Confederacy. Initially, almost one-third of the occupation forces, approximately one hundred thousand officers and men, were from USCT regiments. By the end of 1865, when almost all white volunteer regiments were already discharged from federal service, eighty-five USCT regiments remained on active duty. By the end of 1866, however, only nine USCT regiments remained on active duty.[37] In July 1866, the U.S.

Congress passed an act to expand the size of the peacetime Regular Army. The pre-Civil War Regular Army consisted of only ten regiments of infantry and five regiments of cavalry. An additional nine regiments of regular infantry and one regiment of regular cavalry were organized during the war. In 1866, the U.S. Congress reorganized the Regular Army into twenty-five regiments of infantry and ten regiments of cavalry. Of these two (initially four) regiments of infantry and two regiments of cavalry were manned by African Americans.[38]

During Reconstruction, former members of the Confederacy were prevented from serving in state militias. To fill this void, newly liberated African Americans began to form militias that were loyal to the Republican-controlled Reconstruction state governments. The size and quality of these militias varied widely since they received virtually no support from white Southerners who had military experience. With the rise of the Ku Klux Klan, these militias often had to battle for control of their state. In states with strong Reconstruction governments, militias were used in a law enforcement capacity. Unfortunately, as support from the federal government began to wane during the latter phases of Reconstruction, these African American militias were largely disbanded though a few places retained both white and segregated African American militia formations into the early 20th century.

The period from the end of the Civil War until the entry of the United States into World War I was a formative era for African Americans in the U.S. armed forces. For the first time, African Americans served in the regular armed forces in peacetime. While white prejudice was still the order of the day and Jim Crow laws began to appear in the South during the 1880s, there was more freedom for African Americans during this era than any previous period in American history. Moreover, during these decades, fourteen African American soldiers received the Medal of Honor for extraordinary valor in action.[39] Another four Seminole Indians, who were of mixed racial heritage, serving with the U.S. Indian Scouts also received the Medal of Honor during this era.

From 1866 to 1890, the four African American regiments—9th and 10th Cavalry and 24th and 25th Infantry—spent most of their time in the West defending white settlers, building roads, guarding federal lands, protecting the U.S. Postal Service, and fighting various North American Indian tribes. Despite facing the same deplorable conditions, including outdated equipment, poor rations, isolated locations, low pay, and dangerous situations, the African American soldiers had a lower desertion rate than their white contemporaries. During this period, these African American soldiers acquired the nickname "Buffalo Soldiers" from the North American Indians. Three possible explanations exist for the origins of the nickname. Some historians argue that the North American Indians thought that the African Americans' hair had the same texture as the coat of a buffalo. Others believe that the nickname referred to the buffalo-hide coats issued to soldiers during the severe winters on the Great Plaines. Still, others have asserted that the nickname was a reference to the bravery exhibited by the African American soldiers which compared them to the ferocity of a buffalo. Regardless of the explanation, the nickname was well received both by African American soldiers and also became well-known among the general populace.[40] Despite their many accomplishments, all four regiments were forced to carry the term "Colored" in parentheses on all official government documentation.

The new African American units formed by Congress in the 1860s included African American NCOs and enlisted men, while the officers were all white except for three African Americans. Henry O. Flipper, U.S. Military Academy (USMA) Class of 1877, was dismissed from the Army for "conduct unbecoming an officer and gentlemen" for lying about the missing commissary funds in 1882.[41] John H. Alexander, USMA Class of 1887, died in 1894 from a ruptured aorta.[42] Charles Young[43], USMA Class of 1889, was forced into medical retirement in 1917 to prevent him from possible promotion to general officer during World War I. After riding almost 500 miles on horseback in 16 days to prove his physical fitness, he was finally recalled to active duty on 6 November 1918, five before the war ended. Young died in 1922 from kidney failure while serving as the U.S. Military Attaché to Liberia.

After the closing of the frontier era, African American soldiers remained a vital part of the Regular Army and participated in the Spanish-American War. During that short conflict, five members of the 10th Cavalry Regiment received the Medal of Honor for their actions in Cuba, while one African American sailor received the Medal for his actions aboard the USS *Iowa* (BB-4). In addition to the four Regular Army African American regiments, an effort was made to recruit African American volunteers during the war. A total of twelve regiments (or at least portions thereof)[44] were recruited, but only four saw actual service (6th Massachusetts, 8th Illinois, 9th U.S., and 23rd Kansas) and then only in the occupation of Cuba or Puerto Rico after the end of combat. The roughly six thousand African American soldiers who served in the Spanish-American War included approximately three hundred African American officers. Many of these officers had previously served as enlisted men in the Regular Army while the remainder were generally prominent members of their civilian communities. After the end of the war, the four African American Regular Army regiments served in the Philippines in either or both the later Philippine-American War of 1899–1903 and the Moro Rebellion of 1899–1913.

On 23 March 1907, a detachment of African American soldiers from the 9th Cavalry Regiment was sent to the USMA to instruct white cadets in horsemanship. The detachment eventually grew to squadron-size and these African American soldiers remained responsible for teaching future white officers until horsemanship was abolished at USMA in 1947. It is no small irony that between 1865 and 1917, while African American soldiers served their nation in both wartime and peacetime, they endured prejudice and contempt from the white citizens they served to protect. This animosity even led to a few race riots directed against African American soldiers. One of the ugliest racial incidents of the period took place in Texas.

On 13 August 1906 in Brownsville, Texas, a shooting left a white bartender, Frank Natus, dead and a white police officer, Lieutenant Joe Dominguez[45], wounded (his arm was later amputated).[46] The white residents of Brownsville blamed the murder and maiming on the African American soldiers of the 25th Infantry Regiment who were stationed at Fort Brown, despite white officers arguing that all of their soldiers were in the barracks or otherwise occupied on post during the shooting. BG Ernest A. Garlington, Inspector General (IG) of the U.S. Army, personally investigated the incident. Despite a lack of any real physical evidence, Garlington was convinced of the men's guilt and recommended to President Theodore Roosevelt the dishonorable discharge of 167 men of Companies B, C, and D, 25th Infantry. On 4 November 1906, the 167 African American soldiers were dishonorably discharged.[47] What was particularly perplexing about his decision was that Roosevelt was progressive regarding race, spoke out publicly against lynchings, and even invited African American educator Booker T. Washington to dine at the White House. In 1909, the administration of the new president, William Howard Taft, established a military court of inquiry to review the decision to discharge the 167 African American soldiers from the 25th Infantry. In 1910, the court of military inquiry suggested allowing the dishonorably discharged soldiers to reenlist. Only seventy soldiers were interviewed, fourteen were recommended for reenlistment, and only eleven chose to rejoin the Army.[48] In 1972, the Army overturned the dishonorable discharges against all 167 soldiers. In 1973, the U.S. Congress approved a tax-free $25,000 pension for the only living survivor not permitted to reenlist, Dorsie Willis.[49]

When the United States entered World War I in April 1917, the majority of African Americans wholeheartedly supported the war effort and believed that their service in this conflict would finally gain for them the status of full citizenship. In total, almost four hundred thousand African Americans served in World War I. Ironically, none of the four Regular Army African American regiments saw combat in World War I. In the case of the 9th and 10th Cavalry Regiments, they did not participate for the same reason that almost no American cavalry regiments participated—the nature of trench warfare on the Western Front almost eliminated the cavalry from the battlefield. In the case of the 24th and 25th Infantry Regiments, their manpower was largely raided to produce company grade officers and NCOs for the eight African American infantry regiments recruited from the civilian population. Segregation remained standard operating procedure for the Army during World War I for both officers and enlisted personnel. As a result, the majority of African American commissioned officers were trained in a segregated facility at Fort Des Moines, Iowa.[50]

The overwhelming majority of African Americans who served in World War I served in support units. Their jobs were usually the most physically demanding and least glamorous, such as stevedores unloading ships and engineers building roads. Nevertheless, the Army also recruited and sent into combat two African American infantry divisions (92nd and 93rd Divisions). The 92nd Division was activated in October 1917 at Camp Funston, Kansas. The main combat power of the division came from its four infantry regiments (365th–368th Infantry Regiments) which were made up of African American enlisted men, NCOs, and company-grade officers, as well as white field-grade officers. The 365th Infantry was composed mostly of men from Texas and Oklahoma, while the men of the 366th Infantry came mostly from the mining areas of Alabama. During their stateside training period, the 366th Infantry spent so much time functioning as laborers for non-training tasks that they were derisively called the "fatigue regiment."[51] The 367th Infantry was made up mostly of New Yorkers and, of the 108 commissioned officers in the regiment, only eight were white. The 368th Infantry included men from Tennessee, Pennsylvania, and Maryland, and had ninety-seven African American company-grade officers.[52]

Unlike the training of most white Army divisions during World War I, the 92nd Division never trained as a single unit before leaving for France. The division never trained together because no community in America wanted approximately twenty-five thousand armed African American men stationed near them. The many problems of the 92nd Division, including, "… low and fluctuating strength, large numbers of replacements just before sailing, decentralized control, and shortness of training period," were all noted in an IG report filed by COL Alfred A. Starbird.[53] Virtually all the African American officers in the division's 167th Field Artillery Brigade (349th, 350th, and 351st Field Artillery Regiments) and the 317th Engineer Regiment were relieved and then replaced with white officers before they left for France. The field artillery brigade's commander, BG William E. Cole, grudgingly admitted that the officers in question had never received proper training from the Army.[54] Nevertheless, despite all these problems, beginning in June 1918, the 92nd Division boarded ships for France. The division spent July through September training for trench warfare with French and American veterans as well as learning how to operate as a unit.

In September 1918, the 92nd Division was assigned to the U.S. First Army in preparation for the Meuse-Argonne Campaign. The Meuse-Argonne Campaign began on 26 September and the 92nd Division found itself in reserve attached to the I Corps except for the 368th Infantry Regiment. The 368th Infantry, along with a dismounted French cavalry regiment (11th Cuirassiers), were formed into a special brigade called the *Groupement Durand*. Despite no advanced preparation, a shortage of food, maps, signal flares, grenade launchers, and barbed wire cutters, the regiment was sent into battle. They received no artillery support and, due to the shortage of barbed wire cutters and their unfamiliarity with the terrain, the men of the regiment quickly became lost and disorganized. The regiment's experiences over the next few days were scarcely any better and it was withdrawn from the battle on 30 September. The 368th Infantry lost fifty-eight men KIA and more than two hundred WIA in only five days of combat.[55]

The failure of the regiment was, not surprisingly, blamed on the African American company-grade officers and men rather than their lack of preparation and supplies and/or the incompetence of white field grade officers. During the same battle, the white 35th Division almost collapsed under German artillery fire and sustained horrible casualties—over one thousand KIA in only five days—but received far less harsh criticism. The commander of the 92nd Division, MG Charles C. Ballou, ordered the removal of thirty officers from the 368th Infantry Regiment—all of whom were African Americans. Ironically, the worst examples of officer incompetence in the regiment during the battle were shown by white officers. MAJ Max Elser, commander of the 2nd Battalion got lost on 26 September and ordered his men to withdraw without orders. After the battle, he was hospitalized for "psycho-neurosis"—better known as fear.[56] The 3rd Battalion commander, MAJ B. F. Norris, depending upon which account one believes, either did not accompany his soldiers into battle on the first day or returned to the American trenches and decided to go to bed early while his men were in still combat.[57] Despite this and other examples, it was only African Americans who were blamed. Five African American officers from the 368th Infantry were later convicted of cowardice in the face of the enemy and sentenced to death, though they were exonerated by a War Department investigation.[58]

Based on the first combat experience of one regiment, the entire 92nd Division was removed from the line on 5 October and allowed to do little more than run occasional patrols in no man's land for the next month.[59] On 10 November, the day before the Armistice that ended World War I, the division's 183rd Brigade, made up of the 365th and 366th Infantry Regiments and the 350th Machine Gun Battalion, attacked enemy positions along the Moselle River near the city of Metz. During the attack, the men performed well and captured two and a half kilometers of ground by nightfall.[60] The brigade renewed its offensive at 5:00 a.m. on 11 November and at 11:00 a.m. when the Armistice took effect, it occupied positions closer to Metz than any other Allied units. During its relatively brief period of combat, the 92nd Division sustained 182 KIA and 1465 WIA.[61]

After the war, based solely on the combat performance of a single regiment in its first combat action, the 92nd Division was unfairly tarred as an ill-disciplined formation and the men of the division were unfairly accused of cowardice in the face of the enemy. This unfair criticism of the division stems largely from the institutional racism that pervaded American society of the time. Arguably, the division's greatest problems stemmed from poor white senior leadership, a problem that was mirrored by African American units in World War II. The white officers assigned to African American units were largely drawn from the South in the false belief that they "knew how to handle" African Americans. Ultimately, what resulted from this decision was racist, white senior officers who held African American company-grade officers, as well as African American NCOs and enlisted men, in utter contempt. With no feeling of solidarity between white officers and the rest of the division, unsurprisingly African American troops were not among the most motivated members of the Army during either world war. However, no one in white society was willing to acknowledge that it was racism rather than the African Americans themselves, which was the real problem encountered by the 92nd Division.

After the war, veterans of the 92nd Division struggled against the opinions of white senior officers, especially those who had no experience with the division. One white senior officer epitomized the stereotype more than any other—Lieutenant General (LTG) Robert Lee Bullard. Bullard, a native of Alabama, not only intensely disliked African Americans but was also said to have had a long-running feud with Ballou, the 92nd Division's commander. On 12 October 1918, Bullard became the commander of the U.S. Second Army, and the IV Corps, of which the 92nd Division was a part, was assigned to him. Ballou was certainly talking about Bullard when he later said:

> It was my misfortune to be handicapped by many white officers who were rabidly hostile to the idea of a colored officer, and who continually conveyed misinformation to the staffs of the superior units, and generally created much trouble and discontent. Such men will never give the Negro the square deal that is his just due.[62]

On 1 November, Bullard made the following diary entry:

> The Negro Division seems in a fair way to be a failure. It is in a quiet sector, yet can hardly take care of itself, while to take any offensive action seems wholly beyond its powers. I have been here now with it for three weeks and have been unable to have it make a single raid upon the enemy. Their Negro officers have any inadequate idea of what is expected of soldiers, and their white officers are too few to leaven the lump.[63]

Amazingly, Bullard lied in his diary, which theoretically no one else would ever read. The division was conducting regular raids against enemy positions and Bullard had not yet ordered it on the offensive. Even on the day of the Armistice, Bullard could not keep himself from criticizing the 92nd Division's performance of the previous day. "The poor 92nd Negroes wasted time and dwadled where they did attack, and in some places where they should have attacked, never budged at all."[64] The next day, he added: "Two days ago and again yesterday the 92nd Division would not fight; couldn't be made to attack in any effective sense. The general who commands them couldn't make them fight."[65] He made these statements even though the 92nd Division gave perhaps the best performance of the

American forces involved in the attack on Metz. Unable to completely lie in his official report of the fighting of 10–11 November, Bullard damned the division with faint praise. "… 92nd Division Negroes, under General Ballou, gained a good deal of ground but did the enemy little harm."[66] The 92nd Division was quickly returned to the United States after the end of the war and disbanded at Camp Upton, New York, on 7 March 1919.

The 93rd Division had a far different experience during World War I. The first thing that distinguished the division occurred during its organization. Of the four regiments (369th–372nd Infantry Regiments) that comprised the division, only one, the 371st Infantry Regiment, was composed of draftees. The other three regiments were made up of National Guard units and, therefore, the men of these regiments not only had prior training but also had volunteered for military service perhaps years before the war. Also, not only were there more African American officers in these three regiments, but some of these officers achieved a high rank. For instance, all of the officers and men of the 370th Infantry Regiment were African American, including the regimental commander. This was unprecedented in the history of the Army up to that day. Likewise unique to this division, no field artillery, quartermaster, or any other support units were assigned.[67]

The 369th Infantry Regiment arguably become the most famous unit assigned to the 93rd Division. The regiment began life as the 15th New York National Guard Regiment and ultimately acquired the nickname the "Harlem Hellfighters." The 15th New York originated from a combination of African American desire for greater recognition in American society and the "Preparedness Movement" begun by progressive Republicans like former President Theodore Roosevelt and former Army Chief of Staff MG Leonard Wood. The New York State legislature authorized the formation of what would become the 15th New York in 1913, but it was not until July 1916 that the regiment began formation.[68] While there was no difficulty in finding men willing to volunteer to serve in the enlisted ranks of the regiment, the question of officers was much more complicated. A combination of social status, education, and racial issues made it difficult to find qualified African Americans to serve as officers in the regiment. Thankfully, though the majority of the regiment's officers were white, they were all volunteers, and, therefore, the majority had generally progressive attitudes toward African Americans.

The 369th Infantry Regiment was one of the first American units to arrive in France in January 1918. During their first two months in France, the 369th Infantry performed fatigue duties that involved drainage, road, and railroad construction, as well as other physically demanding jobs. While the rest of the regiment engaged in these decidedly unheroic duties, the regimental band began a goodwill tour of France. The band, led by conductor 1st Lieutenant (1LT) James R. Europe, was largely credited with introducing jazz music to France during the tour. In March 1918, Pershing, as the commander of the American Expeditionary Force (AEF), agreed to attach the 369th Infantry, as well as the three other regiments of the 93rd Division who had not yet arrived, to French control.[69] This decision went completely against Pershing's stated policy of keeping American forces under American control. Many people, then and now, strongly criticized this decision as an example of Pershing "selling out" to pressure both from racists in the War Department and the White House back in the United States as well as the British and French who had long wanted American soldiers as nothing more than cannon fodder.[70] The 93rd Division ceased to exist and its regiments spent the rest of the war under French command.

After a month of training with French veterans, the 369th Infantry was assigned to the French 16th Division and entered combat in April 1918. Regimental commander COL William Hayward nicknamed his unit *les enfants perdus* (the lost infants) since they were separated from the rest of the U.S. Army. While they retained their American uniforms, the men of the regiment were issued with French helmets, rifles, and web gear. In total, the regiment spent almost two hundred days on the front line, one of the longest combat postings of any American unit in the war. The 369th Infantry received the French *Croix de Guerre* as a unit decoration for valor and 153 of the regiment's soldiers were awarded the *Croix de Guerre* individually. Eleven members of the regiment received the Distinguished Service Cross (DSC), the second-highest U.S. decoration for valor, and 1LT George S. Robb, a white officer, received the Medal of Honor. One of the

DSCs was later upgraded to the Medal of Honor. On 15 May 1918, SGT William H. Johnson and one other soldier defended their forward position against twelve German raiders. When his comrade was badly wounded, Johnson engaged in hand-to-hand combat to prevent the capture of his incapacitated comrade. Johnson's Medal of Honor was presented in 2015, ninety-seven years after his actions on the French battlefield.[71] On 12 February 1919, the 369th Infantry returned to the United States and disbanded on 28 February at Camp Upton.

The 370th Infantry Regiment was another former National Guard unit attached to the 93rd Division. Originally known as the 8th Illinois Infantry Regiment, the unit had its origins in African American militia formations founded in Illinois in the aftermath of the Civil War. Unique among the regiments of the 93rd Infantry, the 370th Infantry had no white officers. The regiment did not arrive in France until April 1918 and, like the 369th Infantry, was "loaned" to the French for the duration of the war. The regiment first entered combat in July 1918 and remained on the frontlines until the end of the war in November 1918.[72] Company C, 370th Infantry Regiment, earned the French *Croix de Guerre* for valor as did seventy-one soldiers of the regiment. Also, twenty-one members of the regiment earned the DSC. On 9 February 1919, the regiment returned to the United States and disbanded on 11 March at Camp Grant, Illinois.

The 371st Infantry Regiment was the only regiment from the 93rd Division that was composed almost exclusively of draftee soldiers. Though the regiment was officially organized in August 1917, it did not receive a full complement of soldiers until the end of November. The 371st Infantry was shipped to France in April 1918 and, like the rest of the division, it was "loaned" to the French and served for the entire war with the French 157th Infantry Division.[73] The regiment received the French *Croix de Guerre* for valor as a unit decoration and many of the soldiers received individual commendations, including one French Legion of Honor, 22 DSCs, and 123 French *Croix de Guerres*. One soldier of the 371st, Corporal (CPL) Freddie Stowers, was recommended for the Medal of Honor during the war, but the paperwork was lost. While racism might seem the best explanation for Stowers not receiving the Medal, there was good reason to believe that the paperwork was truly lost. All other Medal of Honor recommendations for African Americans during World War I resulted in at least a lesser decoration for the nominee, while Stowers received no American decoration. Stowers crawled forward leading his squad under heavy machine-gun fire to destroy a machine gun nest which caused heavy casualties in his company. After destroying that position, Stowers urged his men on toward other enemy targets when he was mortally wounded. [74] On 11 February 1919, the 371st Infantry returned to the United States on the transport ship USS *Leviathan* (SP-1326)[75] and disbanded on 28 February at Camp Jackson, South Carolina.

The final regiment of the 93rd Division was the 372nd Infantry. This regiment consisted of various states' National Guard units, as well as a small leavening of draftees. The National Guard formations that comprised the regiment included: 1st Separate Battalion, District of Columbia; 9th Separate Battalion, Ohio[76]; 1st Separate Company, Connecticut; 1st Separate Company, Maryland; Company L, 6th Infantry Regiment, Massachusetts; and Separate Company G, Tennessee.[77] The regiment was organized in January 1918 at Camp Stewart, Virginia, and shipped to France in March 1918. Like her sister regiments, the 372nd Infantry was "loaned" to the French and served for the entire war with the French 157th Infantry Division. The regiment's combat experience was almost identical to that of the 371st Infantry and it also returned to the United States on 11 February 1919 and disbanded on 6 March at Camp Sherman, Ohio.

The Navy was generally more progressive in its attitude toward African Americans than the Army. Though there were no African American naval officers, from the time of the Civil War until World War I African Americans had served relatively freely and in almost all career specialties within the Navy. Then suddenly in 1919, African Americans were completely barred from enlisting in the Navy. While there was no single cause for the Navy's sudden policy change, naval historians generally point the finger at Secretary of the Navy Josephus Daniels. Daniels, who served under infamously racist Democrat President Woodrow Wilson, was a lifelong segregationist and white supremacist, and later ruled largely responsible for the Wilmington

Massacre of 1898[78]. This complete moratorium on African American enlistment remained in place until 1933. President Franklin D. Roosevelt, who served as Assistant Secretary of the Navy under Daniels, allowed African Americans to again enlist in the Navy, but only as mess stewards. This policy remained until 1942 when all career specialties were again opened to African Americans.

Unfortunately, despite the individual valor of African American soldiers in World War I, the attitude of white America regarding race did not change significantly after the war. Even the commander of the AEF, Pershing, whose previous service with the 10th Cavalry Regiment and respect for African American soldiers had earned him the derogatory nickname "Nigger Jack,"[79] did not always support African Americans. At times, he defended the bravery of African American soldiers, while at other times he agreed with white officers' negative opinions of African Americans. Back in the United States, World War I caused great social change as African Americans began to migrate from the Deep South to Northern industrial centers such as Detroit, Cleveland, and Chicago. The war generated a demand for manufacturing which led to an increased demand for labor. African Americans responded to this demand, but they were not welcomed by most whites in the North as they were seen as competition for jobs. In the summer of 1919, with the war over and competition for manufacturing jobs becoming greater, a series of race riots spread throughout America. In most cases, working-class whites attacked African Americans who they believed were stealing their jobs. The riots hit cities such as Baltimore, Washington, DC, Norfolk, Syracuse, New Orleans, Philadelphia, and New York. One of the cities worst hit by the riots was Chicago, where the riots lasted eight days and required the National Guard to restore order.[80] In total, more than 150 people, mostly African Americans, were killed nationwide.

Another racial incident during World War I involved African American soldiers of the 3rd Battalion, 24th Infantry Regiment at Camp Logan outside Houston, Texas. On 23 August 1917, Private (PVT) Alonso Edwards approached two Houston police officers, Lewis Sparks and Rufus Daniels, to ask a question. Sparks and Daniels attacked Edwards because they disliked the tone he used, and they pistol-whipped him repeatedly before arresting him. Later that same day, military police CPL Charles Baltimore approached Sparks and Daniels to ask about Edwards. Sparks and Daniels then fired three shots at Baltimore, before severely beating and arresting him. Word of Edwards and Baltimore's treatment reached the camp, where African American soldiers openly talked about breaking them out of jail. A white officer managed to secure their release from jail, but the battalion's commander, MAJ Kneeland S. Snow, realized that things might deteriorate rapidly and confined all soldiers to post. After dark, Snow discovered soldiers attempting to steal ammunition and ordered the entire battalion to assemble without rifles. At that point, someone yelled that a white mob was approaching the camp and chaos ensued. As the white officers and some African American NCOs tried to reestablish control over the battalion, soldiers began to fire in all directions outside the camp.[81]

One sergeant, Vida Henry, decided to take matters into his own hands. Henry gathered together approximately 150 like-minded enlisted men and marched them into Houston, where they fired on all whites they encountered. Ironically, they encountered few police officers but one of the first they met was Daniels, who was killed immediately. When they saw a car approaching carrying a man in an olive-drab uniform, they assumed he was a member of the Houston Police Department's mounted force. They immediately opened fire, killing the driver, but on closer inspection discovered that the occupant was Captain (CPT) Joseph W. Mattes, an officer of the Illinois National Guard. The killing of Mattes had a sobering effect on them and individual soldiers began to drift away. Henry ordered the remaining men to march back to camp, where he shook hands with each of them before announcing that he planned to shoot himself. His body was discovered the next day.[82] A total of seventeen people died that evening (four police officers, nine civilians, and two soldiers—Henry and Mattes). The city of Houston was then placed under martial law as the 3rd Battalion, 24th Infantry, was disarmed and shipped by rail back to New Mexico under the guard of armed white soldiers.

A massive court-martial ensued on 1 November 1917, during which almost two hundred witnesses testified over 22 days. There was no debate

surprise, on 26 October 1940, only a week before the 1940 presidential election, Davis' name appeared on a list of officer promotions.[90] Many, then and now, have speculated that Davis' promotion was a rather cynical political maneuver by Democratic President Franklin D. Roosevelt, who was then seeking an unprecedented third term in office and courting African American votes.

In January 1941, Davis arrived at Fort Riley, Kansas, where he assumed command of the 4th Cavalry Brigade, 2nd Cavalry Division. In this position, Davis now commanded all of the white officers of the 9th and 10th Cavalry Regiments in the 4th Cavalry Brigade. These white officers showed proper deference to Davis in the official performance of their duties but had almost no dealings with him outside of those duties. Davis was quite isolated while at Fort Riley. Other than his wife, his only companion was his son, 1LT Benjamin O. Davis, Jr., a member of the 1936 Class of USMA, who was appointed his father's *aide de camp* upon the former's promotion to brigadier general. After reaching mandatory retirement in 1941, Davis was asked to remain on active duty to serve as an advisor on African American issues in the Army IG Office. During the three years that Davis occupied this position, he made extensive inspection tours both throughout the United States and in the European Theater of Operations (ETO). In November 1944, he became a special assistant to the commanding general of the ETO, and then, from January to May 1945, he served with the IG in the ETO. In 1946, Davis returned to Washington, DC, and worked with the IG until he became the special assistant to the Secretary of War in 1947. He retired on 14 July 1948, after fifty years on active duty—one of the longest careers in Army history.[91]

The Interwar Period was a bleak time for the Army. In June 1920, less than two years after the end of World War I, Congress passed the National Defense Act, which governed the U.S. armed forces for the next twenty years. The Army remained chronically underfunded and only large enough to serve as a skeleton for future wartime buildups. This legislation created three new branches of the Army (Air Corps, Chemical Warfare Corps, and Finance Corps), while at the same time abolishing one wartime branch (Tank Corps).[92] With no obvious foreign threat and America in an isolationist mood, Congress believed that a small, mostly domestically stationed Army was sufficient.

After the Great Depression began in 1929, even less attention was paid to national defense, as pressing domestic issues claimed the focus of the American government and people. The lack of economic resources caused a state of military limbo throughout the Interwar Period. Between 1921 and 1939, the average yearly strength of the Army was only 126,126, while the average yearly budget was only $318 million (around $5.2 billion in 2019 dollars[93]).[94] The manpower low point for the Army was 1923 when the total strength was only 111,341. In 1939, the manpower high point, the total strength was up to 167,712.[95] The Army's budget low point was 1935 when Congress appropriated only $250 million ($4.7 billion in 2019 dollars). In 1939, the budgetary high point, Congress approved only $449 million ($8.3 billion in 2019 dollars).[96] The manpower and budgetary increases that took place by 1939 were mostly a reaction to the Japanese invasion of China and Germany's blood-less conquest of both Austria and Czechoslovakia. On 1 September 1939, when Germany invaded Poland, the U.S. Army ranked as the 17th largest army in the world, behind smaller and less industrialized nations such as Sweden, Yugoslavia, and Turkey.[97]

For most of the interwar period, planning for African American manpower use was based on a 1922 staff study which later became *de facto* Army policy.[98] The 1922 study argued that African Americans should serve as both combat and support troops otherwise the white population of the United States would suffer disproportionate combat losses. Also, the study stated that an African American was:

> … a citizen of the United States, entitled to it all the rights of citi-
> zenship and subject to all the obligations of citizenship; that than
> the negro [*sic*] constitutes an appreciable part of our best military
> manhood; that while not the best military material, he is by no means
> the worst; that no part of mobilization for the maximum effort can
> afford to ignore such a fraction of the manhood, especially in these
> times of war makes demands upon the physical defectives and the

women; and finally, that in a democracy such as ours political and economic conditions must be considered, and that decision must rest upon these two considerations alone.[99]

The study argued that lower intelligence test scores for African Americans, which were long used as an argument against their military service, were not grounds for discounting all of their manpower. "As a matter of fact, we have to sift our white population for suitable material."[100]

Unsurprisingly, the lessons of the 92nd and 93rd Division's during World War I concerning African American officers were mostly ignored. The study argued that white officers were better suited to lead African American troops but did note the need for the possibility of African American commissioned officers as long as they were "... the same standard of intelligence, grade for grade, as from the white."[101] The study also recommended not grouping African American units into division-size formations. Instead, it argued for smaller African American units attached to otherwise white formations, such as an African American infantry regiment in an otherwise white division. The study said almost nothing about African Americans in the National Guard since those units were completely under state control until they were called up to active duty. As regards the Organized Reserve (then the name of the U.S. Army Reserve), the study called for corps-area commanders to create units exclusively for African American soldiers. The 1922 study was approved by Secretary of War John W. Weeks on 23 December 1922.[102]

During the 1920s and 1930s, the subject of African American participation in a general mobilization of the Army was increasingly seen as a political hot potato. In response, the Army began to classify the sections of their mobilization plans that concerned African Americans. After 1928, to those outside the War Department, it appeared as if the Army had no plan to mobilize African Americans for the next war. The policy of classifying African American mobilization was finally rescinded in 1937. In that year, the War Department personnel division (G-1) again began to study the manpower problem. After much discussion and study, the Army G-1 recommended drafting African Americans at the same rate as their percentage of American society. They argued that the draft policy of World War I created resentment among both whites and African Americans because both believed they were harmed by the policy. African Americans believed they were underutilized, and whites believe they were over-utilized. The most logical solution, therefore, was a proportional draft.[103] While this information was not classified, it was never widely distributed and came as a surprise to many people both in and outside the War Department in 1940. The 1937 G-1 plan omitted any reference to the separate African American combat arms units attached to otherwise white larger formations, effectively rescinding that idea.

As World War II heated up in Europe and Asia, the United States prepared to defend itself with the passage of the Selective Service Act of 1940. This legislation was the first peacetime draft in American history and allowed for the induction of African Americans equal to their percentage of the national populace, which translated into 10 percent at the time. Even though this decision was made three years earlier in 1937, the U.S. armed forces resisted inducting the predetermined 10 percent of African Americans because they argued that the majority of African Americans were of lower intelligence. All incoming servicemen were given the Army General Classification Test (AGCT) an aptitude and/or intelligence test that placed them in one of five classes—Class I was the highest and Class V was the lowest. Almost 50 percent of African Americans ranked in Class V, while approximately a third scored in Class IV. For whites, under 10 percent scored in Class V and approximately 25 percent were in Class IV. On the other end of the spectrum, less than 1 percent of African Americans scored in Class I and less than 5 percent in Class II. For whites, approximately 7 percent scored in Class I and slightly less than 30 percent in Class II.[104] The poor African American scores on the AGCT resulted mostly from the poor quality of education they received in the South, where the majority then still lived. Nevertheless, the Army argued that if 10 percent of all draftees were African American, they would be forced to organize ten combat divisions completely with African American soldiers. The question for the Army throughout the war was how to utilize African American manpower while maintaining inherently inefficient segregationist policies.

The overwhelming majority of the approximately half-million African Americans who served in World War II were draftees.[105] Overall, they demonstrated the same enthusiasm (or lack thereof) for military service as their white counterparts. For many African Americans, their service was filled with irony as they were asked to defeat racism abroad, but they still endured racism at home. Unfortunately, the justified outrage from many white Americans at the word *Jude* (Jew) painted on storefronts in Germany in the 1930s did not carry over to the use of the word *Colored* on public amenities in the American South.

Despite the 1937 G-1 plan, having a policy on the books and executing that policy are two different things. After the draft began, the Army only had enough units designated for African American personnel equivalent to 5.8 percent of all draftees, significantly lower than the 10 percent who were slated for the draft. Likewise, according to the policy, African American and white percentages in combat arms and support units should be the same. However, this was not true, and, at that time, the majority of African Americans found themselves in just three Army branches—infantry, engineers, and quartermaster, while some branches had no African Americans at all. If one did not count the existing African American units in the Regular Army and National Guard there were only two new combat arms units for African Americans—the 94th Field Artillery Regiment and the 44th Coast Artillery Regiment—neither of which was activated.[106]

In the summer of 1940, the War Department Operations and Training Division (G-3) was tasked with correcting the problems of both the 1937 policy and the then-current general mobilization of African Americans. Some units, identified in the 1937 policy, were unnecessary because of motorization/modernization throughout the Army and were therefore eliminated. The G-3 recommended that all branches accept African Americans, except technical branches such as the Air Corps and Signal Corps. They also recommended organizing no African American formations larger than regimental-size. This recommendation was made because they believed that larger African American formations would lead to calls for African American general officers.[107] The G-1 and War Plans Divisions of the War Department disagreed with the G-3 plan regarding branch restrictions. In particular, the G-1 argued for strict maintenance of the 10 percent ratio in all branches of the Army. On 24 October 1940, President Roosevelt ordered U.S. Army Chief of Staff General (GEN) George C. Marshall to make it clear to geographic corps-area commanders that 10 percent of all draftees were African American regardless of their preferences.[108]

The debates about African American percentages and branches continued for a couple of years. On the eve of the attack on Pearl Harbor in December 1941, only 5 percent of all infantrymen and less than 2 percent of the Air Corps, Medical Corps, and Signal Corps were African American. At the same time, however, almost 25 percent of the Engineers, 17 percent of the Quartermaster Corps, and 15 percent of the Chemical Corps were African American.[109] Even a year later on 31 December 1942, only 5 percent of the combat arms but 21 percent of supporting arms personnel were African Americans. The only major positive development was that percentage of African Americans in the Air Corps rose to 8 percent.[110] Perhaps unsurprisingly, the percentage of African Americans in the Army never actually reached 10 percent during World War II. The highest percentage reached was 9.68 percent in September 1945, the month the war ended.[111]

One of the more controversial issues regarding African American representation in the Army was in the officer ranks. All of the prewar planning envisioned African American commissioned officers, but no definite plan for their training existed. Since all African American officer candidates were trained at Fort De Moines during World War I, most people expected something similar in the next war. To nearly everyone's surprise, the Army made two important policy decisions in 1941. First, no quotas were established for the commissioning of African American officers. They were selected the same way as white officers, based on education and ability. Second, none of the Army's Officer Candidate Schools (OCS) were segregated. "The basic and predominating consideration governing selections to OCS," according to the U.S. Army Adjutant General were "... outstanding qualities of leadership as demonstrated by actual services in the Army."[112] When these decisions became public knowledge, there were significant protests from Southerners both in and outside of the U.S. government.

In response, the Army argued that the integration of OCS was necessary on the grounds of efficiency and economy. "Our objection to separate schools is based primarily on the fact that black officer candidates are eligible from every branch of the Army, including the Armored Force and tank destroyer battalions, and it would be decidedly uneconomical to attempt to gather in one school the materiel and instructor personnel necessary to give training in all these branches."[113] This was the first example of intentional integration in the Army's history and proved a complete success. In addition to the success of this limited form of integration, the Army also demonstrated that it was willing to abandon segregation if it was proven to be inefficient and uneconomical.[114]

While President Roosevelt may have favored desegregation of the U.S. armed forces, he believed he was prevented from acting because the Democratic Party, his political power base, received approximately half of its support from white Southerners. If all Southern congressmen and senators withdrew their support from Roosevelt, it was impossible to pass any legislation. The most that Roosevelt believed possible was Executive Order 8802 signed on 25 June 1941, which prevented discrimination based on race, creed, color, or national origin by any corporation possessing a defense contract with the U.S. government.[115] Despite protests by both business owners and workers' unions, too much money was at stake to risk the government's wrath. Ironically, the South was generally less affected by the executive order because it had less industry than the North.

The majority of the U.S. armed forces' segregated units during World War II were found in the Army and, ultimately, African Americans were represented in every one of the Army's combat and support arms. Paradoxically, in the segregated Army, African Americans found opportunities for leadership unparalleled in the rest of American society at the time. This situation was all the more incongruous since there were less than five thousand African Americans in just four units in the prewar Army.

While African Americans had enjoyed a long history of service in the U.S. armed forces, this history was checkered by intolerance. The Army's policy toward African Americans was generally consistent, while restrictive. The Navy and Coast Guard admitted African Americans on and off almost since their beginnings, though policy shifts occurred when the political winds changed. Before World War II, the Marine Corps, on the other hand, never admitted African Americans in its entire existence. The sheer scale of World War II made it a learning experience for all of the U.S. armed forces when it came to African Americans, their potential, and their place in American society.

Section II

Grunts

Chapter 2

Infantry

I n the U.S. Army, the largest number and percentage of African Americans serving as combat soldiers were infantrymen. By the end of the war, more than twenty thousand African American infantrymen had fought in Europe and the Pacific. Not only did many African Americans serve in the infantry, but some of them were part of an experiment that involved the creation of the first racially integrated combat units in American history. This experiment was so successful that it, in part, was used to justify President Harry S. Truman's decision to integrate the U.S. armed forces in 1948. Undoubtedly, African American service in the infantry was the single most important example of their combat arms' service during World War II.

After the outbreak of World War II in Europe and Asia, there was a significant discussion among Army leadership regarding African Americans. While the decision was already made to draft African Americans at a percentage equal to their representation in American society (then 10 percent), the Army had to decide where African Americans could best serve. Overwhelmingly African American soldiers served in menial, physically demanding, support positions. Nevertheless, the African American press and public applied pressure to allow African American representation in every branch of the Army. This representation was token in some branches, the most obvious example was the mere three tank battalions in the Armored Force. However, of all the combat arms branches in the Army, none saw greater African American service than the infantry. By the end of the war, two infantry divisions and five separate infantry regiments were organized with African American company-grade officers and enlisted soldiers.

As National Guard and Organized Reserve units began to be activated before the actual American declaration of war, the Army's inherent racial prejudice quickly came to the surface. Most troubling was the case of the 8th Illinois Infantry Regiment, which served during World War I as the 370th Infantry Regiment. When the 8th Illinois was inducted into federal service on 6 January 1941, it was redesignated the 184th Field Artillery Regiment.[1] This decision came as a shock to the regiment as well as wasted the experience of trained infantrymen, some of whom were even combat veterans of World War I. To compound the problem, the regiment's commander, who was also a member of the Illinois state legislature, was forced to resign his colonelcy and retire from the National Guard because he could not legally both serve on active duty and remain in the legislature. The lieutenant colonel who was the Illinois governor's choice as the new commander was then found physically disqualified for active duty and a disagreement ensued regarding who should command the regiment. The African American community of Chicago, where the regiment was based, feared that the Army would select a white Regular Army officer to command the regiment, as they did during World War I. Ultimately, another African American lieutenant colonel from the regiment was selected to command but the four months of indecision were certainly detrimental to a regiment that was also completely retraining in a more technical military specialty.[2]

On 15 October 1942, the 92nd Infantry Division was reactivated with the 365th, 370th, and 371st Infantry Regiments. The 366th Infantry Regiment was also attached to the division from 21 November 1944 until 25 February 1945.[3] The 366th Infantry was particularly notable because it contained no white soldiers and even the regiment's colonel, Howard D. Queen, was African American. The division's commander from its activation to the end of the war, MG Edward M. "Ned" Almond, was a controversial choice. A native Virginian and a graduate of the Virginia Military Institute (VMI),

Headquarters staff of the 92nd Infantry Division established itself in an ancient Greek temple of Neptune (built about 700 B.C.) in Italy. At the improvised desks (*front to back*): SGTs James Shellman, Gilbert A. Terry, John W. Phoenix, Curtis A. Richardson, and Leslie B. Wood. In front of the desks (*front to back*): TSG Gordon A. Scott, Master Sergeant (MSG) Walter C. Jackson, SGT David D. Jones, and Warrant Officer Carlyle M. Tucker. (NARA)

Almond was highly regarded by senior Army officers, including Chief of Staff and fellow VMI alumnus Marshall. While a certain level of paternalism toward African Americans was common with most whites of the period regardless of what part of the country they originated, the choice of Almond reflected the Army's racist notion that only Southern whites were suitable to command African American units because they were the only ones who "knew how to handle" African Americans.[4] Almond's first command assignment of World War II was as the assistant division commander of the African American 93rd Infantry Division from March to August 1942. While he served in that position, the division commander was MG Charles P. Hall, a native of Mississippi, and the division's senior artillery officer, BG William Spence, was a native of North Carolina—thus maintaining a white Southern senior command structure.

An IG investigation in 1942 stated that the Army was assigning mediocre officers to command African American units, which resulted in problems for these units. Marshall commented on the report:

> Difficulty in handling colored troops almost without exception can be attributed to a lack of knack on the part of officers assigned to this duty. Officers must be carefully selected, with the primary requirement the ability to handle negroes [*sic*]. Such officers can accomplish much, whereas officers who may be better trained in a military way, but without the knack, not only fail in accomplishing the task but create the conditions which breed trouble.[5]

Evidently, white Southerners automatically had the "knack," because no change was made in the Army's unofficial policy of almost exclusively assigning Southern officers to African American units and, unsurprisingly, the quality of those officers never improved.

Even people outside of the African American community questioned Marshall's decision to appoint Almond as a division commander, especially because he had so little command experience. While Almond had proved a successful officer in staff, training, and education settings, his lack of time in command was troubling. While that formula (little command experience but

Combat patrol from the 92nd Infantry Division three miles north of Lucca, Italy. The antitank team, equipped with a bazooka, has just fired a round at a target three hundred yards away. (NARA)

much time in staff, training, and education) proved successful with generals such as Dwight D. Eisenhower and Omar N. Bradley, Almond was the exception that proved the rule. When the 92nd Infantry Division finally entered combat, Almond was a micro-manager, exhibited poor decision-making, and then blamed every failure of himself and other white officers on the African American company-grade officers and/or soldiers. He managed to escape with his reputation largely intact because of white societal contempt toward his African American soldiers. However, Almond's equally poor performance as the X Corps commander during the Korean War finally ended his military career.[6] Almond's racist attitude continued when he commanded the X Corps. He infamously told Lieutenant Colonel (LTC) Don Carlos Faith, commander of the 1st Battalion, 32nd Infantry Regiment, and later posthumous Medal of Honor recipient for his actions in a failed effort to stem the Chinese invasion of Korea, "Don't let a bunch of goddamn Chinese laundrymen stop you!"[7] Interestingly, even Almond's wife, Margaret Crook Almond, was accused of racist behavior—she called an African American Women's Army Auxiliary Corps (WAAC) telephone operator a "nigger."[8]

While the men of the 92nd Infantry Division represented less than 2 percent of the African Americans in the Army, they received more attention in the press, both white and African American, than any other African American servicemen.[9] Unsurprisingly, just as in World War I, no community in America wanted approximately fifteen thousand African American combat soldiers to train near them during World War II. Therefore, the 92nd Infantry Division began training at multiple locations rather than at a single post as almost all white divisions did. The division headquarters (HQ), 600th Field Artillery Battalion, and smaller divisional units trained at Fort McClellan, Alabama. The 365th Infantry Regiment and the 597th Field Artillery Battalion trained at Camp Atterbury, Indiana. The 370th Infantry Regiment[10] and the 598th Field Artillery Battalion trained at Camp Breckenridge, Kentucky. Lastly, the 371st Infantry Regiment and the 599th Field Artillery Battalion trained at Camp Robinson, Arkansas.[11]

To his credit, Almond toured all four training posts even before his troops arrived. Fort McClellan lacked mess halls and barracks for his troops and the post's hospital and laundry were ranked as "sorely deficient." Construction of barracks was five weeks behind schedule at Camp Robinson and the post's quartermaster and ordnance officers had not received orders to issue equipment to the 92nd Infantry's subordinate units. Camp Atterbury had the best situation in both post facilities and the local community as there were African American United Services Organization (USO) Clubs in Indianapolis and Franklin. The worst situation was at Camp Breckenridge as there were few facilities available for the 92nd Infantry's soldiers and the post commander was only listed as merely "cooperative."[12] During the months of separate training, the three regiments developed their own particular unit cultures—some good, some bad—which made things more difficult when the division was finally united. Unfortunately, not until May 1943 was the division finally able to assemble at a single post: Fort Huachuca, Arizona, in the desert away from white communities.

An 81-mm mortar crew of the 92nd Infantry Division in action near Massa, Italy. (NARA)

After nine months of division-level training, the 92nd Infantry took part in maneuvers in Louisiana from February to April 1944. In keeping with Almond's paternalistic attitude toward his men, he was quick to defend them when civilians interfered. One such incident occurred during the Louisiana maneuvers. As one of the division's infantry platoons tried to maneuver through a small town, they were stopped at a roadblock manned by the local sheriff and his posse. Almond was summoned to deal with the situation and was told by the sheriff that his African American troops were not allowed in the town. In response, Almond told his soldiers, "Just run that damn tank through that building over there."[13] Reportedly half the buildings on the town's main street were partially or completely destroyed, which the government was forced to pay for, but no one bothered his troops after that. The division received a grade of "very satisfactory" after the maneuvers, which made it eligible for deployment to combat.

During the 92nd Infantry Division's training, the African American company-grade officers and enlisted men were continually subjected to social discrimination as well as the Army's policy of segregation. Regardless of where they were stationed, African Americans were treated as a threat rather than welcomed by the surrounding white communities. Since the division's white field grade officers were almost all Southerners, there was almost no informal interaction between field grade officers and African American company-grade officers, as well as virtually no interaction between those field grade officers and the African American enlisted men. This separation resulted in a feeling that the white leadership of the division either did not know or did not care what happened to their subordinates. Almond maintained a strict policy that amounted to: "No black officers commanding companies, battalions or regiments and no black staff officers at battalion level or above."[14] As a result, competent African American officers were frequently transferred out of the division when they were promoted to prevent them from becoming commanders.

It is difficult for people who grew up after the Civil Rights movement to understand Almond's paternalism, as it is now viewed merely as racism. Interestingly, Almond removed overtly racist officers. The most senior officer Almond relieved for racism was COL Sterling A. Wood, the commander of the 371st Infantry Regiment. While the regiments were still separated, Almond ordered all officers' messes integrated, but Wood refused to do so and was relieved of command. However, this was the last act in a series of racist incidents involving Wood. He was such an avowed racist that his comments even shocked other white officers, and most infamously stated to his African American soldiers: "You people constitute ten percent of the population of this country, and I'm going to see to it you suffer ten percent of the casualties."[15] Unsurprisingly, despite his relief of command, the Army quickly reassigned Wood and he later commanded the 313th Infantry Regiment, 79th Infantry Division, in combat and then became a brigadier general during the Korean War.

African American BG Benjamin O. Davis, Sr., performed an IG tour of the 92nd Infantry Division in 1943. In his report stated: "General Almond has, in the opinion of the inspector general, overlooked the human element in the training of his Division. ... Apparently not enough consideration has been given to the maintenance of a racial understanding between white and

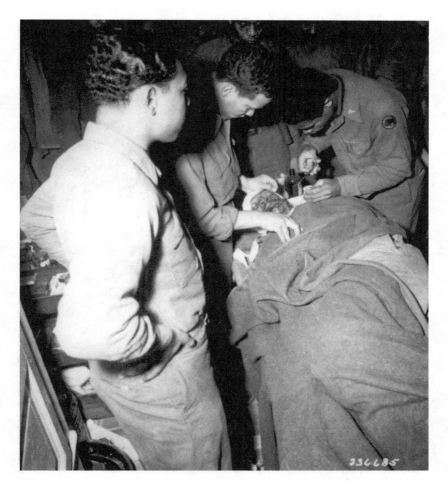

On 10 February 1945, CPT Ezekia Smith, a company commander in the 370th Infantry Regiment, 92nd Infantry Division, received treatment after receiving shell fragments in his face and shoulders near Querceta, Italy. (NARA)

colored officers and men."[16] Davis found that, during the period between 1 January and 1 July 1943, the division's white lieutenants were promoted at a significantly higher rate (39 percent) than African American lieutenants (8 percent).[17] After Davis filed his report, the War Department analyzed the officer promotion rates throughout the Army and found that approximately

On 21 March 1945, PVT Jonathan Hoag, 92nd Infantry Division, was awarded the *Croix de Guerre* by GEN Alphonse P. Juin, commanding general of the French Expeditionary Corps in Italy, for courage while treating wounded, even though he, himself, was wounded. (NARA)

25 percent of African American officers were eligible for, but had not received, a promotion.[18] Based on these findings, the War Department changed its policy regarding African American officers, who could now serve with any unit composed of African American enlisted men rather than only certain types of units.

Another major controversy regarding the 92nd Infantry Division was the question of African American soldiers' intellectual abilities. The division personnel officer (G1), MAJ Carthal F. Mock, Jr., prepared a report in December 1942 entitled, "Analytical Study of the Mentality and Capabilities of Enlisted Men of 92nd Infantry Division." Of the enlisted men on hand at that time, 0.1 percent were ranked in Class I, the highest category of the AGCT. Only 2.5 percent ranked in Class II and 10.4 percent were in Class III. At the lower end of the spectrum, 45 percent ranked in Class IV and 42 percent ranked in Class V. At the same time, the averages in six comparable white infantry divisions (30th, 79th, 80th, 81st, 83rd, and 98th Infantry) were 3.5 percent Class I, 18.8 percent Class II, 32.5 percent Class III, 34.6 percent Class IV, and 10.6 percent Class V. This problem quite clearly stemmed from the poor education system in the American South, where the majority of African American soldiers then came from. In fact, of the 14,939 soldiers then in the division, 2037 were illiterate to one degree or another.[19] These soldiers' lack of education created major problems in preparing the division for combat.

Yet another problem for the 92nd Infantry Division was inadequately trained or sometimes untrainable personnel. On this topic, Mock prepared another memorandum entitled "Analysis of Defective Personnel with Combat Units." The memo argued that "defective" personnel were mistakenly drafted, received basic training, and then passed on to combat units. Mock argued that the burden of dealing with these "defective" personnel was unfairly placed on combat units rather than on the initial reception centers. For the 92nd Infantry, the problem amounted to replacement soldiers who were 9 percent "physically defective," 1 percent "inapt or slow learners," and 12 percent illiterate. Mock believed that resources were wasted dealing with this problem. "Salvage of this personnel requires services of 30 officers and 37 enlisted men. Where salvage is not feasible, additional administrative personnel are required to make necessary disposition."[20] Mock considered the problem of "physical defectives" the greatest problem for the division. "99% of this class personnel, when inducted, should never have been assigned to a combat unit."[21] Interestingly, the issue of race was never mentioned in the memo and white units also experienced some of these same problems during World War II because of the sheer scale of the draft.

A third study prepared by Mock, "Removal of Unqualified Commissioned Personnel," was classified as "Confidential" because of its content. Mock made clear the study's position before the first page has ended. "The negro race mentality is of slower grade than that of the white race."[22] The study then provided statistics based on the AGCT and, interestingly, argued that the soldiers of the 92nd Infantry were less intelligent than the national average of African Americans. "Lack of initiative, lack of interest, lack of ambition, short-visioned, lower standards of living (political, economic, social and religious), distaste for hardships or adventure,—all these tend to create an inertia within the negro individual from which it is difficult to shake him loose."[23] The study then tried to provide proof.

> The present negro [*sic*] race within the US sprang from African tribes which were not aggressive or war-like as were other contemporary tribes. Consequently, these tribes were easily the prey of other tribes who sold them in chains to the slave dealers who sailed to the African coast from the US. ... From the above can be stated that the present negro [*sic*] race is not military minded nor genetically suited for the military.[24]

After making these statements, which certainly were influenced by the Eugenics movement, Mock then seemed to become more thoughtful.

> The military restricts movement and thought along certain lines, which to a people just released from slavery may seem a form of bondage. ... Because of regional outlooks existing in this country, particularly in the South, the negro [*sic*], although given the same liberties as the white, may not enjoy them at the same time and place as the white man. The negro [*sic*] does not understand the reason for the lack of acceptance by the white man. He does not see that the white race also does not accept other races, and frequently does not accept foreigners within the white race.[25]

Finally, Mock got to the point of the study by recommending what type of officer was most effective at leading African American troops.

Rather than recommending white officers and rejecting African American officers, the study recommends four qualifications to look for in the appropriate officers.

(1)   Vigorous physically and mentally
(2)   Aggressiveness and force
(3)   Optimism and cheerfulness
(4)   Sense of justice and fair-play[26]

The study ended by arguing that these qualifications were most often found in young officers. Mock ultimately argued that higher standards were necessary for officers leading African American soldiers than those leading white soldiers, which was generally the complete opposite of the actual selection process.

On 26 June 1944, the first element of the 92nd Infantry Division deployed to Italy—the 370th Regimental Combat Team (RCT), made up of the 370th Infantry Regiment, the 598th Field Artillery Battalion, Company B, 317th Engineer Combat Battalion, Company B, 317th Medical Battalion, and detachments of quartermaster, signals, military police, and ordnance support units.[27] On 30 July 1944, the 370th RCT arrived in Naples, Italy, and engaged in orientation and training until 23 August. The RCT entered combat on 24 August and remained attached to the 1st Armored Division, IV Corps, U.S. Fifth Army, for 42 days until 5 October 1944.[28] The 370th RCT's first major combat operation began on 1 September, when they joined the rest of the IV Corps in crossing the Arno River. The RCT was almost continuously engaged from 1 September until 5 October. During that period, they were often the lead element of the IV Corps, advanced 30 miles against German troops, and continually distinguish themselves by valor. During 42 days on the line, the 370th suffered 19 KIA, 225 WIA, and 19 missing in action (MIA).[29]

On 5 October 1944, the 370th RCT was detached from the 1st Armored Division and redesignated as Task Force 92 (TF-92), the term usually reserved for a reinforced division, because Almond had arrived in Italy and took direct control. Despite its small size, only an RCT with a couple attached units (the 2nd Armored Group functioning as HQ for the white 434th and 435th Antiaircraft Artillery Automatic Weapons Battalions—being used as infantry), TF-92 was now responsible for a six-mile front with the Italian coastline on its left and rugged mountains in the front and right. The next major challenge was an assault against the German-engineered Gothic Line, which extended across the Italian Peninsula from one side to another. The Gothic Line was constructed by Italian laborers and a Slovak technical brigade under German supervision—since the Italian government officially change sides in September 1943.[30] The Germans had constructed this defensive line to allow them to defend the last portion of Italy they still occupied. Initially, TF-92's opponent in the Gothic Line was the 42nd *Jaeger* Division, but they were relieved on 24 October and replaced by the 148th Reserve Infantry Division. There were also Italian units in the Gothic Line and their quality had improved by this point in the war because most were devoted fascists who volunteered to fight rather than draftees.[31] For the next few weeks, TF-92 engaged in aggressive patrolling along the Gothic Line in hopes of disrupting the enemy's defenses and capturing prisoners to gain valuable intelligence.[32]

Beginning on 1 November 1944, the 371st Infantry Regiment entered the line and relieved the 370th Infantry Regiment, who were in combat since August. The final regiment of the division, the 365th Infantry Regiment, began to enter the line on 8 November. TF-92 was now complete. Between 6 and 19 November, the 370th Infantry advanced more than three miles over difficult terrain to seize Castelnuovo. At the same time, the 365th and 371st Infantry Regiments began patrolling their sectors to familiarize themselves with the terrain. On 4 December, the 365th Infantry Regiment was relieved from the 92nd Infantry Division and attached to the 88th Infantry Division. To increase the strength of the 92nd Infantry, the 366th Infantry Regiment, which had spent the previous eight months guarding airbases in southern Italy, was attached to the division.[33] The regiment's African American commander, COL Howard D. Queen, protested in writing that his unit required further training before entering combat because of their long period of military police-style duty, but his request was denied.[34] Almond's attitude toward the regiment was very negative from the first day. Future U.S. Senator Edward W. Brooke related that, in his welcoming speech to the regiment, Almond said: "Your Negro friends and your Negroes Press back home in the

States have been clamoring for you to go into combat. Well, since you ask for it, let's see how you like it. You can believe I will make you fight and suffer your share of casualties."[35] Only two weeks after joining the division, Queen requested relief of his command due to physical and mental strain, a decision which caused frustration among the soldiers of the regiment. While Queen did have legitimate health issues, most of the regiment's officers believed he was driven away by Almond's behavior.

On 26 December 1944, a powerful German counterattack, the lead elements of whom disguised themselves as Italian partisans, caused the 2nd Battalion, 366th Infantry, and the 1st Battalion, 370th Infantry, to retreat from their defensive positions. Many soldiers of these battalions were engaged in desperate fighting, which was at times hand to hand. Most notable of these defenders was 1LT John R. Fox, an officer of the Cannon Company, 366th Infantry. Fox was acting as a forward observer for the 598th Field Artillery Battalion, but when American infantrymen withdrew, he and his observation team remained behind on the second floor of a house to direct defensive artillery fire. He continued to call in artillery closer and closer to his position. When Fox requested what turned out to be the final artillery barrage, the 598th Field Artillery's commander objected because the barrage might hit the American observation team. In his last communication, Fox said, "Fire it! There's more of them than there are of us. Give them hell!" When the bodies of Fox and his team were recovered, approximately one hundred dead Germans surrounded their position. The 92nd Infantry Division's artillery commander, BG William H. Colbern, recommended Fox for the DSC. The paperwork for the decoration never left the division nor was it ever acted upon. Since it seems rather unlikely that someone would lose paperwork initiated by a general officer, it appears that Almond himself stopped the process. Almond personally argued against decorations for "failed missions." After almost forty years of campaigning, Fox's widow finally received his decoration in 1982.[36] Then, in 1997, based on the recommendation of a board of historians, Fox's DSC was upgraded to the Medal of Honor.[37]

Despite the heroism of Fox and many other soldiers, the next day the remainder of the 366th Infantry abandoned its defensive positions, and, in one case, an abandoned American 57 mm cannon was turned against the retreating troops by the Germans.[38] The Indian 8th Division was forced to pass through the retreating Americans to drive back the Germans. This battle highlighted the problems that plagued the 92nd Infantry Division for the remainder of the war—poor leadership, poor training (especially among replacements), and poor planning and preparation (which usually did not include African American company-grade officers and NCOs input). Some units fought well, but their gains were seldom capitalized on, while others fought poorly, but were repeatedly send back into combat to "force" them to get better.

The retreat of the 366th Infantry Regiment and subsequent repositioning of the 92nd Infantry Division caused such disruption in the Fifth Army's lines that the plans for a renewed winter offensive were postponed. As such, both Fifth Army commander GEN Mark W. Clark and IV Corps commander LTG Lucian K. Truscott were quick to blame the 92nd Infantry and their post-war memoirs made their opinions plain. Clark said of the combat struggles by the 92nd Infantry, "... it was a bad performance ..."[39] To his credit, however, he also wrote that it was dishonest and unfair to, "... overlook the serious handicaps which they had to overcome."[40] He cited lack of education and illiteracy as major problems, but also mentioned the bravery of individual African American officers and men as well as various small units within the division. Truscott stated that when struck by the German attack, the soldiers of the 92nd Infantry, "... 'melted away'—a term which was to be frequently used in describing actions of colored troops."[41] Nevertheless, Truscott also acknowledged the problems African American soldiers had to deal with ("... environment, education, economic and social ills ..."[42]) and particularly cited the poor AGCT scores of the division. Truscott argued that at the time there was a consensus among white leadership that some level of integration was necessary, the question was what proportion or ratio that should take.[43] Almond generally agreed with his superiors about the division's performance, but interestingly neither he nor any of his subordinate white officers received any blame. Almond's explanation for what happened was:

The white man ... is willing to die for patriotic reasons. The Negro is not. No white man wants to be accused of leaving the battle line.

The Negro doesn't care. ... People think that being from the south
we don't like Negroes. Not at all. But we understand his capabilities.
And we don't want to sit at the table with them.[44]

Interestingly, the commander of the German 148th Reserve Infantry Division,
Generalleutnant Otto Fretter-Pico, argued that the defeat on 26 December
had nothing to do with the Allied troops and everything to do with their
positioning. "The weakness of your deployment in the Serchio Valley at the
time of my attack on 26 December 1944, was that your troops were deployed
on a front which was too long for the number of men available, and your
reserves were too far in the rear areas which prevented their being deployed
immediately."[45]

On 7 January 1945, the 365th Infantry Regiment returned to the 92nd
Infantry, and, for almost a month, the division trained and reorganized to
go on the offensive. The next major offensive for the division began on
8 February. The plan was to improve the division's positioning by capturing
key features in the hills and then to advance up the Serchio Valley. The four
infantry regiments of the division were to advance in line supported by tanks
from the 758th and the 760th Tank Battalions and tank destroyers from
the 701st Tank Destroyer Battalion. However, from the moment the attack
began the division was hampered by numerous antipersonnel and antitank
mines and deadly accurate artillery fire from well-concealed and pre-sighted
German guns. The terrain caused unit formations to break up during the
advance, especially in the rain and low light conditions. Large numbers of
"stragglers" were a continual problem for the division. "Stragglers" were
individual soldiers who, on purpose or by accident, became detached from
their units. While most legitimately became lost during the offensive, some
became lost intentionally to avoid combat. It is important to note that almost
all of these "stragglers" ultimately returned to the units, and it was not an
issue of desertion. At the same time, individual companies often engaged in
hand-to-hand combat to seize terrain objectives but were then thrown back
by German counterattacks for lack of reinforcement. The tanks and tank
destroyers were particularly hard hit by mines and artillery fire. During the
crossing of the Cinquale Canal, two tanks were disabled almost immediately

by mines, which then blocked the movement of any following tanks. Engineers were prevented from building a bridge over the canal or clearing the minefields because of German artillery.[46] To make matters worse, air support was unavailable because of poor weather.

On 11 February, after four costly and relatively fruitless days of combat, the IV Corps ordered the 92nd Infantry to pull back, largely abandoning their generally untenable positions. Casualties from the four-day offensive were high. The 758th Tank Battalion lost eight tanks,[47] while the 760th Tank Battalion lost sixteen tanks.[48] The 365th Infantry Regiment lost 1 officer and 52 enlisted men KIA and 8 officers and 243 enlisted men WIA.[49] The 370th Infantry Regiment lost 3 officers and 13 enlisted men KIA and 12 officers and 184 enlisted men WIA. The 371st Infantry Regiment lost 4 officers (including the commander of its 3rd Battalion) and 17 enlisted men KIA and four officers and 104 enlisted men WIA. The 366th Infantry Regiment suffered the highest casualties of the four regiments in the division. The regiment lost 347 officers and men KIA (including the commander of its 3rd Battalion), WIA, or MIA, or about a third of the total division casualties.[50] Most disturbing was that the 3rd Battalion, 366th Infantry Regiment lost 260 men as "stragglers" on 10 February alone.[51]

The offensive produced no appreciable gains but caused significant casualties in men and losses in equipment. The number of officers lost in combat was particularly distressing, including two battalion commanders. All of the criticisms of the division's performance centered on the performance of African American soldiers, while no discussion was given to the white leadership's planning and preparations for the offensive. Oddly, the devastating loss of sixteen tanks by the white 760th Tank Battalion received almost no acknowledgment during the excoriation of the division's African American soldiers. There were many parallels between the 92nd Infantry's performance and that of the white 36th Infantry Division at the Rapido River a little more than a year earlier in January 1944. The 36th Infantry was a Texas National Guard unit that suffered more than two thousand casualties during a river crossing operation in Italy also ordered by Clark.[52] Both operations included American divisions fighting on difficult terrain against entrenched German positions with presighted artillery. Likewise, there were comparisons to other operations on the Italian Peninsula involving British Imperial and Polish troops such as the multiple assaults against Monte Cassino. Lastly, once again the commander of the German 148th Reserve Infantry Division, *Generalleutnant* Otto Fretter-Pico, the 92nd Infantry's main opponent, expressed more respect for the division than their commander. He classified the 92nd Infantry as "... a fairly good Division..."[53]

Perhaps unsurprisingly, Almond escaped any responsibility for his division's performance. As at least one historian commented, "Had Almond commanded a white division he surely would have been relieved of command."[54] However, all of his superiors were only too willing to blame the division's African American soldiers and allow the white leadership to escape any scrutiny. Both Almond and Truscott now believed the 92nd Infantry Division was incapable of further offensive action as it was then organized. An after-action review signed by Truscott stated:

> The failure of this operation is marked by the failure of the infantry and engineers of the 92nd division. ... The infantry of this division lacks the emotional and mental stability necessary for combat. I do not believe that further training under present conditions will ever make this division into a unit capable of offensive operation.[55]

Unfortunately, Truscott and Clark were short on manpower and could not afford to get rid of the 92nd Infantry. At this point, the Fifth Army was so desperate for manpower that it included the Brazilian Expeditionary Force (a division-plus-sized formation), the 6th South African Armoured Division, the British XIII Corps, and various Italian formations. Somehow, the 92nd Infantry needed to stay on the battlefield.

One of the biggest problems for the 92nd Infantry Division throughout the war was the lack of adequately trained and available replacements for soldiers killed or seriously wounded in combat. African American replacement soldiers were not considered a priority when it came to shipping. Likewise, when African American replacements did arrive in theater, they were seldom trained as infantrymen. The result was that the 92nd Infantry was usually understrength and often forced to provide additional training before using replacements in combat.[56] Neither of these were problems for white units, especially regarding training, because white replacements were usually trained as infantrymen. This lack of properly trained replacements may help to explain the division's failed offensive in February. Truman K. Gibson, Jr., a civilian advisor on African American issues to Secretary of War Henry L. Stimson, later noted that approximately twenty-six hundred replacements, most of whom came from support units already in the ETO, transferred to the 92nd Infantry in the weeks before the failed offensive. Most had no infantry training and some said they had never fired a rifle before.

> 'No other single observation was repeated [by company officers] in more instances than this one.' ... Furthermore, 89 percent of the replacement troops fell in the two bottom categories of the Army General Classification Test. The Ninety-second was manned by many troops who had the bare minimum of schooling and who were illiterate.[57]

While Almond denied that untrained soldiers were sent into combat, this was disputed by even his white company-grade officers.

In a message to Eisenhower, Marshall incorrectly described the 92nd Infantry's offensive as:

> ... heavily supported if by a year, plentiful ammunition and tanks. It met little opposition in most parts of the front but the infantry will literally dissolved each night abandoning equipment and even clothing in some cases. ... The command and staff are superior. But as matters now stand, the division is not only of little value but weakens the front ... We cannot afford this wastage of effort and jeopardy of the front ...[58]

Marshall then proposed a plan to recycle the men of the 92nd Infantry Division and add some other units to create a more viable division.[59] During March 1945, the division underwent a thorough reorganization. On 28 March 1945, the 366th Infantry Regiment, which was never formally part of the division and was always held in contempt by the division's white leadership owing to the regiment's exclusively African American officers, was disbanded and its personnel used to form the 224th and 226th Engineer General Service Regiments, which effectively reduced the combat veterans of the regiment to nothing more than unskilled laborers. The decision to not even comb this combat-experienced regiment for in its best officers, NCOs, and enlisted men before disbanding the regiment demonstrated the utter scorn for this unit by the white leadership of the 92nd Infantry. The 365th Infantry Regiment became a training unit for replacements before they were sent into combat. The 371st Infantry Regiment became a rear-area security unit, principally guarding German and Italian prisoners of war (POWs).[60] Lastly, the 370th Infantry Regiment, which had performed better in combat than any of the other three regiments, remained as a combat unit but was augmented with the best officers and men from the 365th and 371st Infantry Regiments.[61] Between 24 February and 17 March, 62 officers, one warrant officer, and 1264 enlisted men were transferred out of the 370th Infantry. During that same time, 70 officers, one warrant officer, and 1358 enlisted men were transferred in.[62] Virtually no African American officers over the rank of 1st lieutenant were found in the "new" 370th Infantry. Despite all of these transfers, Almond was not hopeful about the "new" regiment in combat. "… I do not visualize that the combat reliability of the newly revitalized 370th Infantry will be greatly raised."[63] The excellent performance of the 370th Infantry while attached to the 1st Armored Division seems to have been completely forgotten the 92nd Infantry's senior leadership. Perhaps less prejudiced senior white leadership had resulted in superior performance on the part of the regiment. It is also interesting to note that the excellent performance of most of the non-infantry subordinate units of the 92nd Infantry was seldom mentioned, especially given that some units (including two field artillery battalions) were officered and manned entirely by African Americans.

These decisions left the 92nd Infantry Division with only one-third of its authorized infantry strength. The remaining infantry strength for the division came from unlikely sources. The 92nd Infantry added the Japanese American-manned 442nd RCT, made up of the 442nd Infantry Regiment, the 522nd Field Artillery Battalion, and the 232nd Engineer Company. The 442nd RCT was highly respected for its combat performance and became the most decorated unit of its size in the entire Army during World War II. However, no white division commander wanted them in his division. Thus, attaching them to the 92nd Infantry solved two problems—manpower shortage in the division and a home for the Japanese Americans. Some members of the 442nd RCT were sympathetic to the plight of the African American soldiers. Technical Sergeant Al Takahashi said, "You can't blame them for not fighting, the way they treated them. God, they treated them terrible."[64] The final infantry regiment for the division was a completely new formation created expressly for this purpose. The 473rd Infantry Regiment was formed from several units, some of whom had prior experience with the 92nd Infantry. The HQ and HQ Company (HHC), 2nd Armored Group, became the regimental HHC. The white 434th and 435th Antiaircraft Artillery Automatic Weapons Battalions, both of which had previously suffered casualties while serving as infantrymen attached to the 92nd Infantry, were used to form the regiment's 1st Battalion, Cannon Company, and Antitank Company. Lastly, the white 532nd and 900th Antiaircraft Artillery Automatic Weapons Battalions were converted to infantrymen and used to form the regiment's 2nd and 3rd Battalions respectively.[65]

Amid all this reorganization, from 1 to 8 March 1945, Gibson arrived for a visit with the 92nd Infantry Division. Unsurprisingly, all of the information presented to Gibson laid the blame for failure in the division's two combat operations at the feet of African American officers and enlisted men with no mention of the white leadership. Gibson decided to investigate himself by interviewing approximately eight hundred company-grade officers as well as several hundred of the division's enlisted soldiers.

In a preliminary report prepared for MG Otto L. Nelson, the deputy commander of the Mediterranean Theater of Operations, dated 12 March 1945, Gibson argued that one of the most important issues he encountered in his discussions with the officers of the 92nd Infantry was the biased promotion policy for African American officers, a situation which was mentioned to him by both white and African American officers. He noted that the reorganization of the 370th Infantry Regiment resulted in all African American company commanders replaced by white officers. Despite this, the African

American officers who were replaced were not brought before reclassification boards, which should have happened if they were truly incompetent. Gibson also criticized the continued segregationist policies in the division. He related a story of a white captain who attempted to bring two of his African American subordinate officers into a white Officer's Club and was then reprimanded for "an improper social attitude." Another example of this segregation was a lack of African American officers serving in staff positions above the battalion level. Gibson also discussed the problem of "melting away" also known as "stragglers." Both white and African American officers discussed this problem with him and agreed that there was little or no pattern in why this happened. Lastly, Gibson argued that more was necessary to stimulate racial pride among the division's soldiers, most particularly among those soldiers in the lowest two AGCT classes who needed the most encouragement to feel proud of themselves and their status as Americans.[66]

In the "Discussion" portion of his comments, Gibson homed in on the poor quality and training of the replacement troops received by the 92nd Infantry. Of the 2,600 replacements received by the division as of his visit, only 350 men had received infantry training. Additionally, 89 percent of the replacements were in Classes IV or V of the AGCT, with approximately two-thirds in Class V. This lack of training and education/intellectual ability made it very difficult for the division to maintain unit troop strengths and proficiency. Gibson also noted that the Army followed the same training procedures and methods for both white and African American replacements.[67]

In the "Conclusion" portion of his comments, Gibson argued that Almond and his staff were genuinely interested in the success of the 92nd Infantry Division because success would echo to their credit. He once again brought up the disproportionate numbers of soldiers in Classes IV or V of the AGCT and that far too many soldiers were sent to the division without any infantry training. Gibson believed that the normal training procedures used for the rest of the Army were inappropriate in the 92nd Infantry because of the lack of education and/or intellectual ability among the division's soldiers. He blamed this problem on the fact that roughly 75 percent of all African Americans in the Army were from the South and, therefore, had limited educational opportunities. Gibson also argued that the Southern origins of the soldiers greatly affected their sense of racial and national pride. He argued for greater promotion of African American officers, who could then be responsible for developing a program to properly instill racial and national pride in the men of the division.[68]

Unfortunately, on 14 March, Gibson gave a press conference in Rome which caused a severe backlash. During this press conference, he repeated the general narrative of the division's history and its combat performance. Gibson mentioned that the division had experienced problems with "stragglers." Although he mentioned that similar problems were experienced in white divisions and this was only one of roughly fifteen issues he discussed at the press conference, the African American press seized on his comments and almost universally denounced him.[69] African American newspapers in the United States widely called for Gibson's resignation and referred to him as an "Uncle Tom." Adam Clayton Powell, Jr., an African American U.S. Congressman from New York, publicly accused Gibson of smearing the men of the 92nd Infantry Division. Only a few newspapers and authors took Gibson's comments in context. Gibson later received a letter from LTC Marcus H. Ray, the African American commander of the 600th Field Artillery Battalion in the 92nd Infantry Division, regarding his published comments. Ray agreed with Gibson's conclusions about the division and then detailed the reasons he believed they were destined to fail.

It is my considered opinion that the 92d, at the best, was doomed to a mediocre performance of combat duties from its very inception. The undercurrent of racial antipathies, mistrusts and preconceived prejudices made for an unhealthy beginning. The failure to promote worthwhile Negroes and the giving of preferred assignments to white officers made tor logical resentments. I do not believe that enough thought was given to the selection of white officers to serve with the 92d and further, that the common American error was made of assuming that Southern white men understand Negroes. In white officered units, those men who fit into the Southern pattern are pushed and promoted regardless of capabilities and those Negroes who exhibit the manliness, self-reliance, and self-respect which are the 'sine qua non' in white units, are humiliated and discouraged. In the two Artillery Battalions of the Division, officered by Negroes, it was necessary to reduce large numbers of Noncommissioned officers because they held rank only because they fitted the 'pattern.' Their subordinates resented and disrespected them—justly so. I was astounded by the willingness of the white officers who preceded us to place their own lives in a hazardous position in order to have tractable Negroes around them. ... In the main, I don't believe the junior officers guilty of faulty judgment or responsible for tactical failures. Soldiers do as ordered but when plans sent to them for execution from higher headquarters are incomplete, inaccurate, and unintelligible, there is inevitable confusion. The method of selection and the thoroughness of the training in the Officer Candidate Schools weeded out the unfit and the unintelligent with but rare exceptions but the polishing of the officer after graduation was the duty of his senior officers. In mixed units, this, manifestly, has been impossible. I believe that the young Negro officer represents the best we have to offer and under proper, sympathetic and capable leadership would have developed and performed equally with any other racial group. Therefore, I feel that those who performed in a superior manner and those who died in the proper performance of their assigned duties are our men of the decade and all honor should be paid them. They were Americans before all else. Racially, we have been the victims of an unfortunate chain of circumstances backgrounded by the unchanged American attitude as regards the proper 'place' of the Negro. ... I do not believe the 92d a complete failure as a combat unit but when I think of what it might have been, I am heart-sick. . .[70]

When Gibson became aware of the controversy regarding his comments, he stated, "It is hard for me to see how people can, on the one hand, argue that segregation is wrong, and on the other hand, blindly defend the product of that segregation."[71]

Gibson's comments to the press and his preliminary report were so significant that the 92nd Infantry Division's G1, Mock, prepared a 10+ page document (no doubt by order of Almond), which was classified "Secret," to refute and/or respond to them. Mock began by arguing that all officers in the division were promoted based on ability alone. He noted that by that date, 27 March 1945, 308 promotions were given to African American officers. Of these promotions, 235 (76 percent) were from 2nd lieutenant to 1st lieutenant. Of the remaining promotions, 69 (22 percent) were from 1st lieutenant to captain. Only four of the 308 promotions (slightly more than 1 percent) were to field grade ranks, three to major, and one to lieutenant colonel.[72] In his effort to refute Gibson, Mock proved Gibson's original point, African Americans were not welcome in the field grade ranks of the division. Mock next discussed the assignment of African American officers in the 92nd Infantry. As of 2 March 1945, 46 African American officers were assigned as company commanders, but few of these were in the division's infantry regiments with absolutely none in the 370th Infantry Regiment. Likewise, though fifty-two African American officers were assigned to staff duties throughout the division, they were virtually all company-grade officers who had almost no significant role in planning and were little more than gophers for the division's white field grade officers.[73]

Two sections of "Inclosure No. 3" [*sic*] included with Mock's rebuttal provide some interesting points. "Section D" provided a list of the number of "stragglers" in the division from 1 November 1944 to 1 March 1945. A total of 1913 soldiers were listed as stragglers, the overwhelming majority of whom from the division's four infantry regiments. However, no context was provided for these numbers. Did these men eventually return to their units? Were they court-martialed for cowardice? What happened to them? None of these questions are answered by the one-page document. Lastly, "Section E" listed the number of replacements received by the division, broken down by subunit. Tellingly, only eight African American officers arrived to replace officers killed or badly wounded in combat, while at the same time forty-three white officers were received by the 92nd Infantry Division.[74]

On 23 April 1945, Gibson presented the final report on his visit to the 92nd Infantry Division to the Assistant Secretary of War, John J. McCloy. Gibson began by reiterating the division's official report on the failed offensive of February. He then included observations on the division's report, the first of which was that all blame was placed on African American officers and men while white regimental and battalion commanders were noted as excellent. Since no further explanation was provided, therefore, the reader was led to believe that the failure was entirely due to the race of the soldiers involved. Gibson argued that the failed offensive was not a complete failure of the African American officers and soldiers, "… but rather deficiencies of individuals and small units that resulted from a combination of many circumstances and factors."[75]

Gibson's first recommendation was that Class V soldiers, regardless of race, required different training methods. Second, a better selection process was needed for assigning soldiers to combat units, primarily the exclusion of those in Class V, also regardless of race. Likewise, stateside training camps for African Americans needed to be located in places where the surrounding civilian communities were not exceedingly hostile. Gibson again discussed the status of African American officers in the 92nd Infantry Division and argued for a uniform standard for the promotion and performance evaluation of officers. He argued that it was better to have four thousand truly qualified African American officers than for the Army to boast that there were six thousand African American officers, even though many of them were poorly trained or selected. Lastly, Gibson once again attacked the Army's policy of segregation and argued for an integration policy based on a small unit experiment then happening in the ETO in which African American platoons were attached to otherwise white combat units.[76] Unfortunately, at this late stage in the war, Gibson's recommendations had little or no effect on Army policy.

The "new" 92nd Infantry Division entered combat on 5 April 1945 as part of Operation Second Wind. Unsurprisingly, the plan for the attack was not radically different than the previous tries. In addition to the newly reorganized division, supporting troops included the 758th and 760th Tank Battalions and the 679th and 894th Tank Destroyer Battalions. The 365th and 371st Infantry Regiments were still nearby, but they were now under the direct control of the IV Corps rather than the division. Neither of those regiments was expected to engage in combat during this operation.

For Operation Second Wind, the 92nd Infantry Division was divided into "task forces" which centered on an infantry regiment with a field artillery battalion and a battalion of tanks or tank destroyers in support. The 370th Infantry Regiment, supported by the 597th and 598th Field Artillery Battalions, the 760th Tank Battalion, and the 894th Tank Destroyer Battalion, was on the left of the line and the 442nd RCT and their supporting units on the right with the 473rd Infantry Regiment ready to support either force. The lead element of the 370th Infantry was Company C, 1st Battalion, which advanced two miles toward its objective (Castle Aghinolfi) with almost no opposition. One of the platoons in Company C was led by 1LT Vernon J. Baker. During the division's rebuilding, three new white officers were assigned to Company C. Although Baker was the executive officer and *de facto* company commander for months, white CPT John F. Runyon became the new company commander and he assigned one of the other new white officers as the executive officer. Baker was effectively demoted and to make matters worse he became the weapons platoon leader and another new white officer led his old rifle platoon.[77] During the reorganization process, not only did the company get new white officers, but approximately 70 percent of the NCOs and enlisted men were replacements or transfers. When the company went into combat on 5 April, it was made up largely of a group of strangers.

Predictably, as Company C began their assault up the steep slopes leading to Castle Aghinolfi, the soldiers became separated in the early morning darkness. For instance, Baker's weapons platoon, which included two .30 caliber M1919A4 machine guns and two 60 mm mortars, was missing its mortars and their crewmen when they stopped to get their weapons in position to support the rest of the company. Baker later discovered that one of his mortar crews had been stopped by German machine guns and the other suffered casualties when they walked into a minefield. During this initial advance, Baker almost single-handedly destroyed three German machine gun positions and an artillery spotter outpost.[78] Company C finally stopped at a position roughly three miles from their starting point and requested artillery support when they came under German small arms fire. Unfortunately, their supporting field artillery battalion refused to believe that the company had reached the coordinates they provided, and it took several minutes to convince them to provide the fire support. The company also desperately needed reinforcements but was informed by regimental HQ that this was unlikely since two of the four company commanders in the 1st Battalion were already KIA in the assault and, therefore, other companies were in more need of help.[79] At this point, with casualties rising and no reinforcements forthcoming, Runyon ordered his radioman to help him escort the wounded white executive officer to the rear. When he returned to battalion HQ, Runyon reported that his company was effectively wiped out.

With both the company commander and executive officer gone, Baker was again the *de facto* company commander. With only limited fire support and no forthcoming reinforcements, Baker ordered the remainder of the company to make its way back to the day's starting positions. Baker formed a defensive perimeter and armed his eight remaining men and a wounded field artillery forward observer lieutenant with weapons and ammunition taken off dead Americans. After allowing enough time to make sure that the other members of Company C had a good head start, Baker ordered his remaining soldiers to fall back. On the way back, they discovered four German machine gun positions that had been missed on their way up the hill. Once again Baker almost single-handedly eliminated these four positions. By the end of the day, Company C which started the day with four officers and 142 enlisted men had only two officers and 71 enlisted men— exactly half their strength.[80] For his actions that day, Baker received the DSC. Later, like Fox, Baker's DSC was upgraded to the Medal of Honor, which made him the only living African American to receive the Medal of Honor for his actions during World War II.

On 6 April 1945, the 370th Infantry Regiment launched another attack, but the losses of the previous day made success impossible. Interestingly, it was later determined that the 370th Infantry had faced six 152 mm, four 128 mm, and numerous 90 mm guns during their attacks.[81] On 8 April, the white 473rd Infantry Regiment replaced the 370th Infantry, but success was not finally achieved until the 442nd RCT flanked German positions on the right of the American line. After being flanked, the Germans retreated rather than have their whole line overrun.[82] While this was by no means the end of German resistance, the 92nd Infantry Division was now able to make steady progress for the remaining month of the war.

While the 92nd Infantry was performing its mission, the now detached 365th and 371st Infantry Regiments held the western (or left) side of the IV Corps' line. Ironically, the regiments were now performing quite well. The 371st Infantry's commander, COL James Notestein, was particularly proud of his regiment.

> For the first time our troops maneuvered on level ground in superior numbers, with superior supporting fires. While companies had stragglers after the Co's [sic] were hit by artillery and mortar concentrations, each outfit came back with the idea that they were good and that the [Germans] were not invincible. You have told them these same things for six months, but this is the first time they believed it.[83]

There is no small irony that these regiments, now filled with the castoffs from the division's original three infantry regiments, were suddenly performing better once they were no longer under Almond's control.

Even at this late stage of the war, criticism of the 92nd Infantry continued from senior white leadership. In a letter dated 25 April 1945, COL Hans W. Holmer, the engineer member of the Army Ground Forces Board, Mediterranean Theater of Operations, completely mischaracterized the division's 5 April attack. Holmer wrongly stated that the main effort of the attack was led by the 442nd RCT and that the attack by the 370th Infantry Regiment was only secondary. In reality, both regiments were the main effort with the 473rd Infantry Regiment providing support for them. He also wrongly stated that there was almost no German resistance in the 370th Infantry's sector, which was untrue if nothing else based on the German artillery they faced.

> This division has had the advantage of the best equipment and has been nursed along with relatively easy assignments. The results have been

disappointing. It seems clear to me that we should accept these results as proof that colored units do not make front line 'combat troops.'[84]

Another letter, this one dated 7 May 1945 from COL Paul N. Starlings, the president and infantry member of the same board, made largely the same arguments as Holmer. However, Starlings began by stating that the division was "… ably led by its brilliant commander …" Almond and included a long quote supposedly from him.

> I am thoroughly convinced now that colored troops cannot be used for front line action. They are not combat troops and never will be for some time to come. I have worked daily since the arrival of this division in Italy preparing the infantry for front line action. … I was in hopes by this method and also by appealing to the pride of race and what the colored people in America expected of them, that they would go forward in battle. They have failed me and have not only failed to go forward but have run from the enemy in groups as large as a battalion. They throw away their equipment, they will not obey the orders of their officers to advance and seem to have only one thought in mind and that is to get as far from the enemy as they can, mostly by running. They will never make front line infantry soldiers no matter how long and how consciously you train them. This division has had excellent training both in the states and here in Italy and we have been in contact with the enemy for many months but when it comes time for him to advance he just can't do it.[85]

It is difficult to believe that Starlings could remember such a long and detailed quote unless he specifically asked Almond for written comments, which revealed his clear prejudice in favor of the division's commander.

During its combat operations, the 92nd Infantry Division advanced 100 miles and occupied at one time or another an area of roughly 3000 square miles. The division was responsible for the capture of 23,845 German and Italian POWs. At the same time, the 92nd Infantry suffered 444 KIA, 67 died of wounds (DOW) received in action, 62 died from nonbattle causes, 2,152

WIA, and 121 MIA. Lastly, the officers and men of the division received 145 Silver Stars, the third-highest decoration for valor, and 410 Bronze Stars.[86] Interestingly, since the 366th Infantry Regiment, the 442nd RCT, and the 473rd Infantry Regiment were only attached to the division they did not figure into most of those statistics, which means that the number of soldiers in or attached to the division who were killed, wounded, missing, and/or decorated for service or bravery were substantially higher than these numbers. On 16 November 1945, the 92nd Infantry departed Italy for the United States and was disbanded on 28 November at Camp Kilmer, New Jersey.[87] After retiring from the Army as a lieutenant general in 1953, Almond became a vocal critic of the Civil Rights Movement and school integration—most particularly opposing the admission of African Americans to his *alma mater*, VMI.[88]

Just as during World War I, the second division of African Americans also saw combat—the 93rd Infantry Division. The 93rd Infantry was reactivated on 15 May 1942 at Fort Huachuca and included the 25th, 368th, and 369th Infantry Regiments. Interestingly, the 369th Infantry Regiment which served in the 92nd Infantry Division during World War II had no relationship to the same numbered regiment which was known as the "Harlem Hellfighters" during World War I. On 30 August 1940, the New York National Guard's African American 369th Infantry Regiment was converted to the 369th Coast Artillery Regiment. The "new" 369th Infantry Regiment was a draftee unit created from scratch. The basic and advanced training for the men and units of the division took place between May 1942 and March 1943. In April 1943, the 93rd Infantry reported to Louisiana for large scale maneuvers against the 85th Infantry Division. In July 1943, the division arrived at Camp Clipper, California, for desert warfare training. In November and December 1943, the 93rd Infantry again engaged in division-level maneuvers, this time against the 90th Infantry Division. The division arrived in San Francisco for embarkation to the Pacific theater in February 1944. During the stateside training period, the division had three commanding officers, the final of whom, MG Raymond G. Lehmann, led the division through the final phases of training and to the Pacific until August 1944.[89] By the time the division prepared to deploy to the Pacific, the issue of the African American troops in combat had become so controversial that Marshall sent a message, labeled "Secret," to LTG Millard F. Harmon, the commander of Army Forces in the South Pacific Area.

> ... [T]he secretary of war and I both feel it essential that [the 93rd Infantry Division] not be committed prior to adequate preparation on the part of the unit or units involved. The first reports of its conduct inaction undoubtedly will be headlined in this country. It is therefore important that news releases and reports from the theater on the conduct of these troops be strictly factual. The war department has been under constant pressure for a lidded failure to utilize Negros soldiers in a combat capacity. We are very desirous of employing them as soon as practicable and they should have a careful test to determine their battle dependability.[90]

The 93rd Infantry arrived on Guadalcanal aboard the troopships USS *West Point* (AP-23)[91], USS *General John Pope* (AP-110), SS *Lurline*, USAT *Willard A. Holbrook*, and USAT *Torrens*. While the majority of the division offloaded at Guadalcanal, elements were deployed elsewhere.[92] The 2nd Battalion, 368th Infantry Regiment, deployed to Vella Lavella Island. The remainder of the 368th Infantry and the 594th Field Artillery Battalion were garrisoned on Banika Island. Lastly, the 369th Infantry Regiment and the 595th Field Artillery Battalion were posted to New Georgia Island.[93] At this point in the war, all of these islands were peaceful backwater staging and supply areas.

After a month of acclimatization to tropical conditions, the 25th Infantry Regiment, commanded by COL Everett M. Yon, became the first and only unit of the division to see significant combat when it was attached to the Americal Division from 28 March to 12 June 1944 on Bougainville Island. The 25th Infantry was reorganized as an RCT and included the 593rd Field Artillery Battalion, 93rd Cavalry Reconnaissance Troop, and smaller support units. On 3 April, PVT Wade Foggie from Company F became the first member of the division decorated for bravery when he destroyed three enemy pillboxes with a bazooka for which he received the Bronze Star for Valor.[94] On 8 April, during a patrol from Company F, PVT Isaac

Sermon, a Browning Automatic Rifle (BAR) gunner killed at least three Japanese soldiers despite a wound in the neck. After running out of ammunition, he crawled back to retrieve more ammo. Despite three more wounds, Sermon continued to fire on the enemy until he collapsed from exhaustion and loss of blood. He became the first member of the division to receive the Silver Star.[95]

In June 1944, the 25th RCT was withdrawn from Bougainville and redeployed to Nissan Atoll in the Green Islands. Despite the overall positive performance of the 25th Infantry, the regiment spent the next five months performing security and labor details. MG Oscar Griswold, the XIV Corps commander, detailed the perceived problems of the regiment in a written report. First, the regiment had received almost no jungle training before deploying to the Pacific and he argued that, since the African American soldiers' ability to learn and retain information was inferior to white soldiers, it was not worth training them. Second, while the regiment's morale was high overall, the morale of white officers was low, which Griswold blamed on the "lack of responsibility" of the African American company-grade officers and NCOs. Third, African American company-grade officers did not try as hard as white officers and frequently did not have control of their men. Lastly, initiative among all African American personnel was low.[96] Once again, combat-experienced African American soldiers were blamed for all problems and white leadership escaped any attention.

While the 25th RCT was in combat, owing to the Army's segregationist policies and dislike/distrust of African American units, the remainder of the division was performing labor and security duties on Banika, Vella Lavella, and New Georgia islands. On 26 August, after MG Lehmann was medically evacuated back to the United States, MG Harry H. Johnson became the new commander of the 93rd Infantry Division.[97] Johnson had been the commander of the 2nd Cavalry Division during its stateside training and then during its disbandment in North Africa. Johnson fit the Army's mold for a proper white officer for African American troops, he was a Southerner with previous experience commanding African Americans and, since he was a National Guard officer, a Regular Army officer was not "wasted" on this assignment.

From October 1944 until April 1945, most of the 93rd Infantry found itself spread out over various islands performing security and labor duties. The division did not regroup until April 1945 when the majority of the division gathered on the island of Morotai in the Netherlands East Indies. On Morotai, the division relieved the 31st Infantry Division and assumed responsibility for the major supply facility on the island. For the remainder of the war, the 93rd Infantry performed security and labor functions, as well as prisoner of war processing. While largely pacified by the 31st Infantry, approximately five hundred Japanese remained under arms on the island and members of the 93rd Infantry were killed and wounded during occasional skirmishes. The most dramatic incident was a special patrol from the division HQ between 31 July and 3 August 1945. The patrol was led by LTC Jack C. McKenzie, the division operations officers (G3), and acted on information received from an earlier patrol concerning the whereabouts of COL Kisou Ouchi, the commander of the Japanese 211th Infantry Regiment and all remaining Japanese forces on the Morotai. Surprisingly, Ouchi was captured alive, making him the highest-ranking Japanese officer captured at that point in the war. McKenzie, along with two other members of the patrol (African American SGT Alfonsia Dillon and Technician 3rd Grade[98] Stanley Nakanishi—a Japanese American translator) received the Silver Star for their bravery, while Technician 5th Grade (T/5) Albert Morrison, Private First Class (PFC) Robert A. Evans, and PFC Elmer Sloan received the Bronze Star for Valor.[99]

On 1 January 1946, the 93rd Infantry was finally relieved of its various postwar occupation duties and notified of return to the United States. The division was disbanded at Camp Stoneman, California, on 3 February 1946. Since the 93rd Infantry was prevented from seeing any significant combat, the division's wartime casualties amounted to only twelve KIA, five DOW, and 121 WIA—the overwhelming majority of those casualties were from the 25th Infantry Regiment.[100]

In addition to the infantry regiments that served with the 92nd and 93rd Infantry Divisions, four other African American infantry regiments served in World War II. The 24th Infantry Regiment, which like the 25th Infantry was organized after the Civil War, also served in the Pacific during

World War II. As a Regular Army regiment, the 24th Infantry was considered ready for combat far earlier than any other African American infantry units. At the time of the attack on Pearl Harbor, the regiment was stationed at Fort Benning, Georgia, and participated in large-scale maneuvers in the Carolinas between October and December 1941. On 4 April 1942, the 24th Infantry sailed from San Francisco to the New Hebrides Islands where they performed labor and security duties. The regiment was redeployed to Guadalcanal on 28 August 1943 after the battle there was over and, unsurprisingly, they resumed the same duties they had performed in the New Hebrides.[101]

The use of the African American combat units for labor duties or converted to general service engineer units was a controversial issue in the African American community and press, but not until early 1944 did anyone in the white political establishment seem to care. On 9 February 1944, Republican U.S. Congressman Hamilton Fish of New York, who had served as an officer in the 369th Infantry Regiment during World War I, wrote an official letter to Secretary of War Stimson regarding this issue. Fish specifically addressed the situation of the 24th Infantry in his letter. "In the circumstances, I am still wondering whether there is not a deliberate plan to keep Negro soldiers out of actual combat. … If Negro soldiers are trained as combat troops but denied service as such, such discrimination appears to be a violation …"[102] On 19 February 1944, Stimson replied:

It so happens that a relatively large percentage of the Negroes inducted in the Army have fallen within the lower educational classifications, and many of the Negro units accordingly have been unable to master efficiently the techniques of modern weapons. To have committed such units to combat at the dates of conversion would have endangered operational successes as well as submitted the personnel to unnecessarily high casualty rates. Our limitations of manpower and urgent and immediate need for service units of a type whose mission could be efficiently discharged by the personnel concerned left no choice but to include Negro troops in conversions such as those mentioned in your letter.[103]

After receiving the reply, Fish read its entire contents into the Congressional Record and stated that he disagreed strongly with Stimson's comments.

> I do not understand how it is that four separate colored regiments made such gallant fighting records in the last war ... and yet no colored infantry troops have been ordered into combat in this war. The educational standards of colored people have improved in the last 25 years and I cannot agree with the Secretary of War's inference that colored soldiers' efficiency ratings are so low that 'many of the Negro units have been unable to master efficiently the techniques of modern weapons.' I believe many American Negros will resent bitterly this broad indictment of their people and the discrimination against their use in combat units in defense of their country.[104]

Gibson largely agreed with Fish and argued that Stimson's heavy reliance on AGCT scores also damaged the morale of support units, who were characterized as manned with "only illiterates and misfits." "Furthermore, in what regard will combat engineer units be held when it is blandly stated that men too dumb for field artillery for which they have been trained for three years can be sent into combat engineer battalions?"[105] In a reply to Fish, Gibson was able to point out that as of March 1944 five times more white than African American combat units were converted to support units.[106]

In the wake of this controversy, the 1st Battalion, 24th Infantry Regiment, was deployed to Bougainville alongside the 25th RCT from March to May 1944. The combat efficiency of the battalion was initially considered "too low" by Griswold. "In general, the troops of the battalion were inclined to be a bit 'trigger-happy,' but perhaps no more so than those of any other organization which is never had its baptism of fire."[107] As the battalion gained more experience, their confidence and combat ability increased accordingly. By the end of their time on Bougainville, Griswold had changed his opinion about the battalion. "Although this battalion has in the past been employed largely on labor duties to the detriment of its training, its work in combat here has progressively and noticeably improved."[108] During its only real combat of the war, the battalion

SGT John C. Clark and SSG Ford M. Shaw (Company E, 25th Infantry Regiment, 93rd Infantry Division) clean their rifles alongside the East West Trail, Bougainville, in April 1944. (NARA)

suffered eleven KIA, two DOW, and thirteen WIA.[109] The entire regiment was redeployed to the islands of Saipan and Tinian on 19 December 1944 and finally to the Kerama Islands near Okinawa from 29 July 1945 until the end of the war.[110] In these last locations, the regiment again performed labor and security duties.

An example of the odd circumstances that existed in World War II for all units, but most particularly for African American units, was the 367th Infantry Regiment. The regiment was activated on 25 March 1941 at Camp Claiborne, Louisiana.[111] In March 1942, only a year after the regiment was activated, the 1st Battalion was alerted for shipment to Liberia. After arriving at Camp Davis, North Carolina, the battalion anticipated rapid shipping to Africa. However, since the Liberian mission had low priority, the battalion waited for almost a year to get to Africa. On 9 June 1942, since the battalion was unlikely to ever return to the regiment,

Soldiers from the 25th Infantry Regiment, 93rd Infantry Division, cautiously advance through the jungle, while on patrol in Japanese territory off the Numa Numa Trail in May 1944. (NARA)

it was redesignated as the 367th Infantry Battalion and the remainder of the 367th Infantry Regiment was redesignated as the 364th Infantry Regiment to avoid confusion.[112]

On 21 October 1942, after seven months at Camp Davis, the battalion transferred to Camp Jackson. During the seemingly endless months of additional training at Camp Davis and Camp Jackson, the morale of the men plummeted as they began to fear that they, like so many other African Americans, would never see overseas service during the war. Finally, on 8 February 1943, the battalion sailed for Africa aboard the troopships USAT *James Parker* and the British-owned SS *Athlone Castle*. The ships finally arrived in Liberia on 10 March after brief stops at Casablanca, Dakar (French West Africa), and Freetown (Sierra Leone).[113] Most of the units in Liberia were manned by African Americans and the job of the 367th Infantry Battalion was principally guarding supplies and a U.S. Army Air Force base—Roberts Field. After 10 months in Liberia, the battalion was shipped to Oran, Algeria, in January 1944. After a year of guarding supplies and air bases in North Africa, the 367th Infantry was finally disbanded on 10 January 1945 and the soldiers dispersed to support units.[114] Ironically, at that same time, American commanders in Northern Europe were desperately in need of infantrymen in the wake of the German Ardennes Offensive (also known as the Battle of the Bulge) in December 1944.

After losing its 1st Battalion and then redesignating, the 364th Infantry Regiment reconstituted a new 1st Battalion on 10 June 1942. The now full-strength regiment was transferred to Phoenix, Arizona, in that same month, where it trained and guarded the border with Mexico. On 27 May 1943, the 364th Infantry transferred to Camp Van Dorn, Mississippi. It was not until 24 January 1944 that the regiment finally left the continental United States when it arrived for garrison duty in the Aleutian Islands of Alaska for the remainder of the war. The Regimental HQ and 3rd Battalion defended Attu Island, while the 1st Battalion garrisoned Amchitka Island and the 2nd Battalion was posted to Shemya Island.[115]

The final African American infantry regiment of World War II was the 372nd Infantry Regiment. The regiment, which had served in World War I, was composed of African American National guardsmen from the District of Columbia, Ohio, Massachusetts, New Jersey, and Maryland.[116] The 372nd Infantry was called to active federal service on 10 March 1941 and consolidated at Fort Dix, New Jersey. After seven months of training, the regiment reportedly made little progress. The principal issues were the regimental commander, COL Howard C. Gilbert, an African American veteran of World War I, who was then sixty-two years old and "… deficient in basic education, has displayed a decided lack of administrative ability, and appears to be ignorant of modern methods of training."[117] Likewise, the three white National Guard instructors assigned to the regiment were also unqualified. Even after receiving a new commander and other new officers, the 372nd Infantry had to

Soldiers of the 24th Infantry Regiment, then attached to the Americal Division, and a tank prepared to assault Japanese positions along Empress Augusta Bay on Bougainville. (NARA)

both prepare for combat deployment and, at the same time, defend New York City from invasion, which meant that the regiment was usually separated and not training as a unit. Finally, on 20 April 1944, the entire regiment was transferred to Camp Breckenridge to perform proper training. As with so many other African American units, the 372nd Infantry eventually found itself, on 11 November 1944, transferred to Fort Huachuca. The regiment's final move took place on 9 May 1945 when it arrived in Hawaii and remained there until the end of the war.[118]

Perhaps the most unique African American infantry unit of World War II was the 555th Parachute Infantry Battalion. The 555th Parachute Infantry begun as the 555th Test Platoon activated on 30 December 1943 at Fort Benning. The Army authorized the unit with African American officers and enlisted men, all of whom were volunteers. The men who made up the original platoon were largely drawn from the 92nd Infantry Division—sixteen of the first twenty enlisted men and three of the first six officers.[119] By the summer of 1944, enough officers and men had completed airborne training that the platoon was redesignated the 555th Parachute Infantry Company. The original members of the 555th Test Platoon served as the cadre for the company and were duly promoted in rank and position.[120] On 25 November 1944, after almost a year of training, the company moved to Camp Mackall, North Carolina, where it was redesignated as Company A, 555th Parachute Infantry Battalion. Recruiting enough qualified personnel to man a full battalion proved difficult as up to 60 percent of volunteers are ejected, most for failing to meet the strict physical requirements. In fact, at no time did the battalion's manpower exceed 66 percent of the authorized Army table of organization (T/O) strength for a parachute battalion.[121] The manpower shortages which resulted from the Battle of the Bulge appeared to offer the battalion an opportunity to seek combat. Since the battalion was not at full strength, the War Department decided that a "reinforced company" from the 555th Parachute Infantry Battalion would deploy to Europe to augment the 101st Airborne Division. Only the best members of the battalion were chosen to serve in a reinforced company. However, by April 1945, it was obvious that Germany was on its last legs and the reinforced company was discontinued.[122]

In May 1945 with the war in Europe over, the 555th Parachute Infantry Battalion was reassigned to the Ninth Service Command based at Fort Douglas, Utah, but which covered most of the Pacific coast and mountain states. Stationed at Pendleton Army Airfield in Oregon, the battalion's paratroopers were assigned to Operation Firefly whose mission was the recovery and destruction of Japanese balloon bombs. These balloon bombs were released into the jet stream from Japan to create massive forest fires in the Pacific Northwest which would both tie-down American manpower and destroy valuable timber resources. Of the approximately ninety-three thousand hydrogen-filled balloons launched from Japan, however, only around three hundred survived the trip across the Pacific and landed in North America. Nevertheless, American authorities feared the potential destruction from these bombs and were concerned that the Japanese might also try to release bacteriological agents from some of the balloons. Therefore, the existence of these balloons was classified as "Top Secret" during the war. The battalion trained on forest firefighting

S-4384-1

In March 1944, 16 African American soldiers aboard a C-47 transport plane before making one of their required five qualifying jumps before being awarded their jump "wings" at Fort Benning, Georgia. During the war, African Americans would make up the entire strength of the 555th Parachute Battalion. (NARA)

techniques, bomb disposal, and "smoke jumping." "Smoke Jumpers" used maneuverable parachutes to drop into heavily timbered areas, ideally landing in small clearings but often forced by wind and circumstances to land in the trees and then lower themselves down to the forest floor. Between

14 July and 6 October, the 555th Parachute Infantry participated in thirty-six fire missions and though there were many scrapes, bruises, and broken bones, they suffered only one fatality when a man caught in a tree fell 150 feet onto rocks.[123] Though they never saw combat, the men of the battalion were the first African American paratroopers in the Army and ably performed a difficult mission in secret.[124]

After the Normandy invasion in June 1944, the Army began to experience shortages of infantry replacements in Europe. Casualties were beginning to exceed the Army's ability to train replacements and, as a result, enlisted men from other specialties began retraining to serve as infantrymen. The situation was exacerbated further by the Battle of the Bulge, which began on 16 December 1944. Even a week before that battle began, the Supreme Headquarters Allied Expeditionary Forces (SHAEF) estimated that American forces were more than twenty-three thousand riflemen below their authorized strength.[125] The only remaining and relatively untapped source of manpower was African Americans already serving in Europe in large numbers with support units.

As a result of the perceived inferior performance by large African American formations (regiments and divisions), the Army had no interest in deploying those types of units to the ETO. The only other alternative was some form of integration of smaller African American units with existing white formations. This was not as radical of a suggestion as it might first appear, because the same suggestion was made during the Interwar Period when it was proposed to add African American battalions to white regiments. In December 1944, LTG J.C.H. Lee, the senior American supply officer in the ETO, suggested to Eisenhower, the Supreme Allied Commander, the use of African American servicemen as volunteer infantry replacements. Like Eisenhower, Lee was a native Kansan and did not have strong racial views. However, integration was still unacceptable to many senior officers and state-side American politicians, so they were careful about how they approached the issue. Therefore, a request was put out for volunteers from all support units, regardless of race.[126] Eisenhower agreed with proposal and, in a private cable to Marshall on 7 January 1945, stated, "… I cannot deny the Negro volunteer a chance to serve in battle."[127]

The call for volunteers became public on 26 December 1944, and within two months, 4,562 African American soldiers signed up, though ultimately only 2,253 were accepted.[128] Since the volunteers were beginning an entirely new military specialty, they were forced to give up any rank they held in their previous assignments and many senior NCOs now became privates or privates first class to have the chance to serve as infantrymen. Regardless of race, soldiers who scored in Class V of the AGCT were not accepted. As a result, the African American infantry volunteers were generally better educated and more intelligent than the average African American soldier in the ETO. Of the African American volunteers, 22 percent were high school graduates and 29 percent were in AGCT Classes I, II, or III, while among all African American soldiers the numbers were 18 percent high school graduates and 17 percent in AGCT Classes I, II, or III.[129]

In January 1945, the African American volunteers gathered for infantry conversion training, but the question remained how best to utilize these men once they were trained. Initially, the proposal was to group new African American infantrymen into battalions for combat. This proposal almost assuredly had its antecedents in the War Department's interwar proposals. However, the continued "fear" that large formations of African American soldiers were ineffective shot down this proposal. In the end, SHAEF decided to group the African American volunteers into reinforced rifle platoons with white platoon leaders and white NCOs. A total of forty-nine platoons were divided between two armored divisions (12th and 14th) and eight infantry divisions (1st, 2nd, 8th, 9th, 69th, 78th, 99th, and 104th).[130] In most cases, three African American platoons were assigned to each division, who in turn generally assigned one platoon to each infantry regiment.

The most dramatic experience from the African American platoons attached to the infantry divisions came from the 104th Infantry Division. PFC Willy F. James, Jr., was in a platoon attached to Company G, 413th Infantry Regiment, which was assigned to attack the town of Lippoldsberg on 7 April 1945. James was a scout of the lead squad in the assault platoon, making him the point person of his entire regiment. His unit's mission was to seize houses on the edge of the town from which the unit could then launch an attack on the rest of the town. After moving forward approximately two hundred yards over open terrain, James was pinned down by enemy snipers and machineguns.

> Lying in an exposed position for more than an hour, Private First Class James intrepidly observed the enemy's positions which were given away by the fire Private First Class James was daringly drawing upon himself. Then, with utter indifference to his personal safety, in a storm of enemy small arms fire, Private First Class James made his way back more than 300 yards across open terrain under enemy observation to his platoon positions, and gave a full, detailed report on the enemy disposition.[131]

James then volunteered to join in an assault on the key house during which his platoon leader was wounded. As James went to the aid of his platoon leader, he was killed by a burst from an enemy machine gun. For his actions, James received the DSC, but as with Fox and Baker, James' DSC was upgraded to the Medal of Honor in 1997.

Since this experiment represented the closest thing to integration attempted in the Army during World War II, great scrutiny was placed on the combat performance of the African American soldiers and a report was prepared regarding their actions. The report, "Utilization of Negro Infantry Platoons in White Companies," was based on interviews with white officers and enlisted men in seven of the infantry divisions (1st, 2nd, 9th, 69th, 78th, 99th, and 104th). In these divisions, twenty-four infantry companies were visited by the interviewers who asked 250 standardized questions. Also, seventeen hundred other white enlisted men were asked to fill out anonymous questionnaires regarding their attitudes toward using African Americans in combat units. These questionnaires were intended to show the difference of opinion between those who served directly with the African American infantrymen and those who did not.[132] Interestingly, no African American soldiers were interviewed.

The "Main Findings" section of the report detailed several important points. First, white soldiers who served in companies with African American platoons believed those African Americans performed well in combat. Second, white enlisted men who served with African American platoons were "much more likely" than other white soldiers to favor African American soldiers in the infantry. Third, white soldiers who served with African American platoons judged them "at least equal" to white infantrymen. Fourth, white soldiers who served with African American platoons reported that they all got along well together. Fifth, almost all of the officers who served with African American platoons reported that the relations between white and African American soldiers were better than they expected. Sixth, 75 percent of the white soldiers who served with African American platoons reported that their feelings toward African Americans had improved because of their experience. Last, most of the white soldiers who served with African American platoons argued for the use of this model of organization exclusively in the future, rather than organizing larger African American only formations.[133]

The "Detailed Findings" section of the report provided more specific points. None of the officers and only 1 percent of the white enlisted men interviewed gave a negative report of the performance of the African American platoons. Even a company commander from Virginia provided a positive response.

> They have had real battle testing, and have done well. ... Good on teamwork. This colored platoon of 35 man with no prepared positions was counterattacked by 90 Germans. The platoon commander had just been captured. They killed 46 and took 35 prisoners, without losing any ground or having any casualties.[134]

A solid majority (60 percent) of white infantrymen who served with African American platoons reported that they wanted to or were indifferent to continued service with the African Americans. On the other hand, an overwhelming majority (89 percent) of white soldiers who did not serve with African American platoons reported they would "rather not" or "would dislike it very much" serving with the African Americans.[135]

The opinions of both company- and field grade officers were also sought. A captain and company commander from Nevada was very surprised by how good the relationship became in his company.

> Relations are very good. They have their pictures taken together, go to church services, movies, play ball together. For a time there in combat our platoons got so small that we had to put a white squad in the colored platoon. You might think that wouldn't work well, but it did. The white squad didn't want to leave the platoon. I've never seen anything like it.[136]

A report from the 18th Infantry Regiment, 1st Infantry Division, stated that the African American platoon they received performed very satisfactorily and could "… most certainly be considered a battle success."[137] The commander of the 26th Infantry Regiment, 1st Infantry Division, rated his African American platoon as 90 percent efficient and stated that they were, "… capable of successful participation in combat."[138] The 99th Infantry Division reported that their African American platoons were "excellent." "These men were courageous fighters and never once did they fail to accomplish their assigned mission."[139]

As the senior African American officer in the Army, Davis visited some of the African American infantry platoons in April 1945. Davis ultimately visited platoons in the 8th, 9th, 78th, and 104th Infantry Divisions and reported that the African American volunteers were highly thought of by all the white officers he interviewed. One officer, MG Edwin P. Parker, the commander of the 78th Infantry Division, was so pleased with the African American volunteers that he wanted additional platoons.[140]

The only difference of opinion regarding the African American infantry platoons came from the 12th and 14th Armored Divisions. Rather than assigning their twelve platoons to individual regiments as the infantry divisions did, LTG Alexander Patch, the Seventh Army commander of these divisions, decided to organize these platoons into companies. The problem was that the men of the platoons had only the most basic infantry training and were barely qualified to operate in squads and platoons. They had no training at the company level or above and, additionally, they were now assigned to armored infantry battalions and expected to operate in support of tanks for which they also had no training.

The 12th Armored Division already had a negative experience with African American soldiers because of the poor performance of the 827th Tank Destroyer Battalion, so they "objected violently" to accepting any additional African Americans.[141] However, the performance of the African American volunteers changed the white soldiers' perceptions, especially the actions of Edward A. Carter, Jr. Carter's parents were missionaries, and he grew up in India and Shanghai, China. During the Chinese Civil War, fifteen-year-old Carter ran away to join the Chinese Nationalist Army before his parents retrieved him. Later during the Spanish Civil War, he joined the Abraham Lincoln Brigade, a unit composed mostly of American communist volunteers who fought in support of the leftist Spanish Republican government. On 26 September 1941, before the American entry into World War II, Carter voluntarily enlisted in the U.S. Army. Given his experience, he quickly rose through the ranks, and by 1944 he was a staff sergeant.

Unsurprisingly, when the chance came to volunteer for infantry service, Carter jumped at the opportunity. Eventually, he was assigned to the Seventh Army Infantry Company Number 1 (Provisional), which was attached to the 56th Armored Infantry Battalion, 12th Armored Division. On 23 March 1945, near Speyer, Germany, Carter was riding on an American tank which was hit by small arms and *Panzerfaust*[142] fire. Dismounting, Carter led three soldiers to a warehouse where the enemy's fire seemed to come from. Upon reaching the warehouse, he determined that the enemy was approximately 150 yards away across an open field. As soon as they emerged from cover, one of the American soldiers was killed and Carter ordered the other two to return to the warehouse and provide him with cover fire. As they returned, another American was killed and the other seriously wounded. Carter himself was wounded five times in the left arm, left leg, and left hand as he continued to advance.[143] He crawled to within thirty yards of the German position before he was forced to take cover in a position where he waited for almost two hours. Carter remained quiet for so long that the Germans assumed he was dead or incapacitated. As a result, eight German infantrymen approached Carter to take him prisoner or examine his body for possible intelligence. Much to their surprise, instead, Carter killed six of them and captured the remaining two, who provided valuable intelligence on the German positions. For his actions, Carter received the DSC, but as with Fox, Baker, and James, Carter's DSC was later upgraded to the Medal of Honor. Carter remained in the Army after the war but was refused reenlistment in 1949, due to his service in the communist-affiliated Abraham Lincoln Brigade during the Spanish Civil War. He died of lung cancer on 30 January 1963.

In the 14th Armored Division, the African American infantry company was initially known as the "Seventh Army Infantry Company Number 4 (Provisional)," but when it was assigned to Combat Command Reserve of the division it became known as the "CCR Rifle Company."[144] When the African American soldiers arrived at the division they had no officers or NCOs and the division was forced to find the proper individuals. While the division did provide six officers, four were Southerners and the company commander, CPT Derl Hess, was relieved of his previous company when he "... broke down under fire." Of the twenty-seven NCOs required for a company, the division provided only six and official authorization for promoting the African American soldiers to NCO ranks did not come until after the end of combat.[145] The 240 African American soldiers of the "CCR Rifle Company" reported to the division without any weapons or equipment. Unfortunately, almost all weapons and equipment were in short supply throughout the ETO. As a result, most of the weapons and equipment issued to the company were in poor condition. There were not even enough armored infantry half-tracks to equip the company and they received only one per platoon with the remainder of the soldiers mounted on unarmored two-and-a-half-ton trucks.[146]

Despite inadequate training, weapons, and equipment, the soldiers of "CCR Rifle Company" performed well under fire. The company led an advance on the German town of Allersberg on 22 April 1945 and came into close contact with two Mark VI "Tiger" tanks concealed among buildings on the edge of town. The African American soldiers stood their ground while their bazooka teams opened fire. Several bazooka rounds hit the tanks with no effect. When the tanks were a mere fifteen yards from the infantry's positions, PFC Percy Smith finally managed to disable one of the "Tigers" with a bazooka and was then killed by return fire from the tank. In 38 days of combat, "CCR Rifle Company" lost six men KIA, thirty-seven WIA, and one MIA. MAJ (later MG) William E. Shedd, who observed the company in combat, stated that they, "… attacked when ordered to do so, they continue to advance even when they were under heavy enemy fire, they never broke in combat or withdrew from an engagement without orders, and they maintained proper discipline on the battlefield. They were no different than the white soldiers of the division."[147]

The war in Europe officially ended on 7 May 1945. Within a few months, American soldiers began to rotate home based on a points system known as the Adjusted Service Rating Score that considered time in service, time overseas, combat awards, and the number of dependent underage children. Since they had less time in combat, some of the African American infantry volunteers were simply transferred back to support units. Approximately 250 of the former volunteers were reassigned to the 1697th Engineer Combat Battalion after their white divisions returned to the United States. These men refused to work and requested courts-martial so that their situation would come to the attention of senior leadership in the Army. Davis was asked to visit these men and make a report. After interviewing the soldiers, Davis agreed that the Army had "… broken faith with them."[148] Publicly, he urged the men to comply with the orders given to them by their officers and stated that he would report the situation to higher authorities. Privately, Davis wrote to Eisenhower arguing for these men.

> The colored soldier in this theater finds himself in a very embarrassing situation. In his contacts with the inhabitants of this part of the world, he is treated with the same consideration as other individuals. In many instances, the so called 'Jim Crow Practices' have been needed out to him by his white comrades. These practices are bitterly resented. He does not understand why he should be discriminated against in a foreign country free from such costumes by his fellow soldiers from

the homeland. ... It is the opinion of the undersigned that the colored soldier serving in this theater, and especially those who have served in combat against the enemy, is not going to accept without resentment of return to the conditions from what she left. ... It has believed that in view of the promise is implied by the invitation to volunteer for service as infantry replacements, that some special consideration be given tore the activation of a special infantry unit, or that arrangements be made for the assignment of these men to the 92nd Infantry Division, which is now in Europe.[149]

Thankfully, a compromise was worked out for most, but not all, of the infantry volunteers. Most of them who did not have enough points to return to the United States were transferred to the 350th Field Artillery Battalion, which did not redeploy until several months later. In this way, these soldiers remained in a combat arms unit while serving as part of the occupation forces.[150]

The poor combat performance of the 92nd Infantry Division became the defining image of African American infantrymen for the white senior leadership of the Army after World War II, just as the supposed poor combat performance of the 92nd Division had after World War I. However, the African American volunteer infantry platoons, along with other African American infantry units, exploded many racial myths. The authentic lessons for the Army regarding African American infantrymen took several years to penetrate the Army's hidebound culture.

Chapter 3

U.S. Marine Corps

When World War II began, the U.S. Marine Corps did not have a single African American member. From its founding, the Marine Corps' rules explicitly stated that "no Negro, Mulatto or Indian"[1] were permitted to enlist and that policy did not change until ordered to do so by President Franklin D. Roosevelt in June 1942.[2] Therefore, it is unsurprising that there were no African American Marine Corps commissioned officers during the war.[3] Despite these limitations, many African American units were formed and several saw combat in the Pacific. World War II caused fundamental change within the Marine Corps regarding the issue of race. The service went from being known among American minorities as the "white man's service" to including not only African Americans but also the now-famous Navajo Code Talkers.

The initial push for African American service in the Marine Corps was met with opposition by almost all marine officers, but particularly from the Commandant of the Marine Corps, LTG Thomas Holcomb. Holcomb, who grew up in Delaware and Washington, DC, maintained a traditional view of African Americans and saw no need to admit them to the Marine Corps. In January 1942, he testified before the U.S. Navy's General Board that,

"... there would be a definite loss of efficiency in the Marine Corps if we have to take Negroes."[4] Holcomb argued that given the small size of the Marine Corps (sixteen thousand in 1939) too many changes were necessary to accommodate African Americans. "[T]he Negro race has every opportunity now to satisfy its aspirations for combat in the army—a very much larger organization than the navy or the Marine Corps-and their desire to enter the naval service is largely, I think, to break into a club that doesn't want them."[5] He viewed the Marine Corps as a small, elite organization, which he did not want to dilute in any way. Marine officers' notions of white racial superiority resulted from not only general societal racism but also the fact that approximately 40 percent of these officers were from the South, a substantially higher percentage of Southerners in the officer ranks than seen in the U.S. Army.[6]

The General Board released a study on 3 February 1942, soon after America entered World War II, which still supporting Holcomb's perspective on African American service.

1. That enlistment of men of the colored race for unrestricted service is considered by higher authority to be inadvisable.
2. That any practical plan, which would not inject into the whole personnel of the Navy the race question, must provide four:
    (a) segregation of colored enlisted man insofar as quartering, messing and employment is concerned,
    (b) limitation of authority of colored petty officers two subordinates of their own race.[7]

The study went on to discuss the theoretical organization of "colored composite battalions" in the Marine Corps. The study concluded, "Colored battalions could unquestionably be developed in time. While their value generally for field service is gravely doubted, ... Colored composite battalions in the Marine Corps are considered to be practicable, but undesirable, as the wartime project."[8] President Franklin Roosevelt responded to the General Board on 9 February by stating, "This report of the general board I regard as (a) unsatisfactory and (b) insufficient. ... It is my considered opinion that there are additional tasks in the naval establishment to which we could properly assign an additional number of enlisted men who are members of the negro [*sic*] race."[9]

In May 1942, Roosevelt settled the matter once and for all by ordering the inclusion of African Americans throughout the Navy and Marine Corps. On 25 May, a memo was issued by Holcomb's office with the subject line "Enlistment of colored personnel in the Marine Corps." The memo stated that beginning on 1 June, all Marine Corps recruiters were to accept enlistments of African American males between the ages of seventeen and twenty-nine. The memo also discusses the formation of a composite defense battalion in the vicinity of New River, North Carolina.[10] This new facility, a satellite of Camp Lejeune, was eventually located at Jacksonville, North Carolina, and named Montfort Point Camp. On 18 August 1942, the 51st Defense Battalion was activated at Montfort Point under the command of COL Samuel A. Woods, Jr. Unsurprisingly, Woods was a Southerner from South Carolina and a graduate of the Military College of South Carolina (better known as the Citadel). Despite his background, Woods was known almost universally by his African American subordinates for his fairness and was nicknamed the "Great White Father" (though it seems likely that nickname was a somewhat tongue-in-cheek reference to the popular Western films of the time).[11] On 26 August 1942, Howard P. Perry became the first African American to report for active duty in the Marine Corps.

Predictably, after the Marine Corps allowed African Americans to join, not many African Americans were interested, since the Marine Corps had a reputation as the "white man's service." As of 29 October 1942, after almost five months of recruiting, only 647 African Americans enlisted in the Marine Corps.[12] Things changed drastically in January 1943 when one thousand African Americans entered the Marine Corps each month as a result of the Selective Service System and only seventeen-year-olds could voluntarily enlistment. While draftees were allowed to "volunteer" for a specific branch of service, they were given no guarantee of their choice. In anticipation of these draftees, a memo dated 26 December 1942 on this subject of "Colored Personnel" discussed what to do with the African American marines, most particularly how to keep them separated from whites. The memo quickly used statistics provided by the Army to note that African Americans were of inferior intelligence. To absorb approximately one thousand African Americans per month or twelve thousand per year, the memo discussed possible duty assignments. While composite battalions were discussed, the Marine Corps only intended to organize one per year, which would account for just twelve hundred African Americans. An additional thirty-five hundred African Americans were slated for the Messmen's Branch, while the remainder was to be divided among more general service as chauffeurs, messengers, post exchange clerks, janitors, and maintenance. Tellingly, a handwritten note that the bottom of the page circled the reference to Messmen, and it stated, "I don't think we can get away with this type of duty."[13]

The first 198 African Americans to graduate from Marine Corps basic training did so at the end of November 1942.[14] Since the Marine Corps wanted to withdraw all of the white NCOs from Montfort Point and return them to other white marine units, they needed competent African American NCOs to fill those positions. Therefore, the white NCOs were ordered to pay close attention to the initial group of African American recruits and select the best for possible promotion. Most of these first African American NCOs had previous military experience with the Army or Navy. One of the first African American NCOs was Gilbert H. "Hashmark" Johnson, who earned his nickname because he wore so many diagonal stripes ("hashmarks") on his uniform's left sleeve, indicating his six years' service in the Army's 25th Infantry Regiment and nine years as a Navy messman. Since Johnson had infantry experience, he was considered ideal to serve as a marine NCO. After completing basic training, he became an assistant drill instructor under a white NCO for the next group of African American marines and, by January 1945, Johnson was the sergeant major and senior NCO at Montford Point Camp.[15]

On 24 April 1943, MG Charles F. B. Price, the commander of the Samoan Group Defense Force, wrote a letter to BG Keller E. Rockey, the director of the Division of Plans and Policies at Marine Corps HQ in Washington, DC. The Samoan Group Defense Force, which Price commanded, included the 2nd and 7th Defense Battalions and had also previously included the 8th Defense Battalion. Price was deeply concerned about the possibility of receiving an African American defense battalion as part of his command.

Group of African American Marine recruits addressed by their drill instructor, SGT Gilbert H. "Hashmark" Johnson at Montford Point Camp, NC, in April 1943. (NARA)

His concern stemmed from the "primitively romantic" nature of the Polynesian women and fear that:

> ... [T]he introduction of from six hundred to a thousand Negro soldiers into such a community in a short time will infuse enough Negro blood

into the population to make the island in the future predominantly Negro. ... So far as American Samoa is concerned, remember that it is an American possession and that we have both a moral obligation and a selfish interest in protecting the population of that island. ... I suggest, therefore, and if I had to make an official recommendation I would recommend very strongly that we should never repeat never contemplate sending any of our Negro components into any islands of the Polynesian group. If I had to absorb one of these units, I would station it at Wallis Island [a French possession] where the people, although rated as Polynesian, are of a very much lower type than those in the Samoan group, and where a minimum of harm can be done. ... They can do no racial harm in that area, in fact being of a higher type of intelligence, I believe they will actually raise the level of physical and intellectual standards in that area.[16]

As if Price's comments were not bad enough, on 14 May 1943, Holcomb issued "Letter of Instruction Number 421," which remained classified until after World War II. "Letter of Instruction Number 421" stated that while African Americans were receiving rapid promotions, white marines should always outrank them in any given unit. However, Holcomb admonished all marine officers to treat African American marines no differently than white marines.[17]

The first African American Marine Corps combat unit, the 51st Defense Battalion, was originally designated as a composite organization, which was a catchall formation during the early days of African American enlistment. The marine defense battalions were originally organized to solve a problem—defending small islands used as Navy bases. However, by the end of 1942, the purpose of the defense battalion changed from repulsing enemy amphibious assaults to defending against enemy airstrikes. In June 1943, the 51st Defense Battalion was reorganized and contained three groups—a Seacoast Artillery Group (equipped with 155-mm guns), an Antiaircraft Artillery Group (equipped with 90-mm guns), and a Special Weapons Group (equipped with machine guns, 20-mm, and 40-mm weapons).[18]

Antiaircraft gun, christened "Lena Horne" after the famous African American singer, manned by the U.S. Marine Corps' 51st Defense Battalion. (NARA)

The large number of African American draftees in 1943 required the creation of new units. The original proposal to restrict all African American marines outside of the 51st Defense Battalion to messmen, chauffeurs, messengers, post exchange clerks, janitors, and maintenance was no longer feasible. Since the Marine Corps still did not trust African Americans enough to place them in true combat arms units, support units were the only other place for them. While this situation largely mirrored that of the Army, the marine situation was different because marine support units frequently found themselves under fire and often assisted infantry units in combat. This occurred because the island battlefields of the central Pacific were frequently so small there was scarcely any difference between the frontlines and the rear area.

On 8 March 1943, the 1st Marine Depot Company was organized at Montfort Point, and, by the end of the year, a total of sixteen depot companies and three ammunition companies were established.[19] While both types of support companies provided needed labor to move supplies from the rear area to the frontlines there was a significant difference between them.

In June 1944, African American Marines PFC Horace Boykin
(riding captured bicycle) and (*left to right*) CPL Willis T. Anthony, PFC
Emmitt Shackelford, and PFC Eugene Purdy from the 3rd Ammunition
Company, pictured during the Battle of Saipan. (NARA)

Depot companies were responsible for unloading, sorting, and transporting
supplies, but they were not provided with organic vehicles and frequently
were forced to move supplies on foot. On the other hand, ammunition companies unloaded, sorted, guarded, and transported ammunition with their own
trucks and jeeps. Also, marines in ammunition companies received several
weeks of additional training on types of ammunition and fuses as well as their
safe handling. These companies also included explosive ordnance disposal
specialists, but this billet was restricted to whites only. The extra training of
the ammunition companies helped to increase their morale and they tended to

First African American Marines wounded in combat during World War II (*left to right*) SSG Timerlate Kirven and CPL Samuel J. Love, Sr., at the Battle of Saipan, who later received Purple Hearts for their wounds. (NARA)

think of themselves as "elite." In stark contrast, the depot companies frequently experienced problems with morale and discipline from African American marines who felt they were assigned demeaning tasks. Nevertheless, it was the 1st Marine Depot Company, not the 51st Defense Battalion, who were the first African American marines to arrive in the Pacific when they sailed for New Caledonia on 18 April 1943.[20]

In December 1943, the 51st Defense Battalion was notified of their forthcoming transfer to the Pacific theater. Just as the battalion was preparing to leave, the Marine Corps organized the 52nd Defense Battalion on 15 December 1943. To fill the new battalion, four hundred officers and men of the 51st Defense Battalion were transferred to act as a cadre. Thankfully, the 51st Defense Battalion was over strength, and the losses, while not helpful, did not negatively impact the deploying battalion. On 11 February 1944, the battalion sailed from San Diego aboard the SS *Meteor* (MC-262) bound for the Ellice Islands. The 51st Defense Battalion remained in the Ellice Islands for roughly six months during which it had almost no enemy contact. Despite this assignment, there were relatively few complaints from the African American marines because they were some of the only troops on the islands. The most interesting event of their time in the Ellice Islands was the Marine Corps' decision to convert the battalion to a completely antiaircraft organization by eliminating their machine guns, 20 mm, and 155 mm guns, and replacing them with more 40 mm and 90 mm guns. On 8 September 1944, the battalion sailed for Eniwetok Atoll in the Marshall Islands, which proved just as uneventful as the Ellice Islands. The battalion finally sailed back to the United States in November 1945 and was disbanded at Montford Point in January 1946.[21]

On 21 September 1944, after almost eight months of training, the 52nd Defense Battalion, which like the 51st Defense Battalion was converted to a purely antiaircraft formation, boarded the transport USS *Winged Arrow* (AP-170) for the Marshall Islands where they took over the defense of two marine air groups from white antiaircraft units. For six months, from October 1944 to March 1945, the battalion's only encounters with the enemy came from the formation of reconnaissance parties to search nearby smaller islands for Japanese stragglers. The 52nd Defense Battalion deployed to the recaptured island of Guam on 4 May 1945 and remained there for the rest of the war. In November 1945, the battalion relieved the 51st Defense Battalion at Eniwetok and remained until April 1946. After returning to Montford Point, the battalion was redesignated the 3rd Antiaircraft Artillery Battalion on 15 May 1946.[22]

While the 51st and 52nd Defense Battalions, the only African American combat units in the Marine Corps, spent most of the war fighting boredom on isolated Pacific islands, the men of the depot and ammunition companies[23] saw combat on Saipan, Tinian, Guam, Peleliu, Iwo Jima, and Okinawa, and suffered most of the African American marine casualties of World War II. The 18th, 19th, and 20th Depot and the 3rd Ammunition Companies were the first to see combat when they landed on Saipan on 15 June 1944 in support of the 4th Marine Division.[24] One of the 19th Depot Company's squads fought as infantry to reinforce a thinly held section of the frontline and many African American marines were called upon to guard against Japanese snipers and infiltrators during the battle. On Saipan, PVT Kenneth J. Tibbs of the 20th Marine Depot Company became the first African American marine KIA.[25] On the night of 15 June, two hundred Japanese soldiers attempted to use the cover of darkness to launch a counterattack on American positions, which the 3rd Ammunition Company helped to stop. The performance of these four African American marine companies on Saipan was so significant that the new Commandant of the Marine Corps, LTG Alexander A. Vandergrift, stated, "The Negro Marines are no longer on trial. They are Marines, period." Not only did the African American marines receive this vote of confidence from the Commandant, but also they received the Distinguished Unit Citation (DUC, later renamed the Presidential Unit Citation, PUC), the highest unit decoration in the U.S. armed forces, along with the white marines of the 4th Marine Division.[26]

On 21 July 1944, the 3rd Marine Division with the 1st, 2nd, and 3rd Platoons of the 2nd Marine Ammunition Company and the 1st Provisional Marine Brigade with the 4th Marine Ammunition Company and the 4th Platoon, 2nd Marine Ammunition Company began the liberation of Guam.[27] The supply situation for the 1st Provisional Marine Brigade became critical as a result of a lack of sufficient amphibious vehicles. In the end, several expedient methods were attempted to provide the necessary supplies, including the use of rubber boats, rafts, and simply floating 55-gallon fuel drums across shallow areas toward the beach. On the day after the assault, a group of Japanese soldiers assaulted the brigade's ammunition dump but were repelled at the loss of 14 marines from the 4th Marine Ammunition Company. The 4th

During the Battle of Iwo Jima, three African American Marines
(*left to right*) PFCs Willie J. Kanody, Elif Hill, and John Alexander
pause for a meal. (NARA)

Platoon, 2nd Marine Ammunition Company was specifically mentioned
in the DUC awarded to the 1st Provisional Marine Brigade following the
battle, though strangely the 4th Marine Ammunition Company was not
mentioned.[28] After the island was officially declared secure on 10 August,
there were still thousands of Japanese soldiers on the island who refused to
surrender to American forces. Members of the marine ammunition companies were frequently called upon to defend ammunition dumps on the island,
which were a regular target of these Japanese stragglers. In a particularly
notable incident, PFC Luther Woodward of the 4th Marine Ammunition
Company found footprints near an ammunition dump and when he followed
them, he discovered half a dozen Japanese soldiers in a clearing. Woodward
immediately opened fire, killing one and wounding another of the Japanese.
After gathering five other African American marines, they hunted the other
Japanese soldiers—two of whom were eventually killed as well. For his
bravery and initiative, Woodward received the Silver Star.[29]

On 15 September 1944, the 1st Marine Division attacked Peleliu with the 11th Marine Depot Company and the 7th Marine Ammunition Company in support. Despite Peleliu being only approximately five miles long and only a little more than a mile wide at its broadest point, the battle was one of the most intense experienced by the marines during World War II. The Japanese had learned much from their previous defeats and built substantial defenses which the Americans found difficult to overcome. Given the size of the island, often less than hundred yards separated the frontlines from the rear areas and African American marines were heavily engaged in combat while also performing their duties moving supplies and ammunition. As a result, casualties were high—twenty African American marines were WIA and PVT John Copeland from the 7th Marine Ammunition Company died of wounds. Casualties in the 11th Marine Depot Company were the highest of any African American marine company during the entire war.[30] The performance of the African American marine companies, as well as the U.S. Navy's African American 17th Special Naval Construction Battalion, was noted by MG William H. Rupertus, commander of the 1st Marine Division, who wrote almost identical letters to all three units' commanders.

> The Negro race can well be proud of the work performed by the [unit] as they have demonstrated in every respect that they appreciate the privilege of wearing a Marine uniform and serving with Marines in combat. Please convey to your command these sentiments and inform them that in the eyes of the entire Division they have earned a 'Well Done.'[31]

Also, when the 1st Marine Division received the DUC for Peleliu, the 11th Marine Depot Company and the 7th Marine Ammunition Company, who were attached to the division, likewise received the decoration.

The next to last battle in the Pacific was the invasion of Iwo Jima between 19 February and 26 March 1945, which involved the 3rd, 4th, and 5th Marine Divisions. Supporting these divisions were the African American 8th Marine Ammunition and 33rd, 34th, and 36th Marine Depot

Companies.[32] As had been the case on Peleliu, Iwo Jima was so small and had so few terrain features that little to no distinction existed between the frontline and the rear area. African American marines were under almost continual fire along with everyone else on the island. Likewise, African American marines frequently joined the frontline and/or were forced to defend themselves against Japanese attacks, especially at night. Another problem was Japanese artillery, which frequently focused on supply and ammunition dumps. On 2 March 1945, an ammunition dump built by the 8th Marine Ammunition Company was hit by artillery. SGT Haywood McPhatter described the situation that followed.

> We were in foxholes right beside the dump. We raced away and down to the beach for safety and to assemble what we could. It was a disaster. So much ammo was destroyed. We wanted instant supply from Guam and Saipan.[33]

This forced an airborne resupply on 4 March.

> [T]he planes were ... overhead and [the] munitions [floated down] under brightly colored parachutes [that] the Japanese could see very well. The Japanese pop shot at the Marines running helter-skelter anywhere the winds blew the chutes. ... Things got really intense.[34]

In the predawn hours of 26 March, approximately three hundred Japanese launched their final attack of the battle. The three-hour intense and confusing fight resulted in more than 250 Japanese KIA and 18 POWs. Two African American marines, PFC James Davis and PVT James M. Whitlock, received the Bronze Star for Valor for their actions during this final attack. During the battle of Iwo Jima, two African American marines were KIA and eleven WIA.[35]

The last battle of the Pacific was the invasion of Okinawa from 1 April until 22 June 1945, which involved the 1st and 6th Marine Divisions alongside the four divisions of the Army's XXIV Corps. This battle involved approximately two thousand African American marines—the largest

On 17 April 1945, PFC Luther Woodward of the U.S. Marine Corps' 4th Ammunition Company was awarded the Bronze Star for "his bravery, initiative and battle-cunning." The award was later upgraded to the Silver Star. (NARA)

concentration of the war—including the 1st, 3rd, and 12th Marine Ammunition Companies and the 5th, 9th, 10th, 18th, 20th, 37th, and 38th Marine Depot Companies.[36] On a positive note, the frontlines were more distinct from the rear areas on Okinawa than in the previous battles, though small nighttime attacks did still occur. During the initial phase of the battle, the marines were responsible for the northern two-third of the island, which had only one paved road with very few interconnecting roads capable of handling modern military equipment. The Army was responsible for the southern one-third of the island, which was a more populated area with more roads, but had heavily cross compartmentalized terrain ideally situated for stubborn defense. During the later phase of the battle, the marines shifted south to support the Army. Casualties for African American marines amounted to one KIA and eighteen WIA—one of them twice.[37]

After the official end of the war on 2 September 1945, African American marines participated in the occupation of Japan and China. A total of fourteen marine ammunition or depot companies participated in those missions, but these units were soon discharged. Just as in Europe, servicemen in the Pacific rotated home based on the Adjusted Service Rating Score that considered time in service, time overseas, combat awards, and the number of dependent underage children. As a result, some veteran units were discharged even before the end of 1945. By June 1946, forty-eight of the fifty-one depot companies and eight of the twelve ammunition companies were disbanded. Throughout the war, 19,168 African Americans had served in the Marine Corps (more than the entire size of the Marine Corps in 1939), of whom 12,738 served overseas—overwhelmingly in the depot or ammunition companies.[38] Nevertheless, the frequent volunteering of the noncombat trained African American marines to assist their white comrades on the frontlines earned them respect, if sometimes grudging, and guaranteed them a place in the postwar Marine Corps.

Section III

Combat Arms
at a Distance

Chapter 4

Field Artillery

Since the field artillery branch was more technical than the infantry and cavalry, many white U.S. Army officers did not believe that African American soldiers were intellectually capable of manning artillery batteries. Nevertheless, during the Civil War, the USCT included fourteen regiments of artillery, and, during World War I, the 92nd Division included the 349th, 350th, and 351st Field Artillery Regiments. Ironically, artillerymen were some of the only African American veterans of World War I to receive official praise. The Army, therefore, vacillated between doubting the competence of African Americans to serve in field artillery and believing that field artillery was the combat arm best suited for African Americans because it kept them away from direct contact with the enemy. This almost schizophrenic mentality toward African American military service was a byproduct of the Army's institutionally racist policies. Nevertheless, by the end of the war, African American field artillerymen proved themselves both intellectually competent and personally courageous in combat in Europe.

During World War II, the U.S. Army organized African American artillerymen into one brigade, seven regiments, and twenty-eight separate battalions. Of the twenty-eight separate battalions, eleven[1] were assigned to the 2nd Cavalry, 92nd and 93rd Infantry Divisions. Unfortunately, however, nine[2] of the twenty-eight battalions (including the three assigned to the 2nd Cavalry) were later reorganized as engineer, quartermaster, or ordnance units, while the remaining eleven[3] served as separate, usually corps-level, field artillery battalions.

The largest African American field artillery unit organized during World War II was the 46th Field Artillery Brigade. The brigade was activated on 10 February 1941 at Camp Livingston, Louisiana. Several African American field artillery regiments and a few white units were assigned to the brigade during its initial approximately two-and-a-half-year lifespan.[4] On 16 September 1943, the brigade was redesignated the 46th Field Artillery Group and then disbanded on 31 January 1944. Surprisingly, the group was reactivated on 31 December 1944 in France and served as the HQ for the 350th and 377th Field Artillery Battalions. The group was disbanded again on 16 November 1945 at Camp Kilmer.[5]

One of the most peculiar cases regarding African American field artillery regiments was the 184th Field Artillery Regiment. The regiment began life as the 8th Illinois Infantry Regiment and served on active duty during World War I as the 370th Infantry Regiment in the 93rd Division in France. After the war, the regiment reverted to the 8th Illinois and then was inducted into federal service on 6 January 1941 as the 184th Field Artillery Regiment equipped with 155-mm howitzers.[6] The decision to redesignate the regiment required extensive retraining, which was followed by four months of chaos caused by command changes that were certainly detrimental to the retraining process.[7] On 6 January 1943, after two years at Camp Custer, Michigan, the regiment's HQ was disbanded and its two battalions redesignated— 1st Battalion became 930th Field Artillery Battalion and 2nd Battalion became 931st Field Artillery Battalion. More than a year later, the battalions were again redesignated. On 28 February 1944, the 930th Field Artillery Battalion became the 1699th Engineer Combat Battalion, while on 20 March 1944, the 931st Field Artillery Battalion became the 1698th Engineer Combat Battalion.[8] Thus, a trained National Guard infantry regiment, with some combat veterans, was reorganized first as field artillery and then after three years of expensive and extensive retraining redesignated again as engineers.

On 28 June 1944, 155-mm howitzer crew of the 333rd Field Artillery Battalion digging in soon after arriving in France. (NARA)

While the Army attempted to mask their motives by labeling the battalions as "combat engineers," in practice like almost all African American "combat engineers" they were used for little more than physical labor.

The 333rd Field Artillery Regiment was activated on 5 August 1942 at Camp Gruber, Oklahoma, equipped with 155-mm howitzers. After six months, on 12 February 1943, the regiment was redesignated the 333rd Field Artillery Group. This change was made to almost all regiments in the Army, except those in the infantry. The idea was to make everything more modular to attach battalions to any division without having to worry about regimental affiliations. At the same time, the regiment's 1st Battalion became the 333rd Field Artillery Battalion, while the 2nd Battalion became the 969th Field Artillery Battalion.[9] The group and its battalions were shipped separately to the United Kingdom and arrived between 18 February and 7 March 1944. Likewise, they arrived in France in different shipments between 29 June and 9 July 1944.[10] Attached to the VIII Corps, the group and its battalions were used interchangeably with similar white field artillery units. Periodically, white battalions came under the group's control while the group's battalions came under the control of white field artillery groups. Initially, the group and its battalions were heavily engaged during the Allied summer 1944 offensive operations. However, following the failure of Operation Market Garden in late September, the Allied offensive slowed in the fall as a result of shortages of men, equipment, and most particularly gasoline.

When the German Ardennes Offensive (commonly known as the Battle of the Bulge) began on 16 December 1944, the 333rd Field Artillery Group and its battalions were stationed along the Belgian border with France. On the second day of the offensive, 333rd Field Artillery Battalion was flanked and a large number of its men were killed or captured. Eleven members of Battery C attempted to evade capture and eventually arrived in the Belgium town of Wereth, where they were sheltered by farmer Mathias Langer. Unfortunately, approximately a third of the families in the town were ethnically German and one of them informed members of the 1st SS Division that American soldiers were hiding in the town. The SS captured the Americans, then took them to a nearby field where they beat, tortured, and finally murdered them. The 1st SS Division was also involved in the more infamous Malmedy Massacre in which eighty-four American soldiers were similarly murdered. Though the Malmedy Massacre resulted in prosecution, the Wereth Massacre was largely forgotten except by Hermann Langer, the son of the farmer who tried to protect the Americans. Langer built a memorial on the site of the massacre and after a decade of effort, other people, both Americans and Belgians, contributed to purchasing the site and constructing a substantial memorial. During the battle, the 333rd Field Artillery suffered higher casualties than any other artillery unit in the VIII Corps—6 officers (including the battalion commander) and 222 enlisted men were killed or became POWs, which does not even include those wounded or missing.[11]

On 19 December, the 333rd Field Artillery Group was released from the VIII Corps and attached directly to the 101st Airborne Division, which moved to the vicinity of Bastogne, Belgium. That same night, the Germans cut the main road out of the town. The remnants of the 333rd Field Artillery Battalion joined the 969th Field Artillery Battalion and fought on despite having only 450 rounds of high explosive ammunition and cut off from resupply. At times, the frontline was as close as three hundred yards from the group's HQ, and the limited ammunition necessitated firing with great care. Finally, on 26 December, Allied cargo planes dropped artillery ammunition to allow the group to continue its mission.[12] On 28 December, when a route became open out of the besieged area, the group was ordered to move to Matton, France, where the rest of the VIII Corps' artillery outside of the encirclement had established themselves.

After the Battle of the Bulge, the remaining 286 officers and men of the 333rd Field Artillery Battalion were used to fill vacancies in the other battalions attached to the group—578th and 969th Field Artillery. The 333rd Field Artillery Battalion was reformed with replacements and veterans in April 1945 but did not see further combat. The 969th Field Artillery Battalion continued to support the 101st Airborne Division until it was relieved on 12 January. MG Maxwell D. Taylor, the commander of the 101st Airborne, wrote to the commander of the 969th Field Artillery to praise the battalion.

> The Officers and Men of the 101st Airborne Division wish to express to your command their appreciation of the gallant support rendered by the 969th Field Artillery Battalion in the recent defense of Bastogne, Belgium. The success of this defense is attributable to the shoulder to shoulder cooperation of all units involved. This Division is proud to have shared the Battlefield with your command.[13]

MG Troy H. Middleton also commended the battalion, "Your contribution to the great success of our arms at Bastogne will take its place among the epic achievements of our Army."[14] The battalion received the DUC on 7 February 1945. On 21 January, the 969th Field Artillery was attached to the French 1st Division and fired 912 rounds on its first day in combat with that division. Then from 25 January to the end of the war, the battalion was attached in succession to the French 5th Armored Division, U.S. 75th Infantry Division, French 2nd Armored Division, U.S. 30th Field Artillery Group, U.S. XXI Corps, and finally the U.S. 4th Infantry Division. During its ten months of combat, the battalion fought under all four of the American armies in the ETO and fired a total of 42,489 rounds.[15] The 333rd Field Artillery Battalion was disbanded in Germany on 10 June 1945, while the 969th Field Artillery was not disbanded until 15 April 1946 at Camp Kilmer.[16] The 333rd Field Artillery Group was disbanded on 30 December 1945 at Hampton Roads Port of Embarkation, Virginia.[17]

The 349th Field Artillery Regiment was activated on 1 August 1940 at Fort Sill, Oklahoma, equipped with 155-mm howitzers. After almost three years of stateside training, the regiment was redesignated the 349th Field Artillery Group and its 1st Battalion became the 349th Field Artillery Battalion, while its 2nd Battalion became the 686th Field Artillery Battalion.[18] The group and its battalions were shipped to France separately with the group arriving on 21 October 1944, the 349th Field Artillery Battalion arriving on 10 February 1945, and the 686th Field Artillery arriving on 1 February 1945. The three units seldom served together during the war, though all three participated in the Rhineland and Central Europe campaigns. In fact, for most of its time in combat, the group included two completely different battalions—the 754th and 777th Field Artillery Battalions, the first of which was white and the second African American. The group entered combat on 23 February 1945 and completed seventy-seven days of combat with only one minor casualty.[19] The 686th Field Artillery only participated in combat from 1 to 27 April, mostly in support of the 4th Infantry Division. During that brief time, however, the battalion moved twenty-one times as the collapsing German forces retreated rapidly.[20] The group was disbanded on 24 May 1946 in Germany, while both the 349th and 686th Field Artillery Battalions served on occupation duty for more than a year and were disbanded on 20 January 1947, also in Germany.[21]

The 350th Field Artillery Regiment was activated on 10 February 1941 at Camp Livingston, equipped with 155-mm howitzers. The racial attitude of the regiment's officers was made clear by one of the battalion commanders, LTC James H. Leusley.

I doubt if the average negro [sic] soldier is physically as brave and strong as the average white soldier. History shows, however, that there have been individual cases where the negro [*sic*] was just as brave, strong, and courageous as any man. I believe, on the average, he is perhaps a little more obedient, and endures hardship with less growling than the white soldier. On the other hand he is slow to learn, lacks initiative, and I believe would be easily stampeded in case of surprise or heavy concentration of fire. ... I have seen them stay up all night and occasionally lean against a tree or truck and 'cat-nap' rather than go to bed in their tent when we were in the field, simply because they were afraid of the dark. ... I doubt if the negro [*sic*] officer has the qualities needed for successful leadership. ... I firmly believe that a negro [*sic*] unit on strange soil and under new officers, which is bound to happen once combat is joined, will be of little military value. ... I do think that as an aid in solving the negro question, after the war, negro combat units must be given the opportunity to either prove or disprove the fact that they can 'take it' in action.[22]

After more than two years of training on 1 April 1943, the regiment was redesignated the 350th Field Artillery Group and its 1st Battalion became the 350th Field Artillery Battalion, while its 2nd Battalion became the 971st Field Artillery Battalion.[23] The group and the 971st Field Artillery never left Camp Livingston, where they were disbanded on 1 March 1944. The 350th Field Artillery Battalion, however, did see combat. The battalion arrived in France on 22 February 1945 and saw limited combat from 1 March to 5 April attached to the 46th and 351st Field Artillery Groups. During the last month of the war, the battalion guarded thirty-five different positions, including an airfield, an engineering laboratory, a POW hospital, and various supply and ammunition dumps, as well as operated a 245-man motorized patrol.[24] The 350th Field Artillery Battalion was disbanded at Camp Kilmer on 7 August 1946.[25]

The 351st Field Artillery Regiment was activated on 10 February 1941 at Camp Livingston, equipped with 155-mm howitzers. On 1 April 1943, the regiment was redesignated the 351st Field Artillery Group and its 1st Battalion became the 351st Field Artillery Battalion, while its 2nd Battalion became the 973rd Field Artillery Battalion. The 973rd Field Artillery was disbanded on 1 April 1944, but the group and 351st Field Artillery Battalion landed in France on 18 and 25 February 1945 respectively. Understandably, their time in combat was brief, and, after a year of occupation duty, the group was disbanded on 15 June 1946 in Germany, while the battalion was disbanded at Camp Kilmer on 9 August 1946.[26]

The 578th Field Artillery Regiment was activated on 15 June 1942 at Fort Bragg, North Carolina, as the only African American heavy field artillery unit equipped with 8-inch howitzers. On 23 February 1943, the regiment was redesignated the 578th Field Artillery Group and its 1st Battalion became the 578th Field Artillery Battalion, while its 2nd Battalion became the 999th Field Artillery Battalion. While the group was disbanded on 23 February 1944, its battalions saw combat.[27] The 578th Field Artillery Battalion arrived in France on 17 July 1944 and was attached to the 202nd Field Artillery Group, which was responsible for counterbattery fire. By the time of the Battle of the Bulge, in December 1944, the battalion was attached to the 402nd Field Artillery Group. During the first day of the offensive, the battalion fired 774 rounds and was praised by their commander. "The steadiness and determination of all concerned in this trying movement when a heavy artillery battalion was fighting a rearguard action is worthy of the highest praise."[28]

During the chaos of the early days of the battle, units separated, and eventually, the 578th Field Artillery also included a platoon of antiaircraft guns, an extra battery of 8-inch howitzers, and fifty enlisted men from the white 740th Field Artillery tasked as infantry. After two days of retreat, the battalion commander stated, "All concerned were more than anxious to dig in and fight."[29] Nevertheless, the battalion was ordered to move 20 miles south of Bastogne and was attached to the III Corps. As the relief effort moved closer to Bastogne, the 578th Field Artillery moved with it and was attached to two different field artillery groups as needed. Despite frequent tactical movements between 16 and 31 December, the battalion fired 3455 rounds with an excellent rate of effectiveness. While located in Neunhausen, Luxembourg, on 4 January, the battalion was ordered to destroy the entire enemy-occupied village of Berle. The gunners demonstrated their ability by destroying every structure in the village except for one which was marked with a large red cross.[30] Following the defeat of the German offensive, the 578th Field Artillery returned to the VIII Corps for the remainder of the war. In March and April 1945, Allied forces advanced so rapidly that the battalion seldom had the opportunity to fire their guns and were often used as infantry to clear German-occupied positions. By 26 April, the battalion was on the German border with Czechoslovakia. The battalion briefly served on occupation duty after the war and was disbanded on 2 November 1945 in Germany.[31]

The 999th Field Artillery Battalion also served in France, arriving on 17 July 1944. Attached to the XV Corps, the battalion, starting on 4 August, advanced 180 miles over nine days and fired two thousand rounds during that period. During the fall of 1944, the battalion supported American and French divisions in their advance toward the German border. On 21 December, the battalion was attached to the 3rd Infantry Division and performed a sixty-mile night march to occupy new positions in support of the division. On 6 January, the battalion was ordered to Aubure in the Vosges Mountains. Despite steep, icy, winding mountain roads, the battalion successfully moved their heavy guns into place. The 3rd Infantry's artillery commander praised them, saying, "Nevertheless you accepted the mission cheerfully and by an extraordinary display of ingenuity and hard work accomplished the movement in a remarkably short time. The entire matter is a splendid testimony to the efficiency and training of the 999th Field Artillery Battalion."[32]

During the elimination of German positions in the Colmar Pocket in Alsace from 20 January to 9 February, the 999th Field Artillery was attached to two French units until the task was completed. As a reward for their excellent service, the battalion was given the right to incorporate the arms of the city of Colmar into their unit insignia. The battalion then returned to control of the XV Corps. As with the 578th Field Artillery Battalion, the speed of the Allied Spring offensive left little opportunity for the use of 8-inch howitzers. On 8 April, the 999th Field Artillery received a special mission perfectly suited for their large caliber howitzers. The entrance to the port of Bordeaux was still controlled by German-occupied fortifications. After only 10 days of shelling, from the 999th Field Artillery and other battalions, the German positions surrendered on 30 April. After a few months of occupation duty, the battalion returned to the United States and was disbanded on 17 December 1945 at Camp Kilmer.[33]

Four African American field artillery battalions (593rd, 594th, 595th, and 596th Field Artillery Battalions) provided artillery support to the 93rd Infantry Division during World War II. All four battalions were organized on 15 May 1942 at Fort Huachuca, the first three with 105-mm howitzers and the last with 155-mm howitzers.[34] Unfortunately, even though the division and all four of its field artillery battalions were deployed to the Pacific, only one battalion (593rd Field Artillery) saw any real combat. From 28 March to 12 June 1944, the 593rd Field Artillery was attached to the Americal Division on Bougainville Island as part of the 25th Infantry RCT. The battalion was attached to the divisional field artillery and began combat operations on 1 April. Between 1 and 19 April, the battalion fired 7,002 rounds, and then, between 21 April and 20 May, the battalion fired another 4,772 rounds in support of the 25th Infantry and the division. The battalion's efficiency and accuracy were noted and praised by BG William C. Dunckel, the division's artillery commander, MG Robert B. McClure, the division commander, and MG Oscar Griswold, the XIV Corps commander.[35] Unfortunately, the battalion, along with the rest of the 93rd Infantry Division, spent the remainder of the war performing labor and security duties on various already secured Pacific islands. All four of the 93rd Infantry's field artillery battalions were disbanded on 3 February 1946 at Camp Stoneman.[36]

Just as with the 93rd Infantry Division, four African American field artillery battalions (597th, 598th, 599th, and 600th Field Artillery Battalions) provided artillery support to the 92nd Infantry Division during World War II. The battalions were organized on 15 October 1942 at four different Army posts—Camp Atterbury, Camp Breckenridge, Camp Robinson, and Fort McClellan, respectively, the first three with 105-mm howitzers and the last one with 155-mm howitzers.[37] Interestingly, a large number of officers from the 597th and 600th Field Artillery Battalions were originally in the 184th Field Artillery Regiment, which began life as the 8th Infantry Regiment of the Illinois National Guard. As a result, the 597th and 600th Field Artillery were the only all African American combat units in the 92nd Infantry Division.[38] LTC Marcus H. Ray was originally the commander of the 2nd Battalion, 8th Illinois, which originated in Chicago, then of the 931st Field Artillery Battalion. On 5 September 1943, Ray wrote to Truman K. Gibson, Jr., to complain after 484 enlisted men of his battalion were transferred to support units.

> This battalion had passed every test for combat, including the firing of all weapons and physical conditioning tests. The training job accomplished with the group we are losing was possible only because they had in mind release from the insults, discrimination, and segregation by an early move to a combat theater. Ironic, isn't it, that men should be willing to face death for people who hate them. In addition to the racial implications in the transfer of black artillerymen two the quartermaster service, there is a waste of training and education that I can't understand.[39]

Ray later became the commander of the 600th Field Artillery Battalion in the 92nd Infantry. Just a few days after Ray's letter, LTC Wendell T. Derricks, the commander of the 930th Field Artillery Battalion, suffered an almost identical experience. Similarly, Derricks had previously commanded the 1st Battalion, 8th Illinois, then the 930th Field Artillery Battalion, and later the 597th Field Artillery Battalion. The 597th and 600th Field Artillery were highly rated by the division's field artillery commander, BG William H. "Red" Colbern.

> To be perfectly frank, I was very highly pleased with the performance of the battalions having all Negro officers. They did much better than I expected them to do. … It doesn't make a nickel's worth of difference to the general run of Negro enlisted men whether his officer is white or black, just so long as the officer knows his job, is a good disciplinarian, and has the welfare of the man at heart.[40]

While Colbern's comments were intended as positive, his paternalistic tone makes his opinion of African American soldiers clear.

All four of the 92nd Infantry's field artillery battalions saw combat during the war and received praise for their efforts. However, the battalion which saw the most action and the first to enter combat was the 598th Field Artillery which deployed to Italy as part of the 370th Infantry RCT in advance of the rest of the division.[41] The battalion arrived in Naples, Italy, on 30 July 1944, and was posted to the frontline on 24 August where it remained for 42 days until 5 October 1944.[42] The battalion's Battery C fired the first rounds in combat on 29 August.[43] Even when the rest of the division was severely castigated for supposed poor performance, the field artillery battalions continued to receive praise. For instance, during the German counterattack of 26 December 1944, when the 92nd Infantry withdrew from the frontline and the Indian 8th Division was forced to plug the gap in the lines, MG Dudley Russell, who commanded the 8th Division, kept the 598th Field Artillery close by because they continued to fight when the infantry retreated.[44] After the war, all four battalions served for a few months on occupation duty until they returned to the United States and were disbanded at Camp Miles Standish, Massachusetts, on 24 November 1945.[45]

The final African American field artillery unit to see overseas service in World War II was the 777th Field Artillery Battalion, which was organized on 15 April 1943 at Camp Beale, California. The battalion was one of only seventeen in the entire Army organized with 4.5-inch guns. The 4.5-inch gun was a compromise weapon that had superior range to the 105 mm and weighed less than the 155 mm but the Army ultimately decided it unnecessary because of the additional ammunition type complicated logistics. The battalion landed in France on 18 September 1944 but did not immediately enter combat. Since the need for motor transport was so great at that point, from 25 September to 6 October, two officers and seventy-six enlisted men from the battalion were assigned to transport men and supplies to the front, a round trip of 2,100 miles, using a total of thirty-six of the battalion's vehicles. The battalion finally left for Belgium on 25 October and entered Germany on 2 November. Through December, the battalion fired missions in support of the XIII and XIX Corps, though combat tended to last for only short, intense periods.[46] For instance, on 18–19 December, the battalion fired 2,834 rounds, while the next night, they fired 3,284 rounds to repel the German 1st and 5th Panzer Divisions.[47] Near Altfeld, Germany, along the Rhine River between 5 and 10 March 1945, the battalion fired on and destroyed barges, vehicles, and troop assembly points on the east side of the river.[48] On 25 March, the 777th Field Artillery became the first African American combat unit to cross the Rhine River.[49] Only a few months after the end of the war in Europe, on 18 September 1945, the battalion was disbanded in France.

Despite prewar white skepticism, African American field artillery units performed extremely well in combat. Both their technical skill and their courage under fire proved exemplary. By their actions, these African American field artillerymen were able to put another nail in the coffin of racist stereotypes. Also, the frequent mixing of African American and white field artillery battalions in wartime field artillery groups and/or corps-level artillery undermined the segregationist position that required the races to be kept separate. As with almost all other African American combat participation in World War II, these field artillerymen's actions helped to justify President Truman's decision to desegregate the armed forces in 1948.

Chapter 5

Coast/Antiaircraft Artillery

Since coast artillery was about as far from the battlefield as one could get and remain in combat arms and African American field artillerymen had performed well in World War I, some white senior officers believed coast artillery was an ideal branch for African Americans. Nevertheless, as with the field artillery, the Army fluctuated between doubting the competence of African Americans to serve in such a technical branch and believing that coast artillery was well suited for African Americans. However, as the war wore on coast artillery units increasingly became caretakers for stateside installations since they were combat arms units, but their combat utility diminished as the war progressed. At the same time, the African American population and press were concerned that African American soldiers were disproportionately assigned to supporting units rather than combat arms units, so the Army increasingly assigned African Americans to coast artillery units. This allowed the Army to inaccurately inflate its numbers by saying that more African Americans were in combat arms, while at the same time assigning these individuals to stateside coast artillery units who would rarely participate in combat.[1] Then later, as manpower shortages became an issue, these units were often converted into engineer or other support units.

Ultimately, only a small number of African American coast/antiaircraft artillerymen participated in combat, but those who did, proved both their technical
competence and personal valor.

Perhaps no other pre-existing branch of the Army saw more change
(reorganizations, mission modifications, fears of obsolescence/disbandment,
weapons changes, etc.) during World War II than the Coast Artillery Corps
(CAC). While artillery existed in the Army since the time of the American
Revolution, little distinction was made between different types of artillery.
Artillerymen frequently transferred between assignments in light and heavy
or field and coast artillery units. Eventually, the Army's leadership decided
that since the types of weapons used by the two primary forms of artillery
required distinctly different methods of training and employment, then two
separate branches of artillery were necessary. Though the formal legal separation of the branches did not occur until 1907, coast artillery was effectively
separated after 1901.[2]

Coast Artillery was distinctive from field artillery in several ways.
The first difference regarded the issue of mobility—field artillery was
mobile and coast artillery generally was not. Coast artillery guns were
normally mounted in large concrete or stone encasements to protect against
gunfire from enemy ships which could fire shells as large as eighteen inches
in diameter. As a result of the immovable nature of their guns, coast artillery
posts were more permanent and provided better facilities for the soldiers.
The size of the guns used by field and coast artillery was also substantially different. Coast artillery seldom used weapons smaller than six inches
(155 mm), while the largest and rarest caliber used in the field artillery was
eight inches (203 mm).

During its existence, the CAC took on several different missions as
technology evolved. The first of these new missions was the laying or
"planting" of mines at sea. While the coast artillery was involved in this
task as early as 1904, it was not until 1918 that the U.S. Army Mine Planters
Service was officially established and placed under the control of the
CAC. Also during World War I, the CAC manned heavy artillery (155 mm
and above), railroad artillery, and antiaircraft artillery units in France. Railroad
artillery used large-caliber (usually larger than eight inches) guns mounted

on railroad carriages, which allowed these guns a degree of mobility on land than ever before imagined. Given the size of the guns involved, assigning these weapons to the coast artillery or naval shore detachments made sense, since both had greater experience with them. Antiaircraft artillery was a new idea to counter the new threat posed by aircraft. During the war, the CAC organized and manned sixteen antiaircraft artillery battalions.[3]

During the interwar period, coast artillery units were reorganized and wartime practices were standardized. The National Defense Act of 1920 reorganized the CAC with forty-seven Regular Army regiments (twenty-four fixed harbor defense, nineteen antiaircraft artillery, six tractor-drawn 155 mm, five railroad guns, and one trench mortar), but not all of these units were fully manned or even actively organized. Likewise, a large number of coast artillery regiments were organized in the National Guard and the Organized Reserve (36 fixed harbor defense, 162 antiaircraft artillery, 5 tractor-drawn 155 mm, and 4 railroad guns), but like the Regular Army, not all of these units were fully manned or organized on more than paper.[4] Two examples of this were (1) the 1st Trench Mortar Regiment only existed from 1 September 1926 to 1 March 1928, after which it was transferred to the field artillery branch, and (2) the 12th Coast Artillery Regiment (Harbor Defense) only existed from 1 July 1924 to 15 April 1932 when it was disbanded.[5]

During the last years of the interwar period and the first years of World War II, technology evolved and airpower became more powerful and prevalent, which meant that the traditional missions of the CAC became less important. As a result, by the time the United States entered World War II, the only CAC function in great demand was antiaircraft artillery. Additionally, two other types of coast artillery were created during World War II, which were not equipped with any weapons whatsoever. Barrage balloon battalions and searchlight battalions defended American troops and installations by preventing enemy aircraft from making strafing runs or blinding and/or pin-pointing those enemy planes for antiaircraft gunners.

One of the first African American coast artillery units of World War II was originally a National Guard infantry regiment which was converted to coast artillery when inducted into federal service.[6] On 30 August 1940, the 369th Infantry Regiment of the New York National Guard (nicknamed the "Harlem Hellfighters") which won fame for its achievements while fighting alongside the French during World War I, was converted to the 369th Coast Artillery Regiment (Antiaircraft).[7] The 369th Coast Artillery Regiment was called to active duty on 13 January 1941 and moved from New York City to Fort Ontario, New York. After eight months of retraining, the regiment moved to Camp Edwards, Massachusetts, on 5 September 1941. Then after eight months spent guarding Cape Cod, the 369th Coast Artillery left for Camp Stoneman on 5 May 1942, before departing from San Francisco for Hawaii. On 12 December 1943, the regiment was redesignated as the 369th Antiaircraft Artillery Group.[8] The 369th Coast Artillery Regiment maintained its prewar organization of only two battalions and, therefore, the first battalion was redesignated as the 369th Antiaircraft Artillery Gun Battalion and the second battalion was redesignated as the 870th Antiaircraft Artillery Automatic Weapons Battalion. While the group HQ was disbanded on 28 November 1944 in Hawaii, the 870th Antiaircraft Artillery later transferred to Okinawa on 10 May 1945 and became the only part of the old 369th Coast Artillery Regiment to see combat during World War II. The 369th Antiaircraft Artillery Battalion also transferred to Okinawa but did not arrive until after the battle on 12 August 1945.[9] Had the planned-for invasion of Japan taken place doubtless both battalions might have seen considerable combat since Okinawa was a major staging point for the invasion of the Japanese home islands and had already been under both kamikaze and other aerial attacks. After the war, the battalions were disbanded at Camp Anza, California, on 21 January 1946, and Fort Lawton, Washington, on 15 January 1946, respectively.

In addition to the 369th Coast Artillery, eight other African American coast artillery regiments were organized during World War II. The 54th Coast Artillery Regiment (155-mm Gun) was originally an organized reserve unit with white personnel based in Philadelphia, Pennsylvania, from 1927 to 1941.[10] On 10 February 1941, the regiment was activated at Camp Wallace, Texas, with African American personnel. The 54th Coast Artillery moved frequently during its existence—to Camp Davis on 22 May 1941; Fort Fisher, North Carolina, on 21 October 1941; back to Camp Davis on 24 November 1941;

Undersecretary of War Robert P. Patterson inspected the 369th Coast Artillery Regiment during a visit to Hawaii in August 1943. Patterson seen congratulating the regimental commander, COL Chauncey M. Hooper, while the regimental executive officer, LTC Harry B. Reubel, and the commander of the Hawaiian Department, LTG Robert C. Richardson, Jr., look on. (NARA)

to Fort Cronkite, California, on 28 February 1942; to Fort Ord, California, on 5 April 1942; to Capitala CCC Camp, California, on 30 January 1943; and back to Fort Ord on 20 March 1944.[11] On 5 June 1944, the regiment was redesignated as the 152nd Coast Artillery Group. The group moved only moved once to Camp Livingston on 16 July 1944 where it was disbanded on 3 August 1944.[12] After the regiment was redesignated a group, its battalions were given the new designations: 1st Battalion—606th Coast Artillery Battalion (155-mm Gun); 2nd Battalion—49th Coast Artillery Battalion (155-mm Gun); and 3rd Battalion—607th Coast Artillery Battalion (155-mm Gun). The 49th Coast Artillery Battalion arrived at Bougainville on 1 April 1944 where it saw

Members of the S-3 (Operations) section of the 477th Antiaircraft
Artillery Automatic Weapons Battalion study maps at Oro Bay,
New Guinea, in November 1944. (NARA)

combat. The battalion later transferred to New Guinea on 18 March 1945 and
the Philippines on 27 August 1945, both times after the end of combat operations, and was disbanded on 20 January 1946 in the Philippines.[13] The group's
other two battalions remained stateside and were disbanded on 3 August and
31 July 1944 respectively.[14]

The 76th Coast Artillery Regiment (Antiaircraft) was activated on
10 February 1941 at Fort Bragg. Oddly, the regiment's first battalion was
already activated on 1 August 1940. The regiment moved to Philadelphia,
Pennsylvania, on 11 December 1941 and then transferred to Camp Stoneman
on 30 July 1942 before shipping to Espiritu Santo, New Hebrides, where
it arrived on 2 September 1942. On 1 November 1943, the regiment was
redesignated the 76th Antiaircraft Artillery Group and its battalions were also
redesignated: 1st Battalion—76th Antiaircraft Artillery Gun Battalion; 2nd
Battalion—933rd Antiaircraft Artillery Automatic Weapons Battalion; and
3rd Battalion was disbanded.[15] The group HQ moved to the Russell Islands

on 10 June 1944, then to New Guinea on 2 January 1945, then to the Philippines on 17 August 1945, and finally back to Camp Stoneman, where it was disbanded on 27 January 1946.[16] After the regiment was reorganized, its former battalions continued to serve in the Pacific. The 76th Antiaircraft Artillery Gun Battalion arrived at New Georgia on 4 February 1944, then to Los Negros Island on 8 January 1945, and finally to Camp Anza where it was disbanded on 31 December 1945.[17] The 933rd Antiaircraft Artillery Automatic Weapons Battalion transferred to the Russell Islands on 12 December 1943, then the Admiralty Islands on 12 December 1944, and finally to Camp Anza, where it was also disbanded on 31 December 1945.[18]

The 77th Coast Artillery Regiment (Antiaircraft) was also activated on 10 February 1941 at Fort Bragg and like the 76th Coast Artillery, its first battalion was activated on 1 August 1940. The regiment was moved to Windy Hill, South Carolina, on 14 July 1941, then back to Fort Bragg on 27 October 1941, and finally to Hartford, Connecticut, on 11 December 1941. On 9 May 1942, the regiment arrived at Tongatabu Island, Kingdom of Tonga. Almost a year later on 18 April 1943, the regiment moved to the New Hebrides Islands, where on 1 November 1943 it was redesignated as the 77th Antiaircraft Artillery Group. The regiment's battalions were also redesignated: 1st Battalion—77th Antiaircraft Artillery Gun Battalion; 2nd Battalion—938th Antiaircraft Artillery Automatic Weapons Battalion; and 3rd Battalion—374th Antiaircraft Artillery Searchlight Battalion.[19] The group accompanied by the regiment's former battalions moved to New Georgia on 13 December 1943 and then to Los Negros Island on 8 February 1945. The group HQ and the 77th Antiaircraft Artillery Battalion were disbanded at Camp Anza on 31 December 1945.[20] The 374th Antiaircraft Artillery Searchlight Battalion and the 938th Antiaircraft Artillery Automatic Weapons Battalion arrived on New Guinea on 6 March 1945, where they were disbanded on 25 June 1945 and 15 February 1946, respectively.[21]

The 90th Coast Artillery Regiment (Antiaircraft) was activated on 1 May 1942 at Camp Stewart. On 12 April 1943, the regiment landed in North Africa, and, a year later on 25 May 1944, it was redesignated as the 90th Antiaircraft Artillery Group, before disbanding on 5 December 1944.[22]

The regiment's battalions were likewise redesignated: 1st Battalion—90th Antiaircraft Artillery Gun Battalion; 2nd Battalion—897th Antiaircraft Artillery Automatic Weapons Battalion; and 3rd Battalion—334th Antiaircraft Artillery Searchlight Battalion. As so often happened with African American units in the ETO, all three of these battalions were later broken up and their troops used to create engineer and quartermaster units on 4 December 1944, 15 September 1944, and 9 December 1944, respectively.[23]

The 99th Coast Artillery Regiment (Antiaircraft) was activated on 15 April 1941 at Camp Davis. On 10 May 1942, the regiment arrived at Fort Reed, Trinidad, where it remained until 9 December 1943 when it transferred to Camp Stewart.[24] The posting of the 99th Coast Artillery to Trinidad was largely a public relations mission, both to show American commitment to the nations of the Caribbean and an overseas posting for an African American unit. On 29 February 1944, the regimental HQ was disbanded and its battalions redesignated: 1st Battalion—99th Antiaircraft Artillery Gun Battalion; 2nd Battalion—871st Antiaircraft Artillery Automatic Weapons Battalion; and 3rd Battalion—338th Antiaircraft Artillery Searchlight Battalion. While the 99th and 338th Antiaircraft Artillery were then disbanded on 28 August and 31 July 1944 (respectively), the 871st Antiaircraft Artillery transferred to New Guinea on 4 February 1945, where it was promptly disbanded on 18 March.[25]

The 100th Coast Artillery Regiment (Antiaircraft) was activated two days after its sister regiment, the 99th Coast Artillery, on 17 April 1941 also at Camp Davis. The regiment moved to Fort Brady, Michigan, on 8 April 1942, where a remained until 28 April 1943 when the regimental HQ was disbanded. The battalions were then redesignated: 1st Battalion—100th Antiaircraft Artillery Gun Battalion; 2nd Battalion—538th Antiaircraft Artillery Automatic Weapons Battalion; and the 3rd Battalion was disbanded.[26] While the 538th Antiaircraft Artillery was disbanded on 24 April 1944, the 100th Antiaircraft Artillery transferred to Australia on 18 November 1943 and finally to New Guinea on 18 February 1944 where they participated in combat before being disbanded on 4 December 1944.[27]

The final two African American coast artillery regiments organized during World War II share extremely similar histories. The 612th Coast

Artillery Regiment (Antiaircraft) was activated on 1 September 1942 at Camp Stewart. Redesignated as the 121st Coast Artillery Group on 20 January 1943, but then disbanded on 2 April 1943. The 612th Coast Artillery's battalions became: 1st Battalion—741st Antiaircraft Artillery Gun Battalion; 2nd Battalion—207th Antiaircraft Artillery Automatic Weapons Battalion; and 3rd Battalion—234th Antiaircraft Artillery Gun Battalion. The 207th Antiaircraft Artillery transferred to Australia on 29 September 1943 and then to New Guinea on 3 December 1943 before arriving at Camp Stoneman where it was disbanded on 20 January 1946. The 234th Antiaircraft Artillery arrived in India on 23 January 1945 before transfer to Saipan on 9 June 1945 where it was disbanded on 15 June. The 741st Antiaircraft Artillery transferred to Australia on 1 October 1943 and then to New Guinea on 14 October 1943 where it was disbanded on 30 January 1946.[28]

The 613th Coast Artillery Regiment (Antiaircraft) was activated at Camp Stewart on 10 December 1942. Then on 20 January 1943, the 613th Coast Artillery was redesignated the 122nd Coast Artillery Group before disbanding on 2 April 1943.[29] The 613th Coast Artillery's battalions became: 1st Battalion—742nd Antiaircraft Artillery Gun Battalion; 2nd Battalion—208th Antiaircraft Artillery Automatic Weapons Battalion; and 3rd Battalion—235th Antiaircraft Artillery Gun Battalion. The 235th Antiaircraft Artillery was disbanded on 12 December 1944 at Camp Livingston. However, the 613th Coast Artillery's other two battalions saw service in the Pacific. The 208th Antiaircraft Artillery transferred to Australia on 23 September 1943 and then to New Guinea on 1 February 1944 where it was disbanded on 4 December 1944. The 742nd Antiaircraft Artillery arrived on Espiritu Santo on 16 October 1943, then transferred to New Britain on 20 May 1944 before finally arriving at New Guinea on 21 November 1944. After transferring to the Philippines, the battalion was disbanded on 11 February 1946.[30]

In addition to the former regimental battalions, another eighteen African American antiaircraft artillery battalions were organized during World War II. However, only ten of these eighteen battalions saw overseas service and only two have a well-documented enough history to discuss in detail.[31] The 320th Antiaircraft Artillery Balloon Battalion (Very Low Altitude) was activated on 10 December 1942 at Camp Tyson, Tennessee. All Army barrage balloon units were trained at Camp Tyson because the location of the camp isolated it from military and commercial aviation lanes making accidents less likely. While barrage balloons were first developed during World War I and were used extensively in Europe during World War II, they were largely unknown to Americans. Filled with hydrogen, these balloons could reach altitudes up to ten thousand feet. The balloons were tethered with steel cables and placed at important points to deter low flying aircraft, which could have their wings sheared off by the cables. Ultimately, the Army organized twenty-one barrage balloon battalions of which only two left the continental United States during World War II—the 305th Coast Artillery Barrage Balloon Battalion, which transferred to Hawaii and was later redesignated as the 861st Antiaircraft Artillery Automatic Weapons Battalion[32], and the 320th Antiaircraft Artillery.[33]

After almost a year of training at Camp Tyson, the 320th Antiaircraft Artillery arrived in the United Kingdom on board the British ship RMS *Aquitania* on 24 November 1943. The African American soldiers of the battalion were quite shocked by the reception they received in the UK. The average Briton made no distinction between Americans by color—they were all "Yanks." African American soldiers were treated as equals and invited to homes, pubs, and dances. These soldiers were pleasantly surprised by the positive treatment from strangers, while white American soldiers, especially those in the South, were outraged at the same positive treatment of their countrymen. When racial incidents occurred in the United Kingdom, they were usually caused by white American soldiers. White Americans typically refused to eat or drink with African Americans, and this often led to angry exchanges and fistfights. The worst racial incidents were caused by white American indignation when seeing African Americans with British women.[34] Oddly enough, the British generally preferred African Americans to white Americans. George Orwell, the famed British writer, said, "The general consensus of opinion seems to be that the only American soldiers with decent manners are the Negroes."[35]

On 2 June 1944, the 320th Antiaircraft Artillery boarded landing craft in preparation for the invasion of France. When the battalion landed on D-Day, 6 June, they became the first African Americans to arrive in France. The battalion HQ and Battery A were attached to the 1st Infantry Division, which landed on Omaha Beach, while Battery C was attached to the 4th Infantry Division which landed on Utah Beach.[36] Battery B did not begin to land until 7 June. Ironically, the 320th Antiaircraft Artillery's balloons were pre-inflated and brought across the English Channel on landing craft on 7 June, because no hydrogen supplies were brought to France until later in the campaign. The first twelve balloons arrived on Omaha Beach by the evening of 7 June, but all were destroyed by enemy fire. On Utah Beach, twenty-five balloons came ashore on that same day, but it was soon determined that the balloons were used by German artillery as aiming points, so they were all cut loose and replaced later.[37]

As a "Very Low Altitude" unit, the 320th Antiaircraft Artillery's balloons were about the size of a modern compact car. More balloons were brought over until the battalion reached full strength of 141 balloons on 21 June.[38] The battalion was crucially important to defending the landing beaches from German aerial attack since most enemy planes would not approach the beach once they saw the balloons. However, only once was the battalion able to confirm the destruction of a German aircraft. On 16 June, a Junkers Ju 88 twin-engine bomber caught the wire of a balloon from Battery B and then crashed into the ocean immediately off the beach.[39] After the Allies captured the French port of Cherbourg, Battery A was moved to the harbor to provide defense from German attack. Later, that battery was ordered to protect the ports on the Brittany peninsula. Battery B remained on Omaha Beach until late October, while Battery C also remained at Utah Beach. The battalion left France on 24 October 1944 and returned to the United Kingdom. During their service in France, three members of the 320th Antiaircraft Artillery were KIA[40] and another seventeen were WIA, while the battalions' commander and four enlisted men received the Bronze Star for their actions.[41] The battalion was commended in writing by its immediate superior BG Edward W. Timberlake, commander of the 49th Antiaircraft Artillery Brigade, as well as MG Hoyt S. Vandenberg, commander of the Ninth Air Defense Command, LTG Leonard T. Gerow, commander of the V Corps, and GEN Dwight D. Eisenhower, the Supreme Allied Commander.[42]

On 13 November, the battalion boarded the troopship USAT *Excelsior* and returned to the United States. After five months of training at Camp Stewart, the battalion boarded the troopship USAT *Aconcagua* on 24 April 1945 bound for Hawaii.[43] This made the 320th Antiaircraft Artillery the only barrage balloon unit to serve in both Europe and the Pacific during World War II. The battalion was scheduled to participate in the invasion of Japan, but the Japanese surrender negated that mission and the battalion was disbanded in Hawaii on 14 December 1945.

The other African American antiaircraft artillery battalion to see significant overseas service during World War II was the 452nd Antiaircraft Artillery Automatic Weapons Battalion. The battalion was activated on 1 August 1942 at Camp Stewart, where they conducted initial training before transferring to Camp Atterbury on 10 January 1943. After nine more months of training, the battalion embarked from New York on 21 October 1943 for the United Kingdom.[44] The batteries of the battalion were deployed in defense of four different locations around the United Kingdom for the next seven months. On 23–24 June 1944, the battalion landed on Utah Beach and again individual batteries were deployed to defend American ammunition and fuel dumps. Then from 8 to 16 August, the batteries were assigned to defend important road junctions, bridges, and crossroads along the Third Army's supply route.[45]

From 17 August to the end of January 1945, the 452nd Antiaircraft Artillery Automatic Weapons Battalion's batteries were further broken down into platoons and assigned to protect American field artillery battalions. During the early part of this period, the Luftwaffe remained active and the battalion's weapons engaged them on 23 separate occasions with one confirmed shootdown—a JU-52 transport aircraft that resulted in 26 POWs (nine airmen and 17 nurses). The battalion even had the opportunity to engage a ME163 "Komet" rocket aircraft and two V1 "Buzz bombs."[46] During these assignments, six enlisted men were KIA, and one officer and twenty-one enlisted men WIA. For their actions, five enlisted men received the Silver Star, while eight officers and seventeen enlisted men received the Bronze Star, but only one of these for valor.[47]

In March 1945, when the 452nd Antiaircraft Artillery Automatic Weapons Battalion accompanied Third Army units into Germany, Luftwaffe activity increased dramatically. During that month alone, the battalion had 133 engagements and claimed 42 aircraft destroyed with another 23 probably destroyed. On 17 March, the battalion engaged 53 Luftwaffe FW190s and ME109s and destroyed four with four probables. The next day, on 18 March, the battalion accounted for six destroyed with two probables. On 20 March, the battalion engaged a total of 248 aircraft and destroyed 12 with four probables. On 23 March, the battalion was protecting a pontoon bridge that was attacked by fifty-eight German aircraft, of which the battalion destroyed ten. In the last few days of the war in May 1945, the battalion had thirteen engagements and destroyed four aircraft. The battalion's final total was sixty-eight destroyed, nineteen probably destroyed, and eleven damaged.[48] During the period from February to May, one enlisted man was KIA when his vehicle was ambushed and wrecked, while four others were WIA.[49] After the war, the battalion served on occupation duty until they were disbanded on 17 November 1945 at Camp Miles Standish.[50]

As with field artillery, despite prewar skepticism on the part of some white officers, African American coast/antiaircraft artillery units performed extremely well in combat when they were given the opportunity. Nevertheless, they were seldom given that chance. Unfortunately, all of the African American coast/antiaircraft artillery units disbanded during the war were cannibalized to form support, usually general service engineer, units. Once again, the Army establishment wasted money, resources, and trained/skilled personnel on unskilled labor simply because they were African Americans.

Section IV

Mobile Warfare and Mechanical Proficiency

Chapter 6

Cavalry

African American service in the cavalry began during the Civil War with the six cavalry regiments (1st–6th U.S. Colored Cavalry) of the U.S. Colored Troops. Then almost immediately after the war, the U.S. Army formed two African American cavalry regiments—9th and 10th Cavalry. These regiments, who acquired the storied nickname "Buffalo Soldiers," saw extensive combat on the American frontier, as well as the Spanish American War, the Philippine Insurrection, and Moro War. Unfortunately, American cavalrymen played almost no role in World War I, and the 9th and 10th Cavalry, like their white counterparts, spent the war either guarding the Mexican border or serving with wartime infantry or field artillery formations. By World War II, African American cavalrymen faced two different prejudices—one regarding their race and the other as members of a branch that was by then generally derided as outmoded.

After World War I, the Army reorganized the cavalry into divisions for the first time since the Civil War and one of those divisions, the 2nd Cavalry, became important in the history of African American cavalrymen. The 2nd Cavalry Division was organized on 20 August 1921, but not brought to full strength until 1 April 1941.[1] The division was structured as a "square division" containing two brigades with two regiments each. During the Interwar Period, other than the four active-duty cavalry regiments, most of the division's supporting units were either not fully organized or existed only on paper. On 24 March 1923, the African American 10th Cavalry Regiment was assigned to the division's 3rd Cavalry Brigade. The 10th Cavalry was stationed at Fort Huachuca and spent years patrolling the border with Mexico. On 15 August 1927, the 10th Cavalry was reassigned to the 3rd Cavalry Division, an organization which, like the 2nd Cavalry Division, existed largely on paper except for four active-duty cavalry regiments. From 1931 to 1941, the 10th Cavalry was divided between three posts. The regimental HQ, 1st Squadron, and Service Troop transferred to Fort Leavenworth, Kansas, on 12 October 1931. At the same time, the 2nd Squadron transferred to the U.S. Military Academy at West Point, New York, and the Machinegun Troop transferred to Fort Myer, Virginia. Later, on 1 November 1940, the troopers of the 2nd Squadron were redesignated as the U.S. Military Academy Cavalry Squadron, while the 2nd Squadron, at least on paper, returned to the regiment. After 1931, the squadron's troopers trained the almost entirely white Corps of Cadets in horsemanship until equestrian courses were abolished from the Academy's curriculum and the unit was disbanded on 1 September 1947.[2] On 1 February 1941, the regiment was reassigned to the 2nd Cavalry Division and, on 12 March 1941, transferred to Fort Riley.[3]

The Army's other African American cavalry regiment, the 9th Cavalry, was transferred from Fort Stotsenberg, Philippines, to Fort Riley on 15 November 1922. Upon arrival at Fort Riley, the regiment absorbed more than two hundred African American cavalrymen already assigned to the post. From 1922 to 1940, the regiment served as the support and demonstration unit for the Cavalry School. While this assignment was certainly necessary and important, it reinforced the notion that African Americans were not suitable for combat service but existed only to support white soldiers. On 18 August 1933, the regiment, while still assigned to the Cavalry School, was also listed on the order of battle of the 3rd Cavalry Division. After seven years with the 3rd Cavalry Division, on 10 October 1940, the regiment was reassigned to the 2nd Cavalry Division.[4]

By March 1941, all four regiments of the 2nd Cavalry Division were now concentrated at Fort Riley. The division's 3rd Cavalry Brigade included the 2nd and 14th Cavalry Regiments, while the 4th Cavalry Brigade included the 9th and 10th Cavalry Regiments. Oddly, this made the 2nd Cavalry Division the first integrated division-sized formation in the Army. From January to June 1941, the 4th Cavalry Brigade was commanded by the Army's first, and at that point only, African American general officer—BG Benjamin O. Davis, Sr. Although the 2nd Cavalry Division had all four regiments at the same post, it was not until November 1941 that all of the necessary support units were finally activated and/or attached to the division. After the attack on Pearl Harbor in December 1941, the 3rd Cavalry Brigade was sent to Arizona to guard the border with Mexico. The 4th Cavalry Brigade remained at Camp Funston, a subcamp of Fort Riley, preparing for combat.[5]

In early 1942, the Army realized both that they needed to create more armored divisions and that horse cavalry would most likely have little role in World War II. As a result, the 3rd Cavalry Brigade, as well as all of the other "white" formations of the division, was removed and used to organize the 9th Armored Division. Even the division HQ was disbanded on 15 July 1942, thus all that remained of the 2nd Cavalry Division was the African American 4th Cavalry Brigade.[6] The orphaned 4th Cavalry was seen as nothing more than a nuisance at Fort Riley. As a result, the brigade HQ and 10th Cavalry Regiment were transferred to Camp Lockett, California, on 28 June 1942. At the same time, the 9th Cavalry Regiment was sent to Fort Clark, Texas.[7] While ostensibly both units were engaging in border security missions, in actuality no one knew what to do with the brigade, its African American troopers, or its horses—all of whom were seen as unnecessary. Many senior officers in the Army wanted to disband both the brigade and its regiments, but that was politically impossible for the Roosevelt Administration, then courting African American voters for the Democratic Party in the midterm congressional elections of 1942.

After the election, on 25 February 1943, the 2nd Cavalry Division was reactivated at Fort Clark with the 4th and 5th Cavalry Brigades. The 5th Cavalry Brigade contained two new African American cavalry regiments— the 27th and 28th Cavalry. In addition to the two cavalry brigades, all of the other formations of the division were manned by African Americans, including three field artillery battalions, an engineer squadron, a medical squadron, a mechanized cavalry reconnaissance squadron, a quartermaster squadron, an ordnance maintenance company, and a military police platoon.[8] The commander of the division, MG Harry H. Johnson, was a Texas National Guard officer.[9] The Army viewed Johnson as perfect to command the division because he was both a Southerner, who obviously "knew how to handle" African Americans, and a National Guard officer, so a Regular Army general officer did not have to be "wasted."

Despite the reactivation of the 2nd Cavalry Division, the Army made no effort to assemble the division in a single place to conduct thorough training. The division remained divided between Camp Lockett and Fort Clark. Unlike virtually every other American division, the 2nd Cavalry did not participate in large-scale maneuvers before deploying to a combat zone. Also, the division remained horse-mounted until notified for overseas shipment and never retrained as infantry like the 1st Cavalry Division. On 4 February 1944, almost a year since its reactivation, the 2nd Cavalry began arriving at Camp Patrick Henry, Virginia, bound for the ETO.[10] After arriving in North Africa, the junior officers, NCOs, and enlisted men anticipated additional training and maneuvers before deploying to Italy. Only the more senior officers of the 2nd Cavalry were informed of the truth—despite the desperate need for American combat troops in Italy, the division was disbanded and its personnel used to create support units.

On 22 February 1944, the first unit of the 2nd Cavalry Division was disbanded—the 9th Cavalry Regiment, which was originally organized in 1866 with Civil War veterans, some of whom were freedmen and some former slaves. These men and their descendants policed the American frontier, charged up San Juan Hill alongside Theodore Roosevelt's "Rough Riders," and counted no less than 13 Medal of Honor recipients on the historic roles of the regiment. Despite all of these past achievements, the regiment was broken up and its subunits converted to a long list of dump truck companies, provisional port companies, and quartermaster truck companies.[11] On 29 March 1944, the same fate befell the 10th Cavalry Regiment, whose historic accomplishments mirrored those of the 9th Cavalry and historic rolls of which included five Medal of Honor recipients. The subunits of the 10th Cavalry were converted to an engineer construction battalion, engineer dump truck company, and quartermaster truck company.[12] Similar fates awaited all of the other subunits of the 2nd Cavalry Division.

The Army's decision to break up the 2nd Cavalry Division was unprecedented. At no other time and to no other division in the Army did such an event occur. Just across the Mediterranean from where the division was disemboweled, the U.S. Fifth Army was in desperate need of combat troops as the imminent invasion of France siphoned off all of the best combat units and the Italian campaign increasingly became the redheaded bastard stepchild of the Army. Nevertheless, a trained combat division was reduced to nothing more than truck drivers and stevedores.

Apologists have since argued the 2nd Cavalry Division's fate was predetermined when the Army abandoned horse cavalry. Unfortunately, that argument does not hold water when one considers the completely different fate of the 1st Cavalry Division. The 1st Cavalry, a white unit, was unhorsed and retrained in infantry tactics while retaining its cavalry designation and unit organization. The division spent World War II in the Pacific where it participated in the New Guinea, Bismarck Archipelago, Leyte, and Luzon campaigns, and ended the war as one of the main occupation units of Japan.

Other than the 2nd Cavalry Division and the U.S. Military Academy Cavalry Squadron, there were only two other small African American cavalry formations during World War II. A few African American cavalrymen traded their horses for armored cars, light tanks, and jeeps and saw combat in Italy and the Pacific as the division reconnaissance troops of the 92nd and 93rd Infantry Divisions. The 92nd and 93rd Reconnaissance Troops (Mechanized) had very different experiences during the war.

The 92nd Cavalry Reconnaissance Troop was organized on 15 October 1942 at Fort McClellan with a cadre of eighteen enlisted men from the 93rd Cavalry Reconnaissance Troop.[13] The remainder of the troop's personnel were obtained from existing units and recent graduates of the Cavalry Replacement Training Center at Fort Riley. The troop spent the end of 1942 and the first four months of 1943 at Fort McClellan training in mechanized cavalry operations.

On 4 May 1943, the troop, then numbering 13 officers and 268 enlisted men, was transferred to Fort Huachuca to join the rest of the 92nd Infantry Division.[14]

On 15 July 1943, the Army issued a new T/O for division reconnaissance troops. This resulted in a change of both equipment and personnel strength, and the 92nd Cavalry Reconnaissance Troop was reduced to six officers and 143 enlisted men.[15] After participating in two major maneuvers and spending months training to eliminate deficiencies, the troop, along with the rest of the division, was shipped to Italy. After arriving at Livorno, Italy, on 5 November 1944, the troop moved to the front lines and for more than two months established a routine of providing security for the 92nd Infantry as well as engaging in normal patrol activities along the front lines.[16]

On 26 December 1944, a strong German attack hit the 92nd Cavalry Reconnaissance Troop's outposts. During this first combat action, two troopers were killed (T/5 Wallace Hobbs and PFC Harold Stern) and another wounded, but the troop performed their duties with such efficiency that two men, Staff Sergeant (SSG) William F. Maurice and CPL Jefferson Hilliard, received the Silver Star and another two troopers received Bronze Stars for Valor. From 28 December 1944 to 19 April 1945, the troop performed all of their patrols on foot in enemy-held areas. These were combat operations for which the troopers were not trained nor equipped. They had never received training in small unit infantry tactics and did not have the more powerful weapons issued to infantry soldiers. For instance, rather than the standard M1 Garand infantry rifle, Browning Automatic Rifle (BAR), and Browning M1919 light machinegun, cavalry troopers were generally equipped with the M1 Carbine, Colt M1911A1 pistol (or sometimes even the M1917 revolvers manufactured by Colt and Smith & Wesson during World War I), and submachine guns—either the M1 Thompson or the M3 "Grease Gun." Even discounting the lack of training in infantry tactics, the relative lack of firepower from small arms put dismounted cavalrymen at a distinct disadvantage when facing German infantry formations. Despite these limitations, the men of the troop performed with valor and distinction. For instance, during an 11 March patrol, six troopers made a raid on enemy positions near Gallicano, Italy, and knocked out several machinegun positions—killing or capturing fifteen Germans at the loss of only three wounded Americans. Two members of the patrol, T/5 Theodore Archibald and PFC Emanuel Gardner, both received the Silver Star.[17]

On 19 April 1945, with the enemy now in rapid retreat in the final days of the war, the 92nd Cavalry Reconnaissance Troop was remounted with armored cars, light tanks, and jeeps, and conducted mechanized cavalry operations in support of the 92nd Infantry. On 25 April, the troop's commanding officer, CPT Murray L. Steinman, who had led the troop since before they left the United States, was killed by German artillery fire. Despite their commander's tragic death, the men of the troop continued to skillfully execute their missions until hostilities in Italy ended on 2 May 1945. Ironically, Steinman was one of only three KIAs from the troop.[18]

In late March or early April just before his tragic death, Steinman prepared a ten-page single-spaced report on the operations of his troop since their arrival in Italy. He began by pointing out that the troop was not used for the purpose in which it was trained, organized, armed, or equipped. It is important to note that the terrain of Italy was the cause of this decision rather than any racism on the part of the Army. For most of the four months that the troop fought dismounted, their missions consisted of providing security and early warning for the division. As such, the troop created an outpost and observation system to provide a constant flow of information.[19]

On the topic of the troop's organization, Steinman argued that the Army's T/O for the infantry division reconnaissance troop was poorly thought out. The T/O had too few officers and required each officer to do too much. Likewise, several enlisted positions needed reconsideration. The HQ radio sergeant, who truly required training as a communications specialist who could coordinate all communications for the troop, was nothing more than a glorified radio operator. Steinman also argued that there were problems with the administration and supply subsections of the troop. Lastly, he contended that a combat engineer detachment was required for small-scale repair and demolition operations. It is interesting to note that virtually none of his comments centered on the combat platoons of his troop.[20]

Steinman discussed individual and unit equipment down to the level of troopers' boots. Regarding small arms, he mentioned the lack of M1 Garands as well as a desire for BARs, which were not issue weapons for the cavalry troop. He was particularly dismissive of the M3 "Grease Gun" which he stated had "... proven an unstable weapon."[21] Regarding the vehicles of the troop, he was especially critical of the M8 "Greyhound" armored car, which he argued lacked sufficient horsepower, was equipped with a poorly designed engine (making most repairs difficult, especially in the field), had tires unsuitable for off-road operations (a requirement in a combat vehicle), and possessed a poorly laid out interior.

On the topic of training, Steinman believed that the men of the troop received adequate basic and advanced individual training but still found some shortcomings. He listed four areas that were in most need of training readjustment: mine and booby trap training; map reading; artillery fire support training; and small unit tactics. On the issue of map reading, it was not that the training itself that was a problem, but it was perhaps "... taught along the wrong lines."[22] In stateside training, photographic and full-color maps were used, but in theater, maps were exclusively black and white with foreign signs and symbols and used the metric system (which Americans of the era were completely unfamiliar with). Regarding artillery fire support, he noted that neither he nor his troopers were trained on how to adjust artillery fire. This meant that ammunition was wasted and Allied soldiers were needlessly endangered. The issue of small unit tactics referred almost exclusively to dismounted (or infantry) tactics which were the troop's bread and butter missions in Italy where the terrain did not support mechanized reconnaissance.

The final topic of Steinman's report, to which he devoted two pages, was the use of mules. While the Army had abandoned the use of horse cavalry during World War II, animals were still used as "prime movers" to transport equipment, supplies, rations, ammunition, and to evacuate wounded in terrain where motorized vehicles could not operate. The mules in question were procured through local Italian sources and he complained about their relatively small size and, therefore, their small carrying capacity.[23] Also, Italian muleskinners were secured because few Americans had sufficient familiarity or training to work with the animals. The 92nd Infantry Division eventually attempted to solve the problem by creating the 92nd Provisional

Mule Pack Battalion, which ultimately grew to a strength of 372 mules, 173 horses, and 600 Italians.[24] As with some earlier issues, the use of mules by the 92nd Infantry was a solution to the problem of the Italian terrain and not the result of racial prejudice.[25]

While this unpublished and, quite possibly unread, report by Steinman might seem unimportant, it is interesting for a few reasons. First, the report speaks well to the professionalism of both Steinman and the members of his troop who did whatever it took to achieve success. Second, the Italian campaign brought unique problems for American units as illustrated by the host of issues mentioned in the report. Last and perhaps most importantly, nowhere in the report is the issue of a race mentioned. By all appearances, Steinman simply saw his troopers as American soldiers—nothing more and nothing less.

The 93rd Cavalry Reconnaissance Troop experienced a very different war in the Pacific. The troop was organized along with the rest of the 93rd Infantry Division in May 1942 at Fort Huachuca. Between May 1942 and March 1943, the 93rd Cavalry completed basic and advanced training and, in April 1943, along with the rest of the division reported to Louisiana for large-scale maneuvers against the 85th Infantry Division. Then, in July 1943, the troop arrived at Camp Clipper for desert warfare training. Finally, in November and December 1943, the division participated in maneuvers against the 90th Infantry Division.

On 23 January 1944, the 93rd Cavalry Reconnaissance Troop boarded the troopship USS *General John Pope* (AP-110) and arrived at Guadalcanal on 6 February 1944. After less than two months on Guadalcanal, the troop boarded the attack transport USS *Harry Lee* (APA-10) on 25 March 1944 bound for Bougainville alongside the 25th Infantry Regimental Combat Team. On Bougainville, the 93rd Cavalry was placed under the direct control of the XIV Corps HQ.[26] After familiarizing themselves with jungle scouting and patrolling, their first duty was providing security for engineer units who were building roads. Next, the troop began to perform reconnaissance and mapping missions for several days at a time in enemy-controlled territory.

On 14 May, a patrol from the 93rd Cavalry Reconnaissance Troop, led by 1LT Charles Collins and his platoon sergeant, SSG Rothschild Webb, departed on a mission to reconnoiter all river crossings between the Saua and Reini Rivers. On 16 May, the patrol made contact with Japanese soldiers three times and was forced to call in artillery support. The next day, they were ambushed and forced to withdraw toward the Reini River under fire and were then hit by another enemy ambush, this time armed with machine guns and mortars. Three members of the patrol were killed (SGT Nehemiah Hodges, T/5 Moses Davis, and PVT Deormy Ray) and three wounded, including Collins who received severe head wounds from enemy mortar fire. Collins' wounds were so severe that he was left behind, but Webb volunteered to stay with him.[27] As the rest of the patrol withdrew from the ambush, T/5 Sanders V. Williams was also severely wounded and two of his friends, T/5 Clarence Reece and PFC Walter J. Jeffress, remained behind with him. When Company I, 25th Infantry Regiment, was dispatched to recover the bodies of those killed or missing (and assumed dead) on the patrol, they were surprised to discover all five of the men alive. Webb, Reese, and Jeffress cared for and protected the Collins and Williams for two days before rescue. For their actions during and after the ambush, Webb received the Silver Star, while Collins, Reece, and Jeffress received the Bronze Star for Valor.[28]

In June 1944, the 25th Infantry Regimental Combat Team was withdrawn from Bougainville, but the 93rd Cavalry Reconnaissance Troop remained on the island and continued to perform reconnaissance missions in enemy territory while attached to the American Division until October. In one particularly intense fight, the entire troop attacked a Japanese-controlled terrain feature known as Horseshoe Ridge, while in support of the 182nd Infantry Regiment (Massachusetts National Guard). All three platoons assaulted Horseshoe Ridge simultaneously from the front, rear, and flanks. Despite fierce combat, the troop was unsuccessful and pulled back with five soldiers seriously wounded. At twilight, 2nd Lieutenant (2LT) Glenn A. Allen and a handful of men attempted to climb the ridge without any supporting fire in the hopes they would surprise the enemy. Luckily, the Japanese were in the process of evacuating their positions and Allen and his men were able to establish a defensive position, engage the enemy, and hold out until reinforcements arrived. Allen received the

Bronze Star for Valor and six other members of the troop also received the Bronze Star for service or valor. The attack resulted in commendations for the 93rd Cavalry from both MAJ James W. Harris, the commander of the 3rd Battalion, 182nd Infantry Regiment, and MG Robert B McClure, the commander of the Americal Division.[29]

During August 1944, the 93rd Cavalry Reconnaissance Troop performed regular reconnaissance missions in support of the 164th Infantry Regiment (North Dakota National Guard). Their missions often involved ambushes against the Japanese supply line and establishing observation posts to direct mortar and artillery fire on enemy locations. From 1 to 11 September, the 93rd Cavalry performed similar missions in support of the 182nd Infantry Regiment. Numerous Bronze Stars were presented to the officers and men of the troop for valor or service after these various missions. The troop was so successful that the regimental commander of the 182nd Infantry officially requested that the 93rd Cavalry remain attached to his regiment. Instead, on 25 October 1944, the troop boarded the SS *Lew Wallace* (MC-485) bound for New Guinea. At Finschhafen, New Guinea, the 93rd Cavalry was placed on military police duty and attached to the 720th Military Police Battalion until 30 March 1945 when the troop set sail for Morotai Island, Netherlands East Indies.[30] At Morotai Island, the 93rd Cavalry rejoined the 93rd Infantry Division. While the rest of the division performed labor duties, the 93rd Cavalry provided security from the approximately 500 Japanese soldiers who remained under arms on the island. During the most dramatic event of the period, Japanese COL Kisou Ouchi, the commander of the Japanese 211th Infantry Regiment and all of the remaining Japanese forces on the Morotai, was captured in early August 1945. The scouts who guided the American expedition into Japanese-held territory were all members of the 93rd Cavalry. For their efforts, those four cavalrymen were all decorated—SGT Alfonsia Dillon received the Silver Star, while T/5 Albert Morrison, PFC Robert A. Evans, and PFC Elmer Sloan received the Bronze Star for Valor.[31]

Since the 2nd Cavalry Division was disbanded in February and March 1944 in North Africa, the 92nd Cavalry Reconnaissance Troop was disbanded on 28 November 1945 at Camp Kilmer and the 93rd Cavalry Reconnaissance

Troop was disbanded at Camp Stoneman on 3 February 1946, the men of the U.S. Military Academy Cavalry Squadron were the final African American cavalrymen in the Army. Then in 1947, the U.S. Military Academy decided to abolish equestrian courses from its curriculum for the incoming Class of 1951 and, on 1 September 1947, the U.S. Military Academy Cavalry Squadron was disbanded.[32] An era of American history came to an end—African American cavalrymen, the famed "Buffalo Soldiers" of the American West, ceased to exist.

Chapter 7

Armored Force

T he Armored Force was a temporary "branch" in the U.S. Army during World War II and African Americans were not initially welcome to join. The general belief among white Army officers was that while African Americans might serve well as infantrymen, the mechanical nature of tanks made them too technically difficult for African Americans to operate. This was another manifestation of the general belief that African Americans were inherently less intelligent than whites. The performance of African American tankers during World War II was critical to proving their value in modern mechanized warfare and dispelling white stereotypes that reinforced segregation within the Army.

During World War I, the Army had created the Tank Corps for a then-new weapon—the tank. Though the tank was an amazing weapon, its early manifestations were less than dependable. These early tanks were slow, mechanically unreliable, underpowered, and easily disabled in difficult terrain. As a result, less than two years after the end of the war, the U.S. Congress abolished the Tank Corps, transferred all of the Army's tanks to the infantry, and prohibited the cavalry from possessing any tanks.[1] The dominant belief was that tanks were nothing more than armored machine gun carriers to support slow-moving infantrymen. While that view was more true than false in 1920, it failed to take into consideration the potential development of the tank. The cavalry, the branch of the Army most interested in rapid maneuver and the natural home for the tank, had a difficult time asserting their role in the development of tanks during the Interwar Period. To circumvent the law, the cavalry referred to tanks as "combat cars" so that they could procure some and begin experiments.

Infighting between the infantry and cavalry over "ownership" of the tank continued into World War II. In May 1940, the final act regarding the future of the tank in the Army occurred immediately after the Third Army Maneuvers in Louisiana. During the maneuvers, the IX Corps was supported by the 7th Cavalry Brigade (Mechanized)[2], commanded by BG Adna R. Chaffee while the IV Corps was supported by the Infantry's Provisional Tank Brigade[3], commanded by BG Bruce Magruder. During the second phase of the maneuvers something truly revolutionary happened, the 7th Cavalry Brigade was combined with the Provisional Tank Brigade to form an *ad hoc* division—the first division-sized mechanized formation in Army history. During the last exercise of the maneuvers, the provisional mechanized division launched an attack on a prepared enemy infantry position. The mechanized force penetrated the position and was thoroughly routing its opponents when the maneuvers were ended for a time.[4]

On 24 May 1940, at the end of the final day of the maneuvers, Chaffee, Magruder, MG Stanley D. Embrick (commander of the Third Army), BG Frank M. Andrews (Assistant Chief of Staff of the U.S. Army for Operations and Training—G3), and COL George S. Patton (an umpire at the maneuvers) met in the basement of the Alexandria (Louisiana) High School to discuss the future of mechanization. All of the impromptu conference participants agreed that, if mechanization were to succeed in the Army, it needed to become a separate organization. In the opinion of the participants, the cavalry and infantry branches both continued to view mechanization as only an auxiliary to their existing forces, rather than as a revolutionary new weapon.[5] The supporters of mechanization believed that while mechanized doctrine and vehicles evolved during the interwar period in other nations, the opponents of mechanization within that the infantry and cavalry branches had prevented a similar evolution in the United States.

After the maneuvers, Andrews returned to Washington, DC, and presented the recommendations to Chief of Staff Marshall. A second and more formal conference was held in Washington on 10 June 1940, which involved most of the original participants, along with the Chiefs of Cavalry and Infantry. For several hours, the branch chiefs argued they were the proper individuals to develop tanks, but their lack of progress in comparison with the tanks of other nations of the world ultimately betrayed them. On 24 June 1940, Marshall announced his decision to create a separate Armored Force[6] with Chaffee as its first chief.[7] The term "Armor" was chosen for the new force to avoid using the terms "Mechanized," used almost exclusively by the cavalry, or "Tank," which was used almost exclusively by the infantry.

In March 1941, after more than six months of lobbying by First Lady Eleanor Roosevelt, former federal Judge William H. Hastie, Jr., the civilian assistant on African American issues to the Secretary of War, and the African American press, ninety-eight soldiers became the first African Americans in the Armored Force.[8] These first African American soldiers were assigned to the newly organized 78th Tank Battalion (Light) at Fort Knox, Kentucky. At Fort Knox, they received advanced individual training on tanks and armored warfare, as well as technical training related to the repair of the engines, tracks, and other mechanical issues related to the M5 "Stuart" light tanks. In June 1941, the 78th Tank Battalion was redesignated as the 758th Tank Battalion (Light) and a few months later transferred from Fort Knox to Camp Claiborne.[9]

While the situation in Kentucky was not particularly good, the situation in Louisiana was even worse. At Camp Claiborne, the soldiers of the 758th Tank Battalion helped to build a camp that when they arrived was little more than a series of tents with only a few permanent buildings. The battalion's soldiers had almost no free time since they were either working on infrastructure for the camp or training with their tanks.[10] Camp Claiborne began life in 1930 as a camp for the Civilian Conservation Corps, a Great Depression-era New Deal program. Camp Evangeline, as it was originally known, was established to help reforest a large swath of Louisiana land that had suffered from mismanagement. When the Army took over the camp in 1940, it renamed the camp after William Claiborne, the first U.S. governor of Louisiana.[11]

Ironically, the first African American member of the Armored Force to die fighting for the United States during World War II did so without anyone knowing who he truly was. The soldier in question, PVT Robert H. Brooks, was born and raised in Kentucky but moved to Cincinnati as an adult where the light-skinned man "passed" as white. Drafted in 1940, Brooks was assigned to the 192nd Tank Battalion, which, after participating in the Louisiana Maneuvers, was selected to reinforce the American garrison in the Philippines. Unfortunately, this placed Brooks in the Philippines at Fort Stotsenburg on 8 December 1941 when the Japanese attacked, and he was killed by a Japanese bomb during the first aerial attack. Upon learning of his death, MG Jacob Devers, the then-Chief of the Armored Force, decided to name the main parade field at Fort Knox after him as the first Armored Force casualty of the war. Devers' aide contacted Brooks' parents in Kentucky and discovered his true identity. When Devers was informed, he said, "It did not matter whether or not Robert was black, what mattered was that he had given his life for his country."[12] The ceremony took place in the presence of Brooks' parents, though they were not introduced publicly.

In May 1942, the Army organized the 5th Tank Group[13] at Camp Claiborne to administer African American tank battalions. In July 1942, the 758th Tank Battalion was selected to participate in extensive maneuvers in what was then known as the Tennessee Maneuver Area, which covered twenty-one counties of the state of Tennessee.[14] Almost as importantly, that same month the first African American Armored Force officers began to arrive. The arrival of these new officers allowed for the promotion and/or transfer to white units of the white platoon commanders.[15] In September, the battalion traveled by train to Murfreesboro, Tennessee. From September to November 1942, the battalion received intense and realistic battlefield training in Tennessee. When it was time to return home, however, neither the battalion nor the white residents of Alexandria, Louisiana, wanted them to return to Camp Claiborne. The battalion then found itself shuttled from Camp Jackson to Camp Gordon, Georgia, and even briefly to Fort Leonard

Wood, Missouri, before finally returning to Camp Claiborne. It was not until September 1943 that the 758th Tank Battalion finally left Camp Claiborne for good.

In September 1943, the 758th Tank Battalion was transferred to Camp Hood, Texas. While the African American soldiers of the battalion were happy to permanently leave Louisiana, they found Texas scarcely more welcoming but at least mercifully less swampy. Camp Hood's location in Central Texas contained hills, valleys, woods, and otherwise open areas perfectly suited for maneuver warfare training. While the 5th Tank Group and its two other battalions remained at Camp Hood, the 758th Tank Battalion was quickly transferred to Fort Huachuca in late October 1943 and attached to the 92nd Infantry Division.[16]

Fort Huachuca was established as a temporary encampment in 1877 and became a permanent Army post in 1886. Throughout most of its existence, the post was home to African American soldiers from the 9th and 10th Cavalry Regiments as well as the 24th and 25th Infantry Regiments. The Army saw the isolated desert location as an ideal site for the African American units to avoid friction with white civilian populations—principally because there were almost no white civilians anywhere near the post! Now that the 758th Tank Battalion was attached to the 92nd Infantry Division, the battalion's training emphasized combined arms coordination between infantry, artillery, and tanks.[17] Since most of the soldiers at Fort Huachuca were African American there were virtually no racial incidents on the post. While the soldiers were completely isolated in the Arizona desert, the lack of racial animus and a vigorous recreation program on the post made life far more bearable than at Camp Hood or Camp Claiborne.

After more than six months of training with the 92nd Infantry Division, the 758th Tank Battalion returned to Camp Hood in July 1944 to undergo their final tank qualifications.[18] On 30 September 1944, the battalion left Texas bound for Camp Patrick Henry. Camp Patrick Henry was a staging point from which hundreds of thousands of American soldiers boarded troopships bound for the ETO. After arriving at Camp Patrick Henry on 3 October, the men of the battalion had to endure more than three weeks of boredom as they awaited their ships for overseas transport. On 6 October, a riot broke out between the men of the battalion and a group of paratroopers. While racism was the most likely explanation for the riot, another possible reason was that the paratroopers may have mistaken "tanker boots" for "jump boots" and resented the idea of unauthorized personnel wearing "their" boots. Regardless of the explanation, the only fatality was a white Air Corps enlisted men, but strangely no charges were brought against anyone.[19]

Finally, on 21 October, the 758th Tank Battalion left for Europe aboard two liberty ships, the SS *John W. Brown*[20] and the SS *Joseph Warren*. After a little more than a month at sea, the battalion arrived in Italy and began to prepare for combat in the last week of November 1944.[21] The battalion remained attached to the 92nd Infantry Division for its entire time in combat, but never served together as a single unit, rather it was broken up and attached to different subunits of the division. Unfortunately, the battalion remained a light tank unit equipped with M5 tanks, which meant that their utility in combat was minimal against anything other than enemy infantry. M5 tanks were well-made, rugged, and easy to operate, but they were not suitable for use in anything other than reconnaissance units where mobility rather than protection gave them an advantage. The light armor and small main gun (37 mm) of the M5 tank meant that they were both under-armored and under-gunned compared to most German tanks they faced in combat. In fact, by 1944 these tanks were seldom found in independent tank battalions like the 758th Tank Battalion. Instead, they were usually assigned to divisional cavalry reconnaissance troops and corps-level cavalry reconnaissance groups. It is not clear why the 758th Tank Battalion was not converted to a medium battalion with M4 "Sherman" tanks like the other two African American tank battalions.

Throughout the Italian Campaign, subunits of the 758th Tank Battalion found themselves providing fire support for the 92nd Infantry Division. Ironically, the small size and main gun of the M5 light tank made it very popular while fighting in villages throughout Italy.[22] The larger M4 medium tanks often could not fit down the narrow streets of the small villages and their longer main guns frequently had trouble traversing without hitting walls.[23] This might represent one of the very few instances in which the M5 tank had an advantage over its bigger brother! In addition to the 758th Tank Battalion, the 92nd Infantry was also supported by the 760th Tank Battalion, a white unit equipped with M4 medium tanks, which likewise found itself broken up and parceled out within the division.[24] Throughout December 1944 and January 1945, elements of the battalion engaged in sporadic combat in the mountains of Italy. On 8 February, the 92nd Infantry launched a major attack against the Germans, principally the 148th Reserve Infantry Division. The attack, which lasted four days, was only the second substantial combat operation for the 92nd Infantry. Things did not go according to plan and, as other Allied units had already learned, combat on the Italian Peninsula tended to favor the defender. The 758th Tank Battalion lost eight tanks during the offensive—five were destroyed by mines while three others were only disabled by mines and then destroyed by their crews to avoid enemy capture.[25]

The next major offensive, Operation Second Wind, for the 92nd Infantry and its supporting units did not begin until 5 April 1945. While the springtime certainly made temperatures more pleasant, it also meant that the unpaved roads of Italy quickly turned muddy. Even the light tanks of the 758th Tank Battalion quickly bogged down under these conditions. Nevertheless, the battalion's tanks continued supporting the division's infantry formations as they pushed forward. The majority of the battalion's casualties during the offensive were sustained as a result of tanks damaged or destroyed by antitank mines or *Panzerfausts*. During this period, only four members of the battalion were KIA, all of whom were members of Company B. Two of these losses occurred during a failed attempt to cross the Cinquale Canal, during which the 1st Platoon of Company B supported an infantry task force. The tank belonging to the platoon's leader, 1LT William Hannah, was hit by a *Panzerfaust* and disabled. The tank's driver, T/5 Samuel Berry, was killed instantly while Hannah and the two other tankers were wounded but escaped the vehicle. After carrying the two wounded soldiers to safety, Hannah was killed by enemy gunfire and later received a posthumous Silver Star for his actions.[26]

After the war ended, the 758th Tank Battalion was disbanded in Italy on 22 September 1945 and the men of the battalion rotated home based on the Army's point system rather than as a unit.[27] In June 1946, the battalion was reactivated at Fort Knox as a training battalion at the Armored Force's school. In November 1949, the by-then integrated battalion was redesignated as the 64th Tank Battalion. Finally, in January 1963, the battalion was redesignated as the 64th Armor Regiment and some of its battalions remain on active duty as of this writing.[28]

The second African American tank battalion activated during World War II was the 761st Tank Battalion. The battalion was activated in April 1942 at Camp Claiborne along with the 5th Tank Group to which both it and the 758th Tank Battalion were attached.[29] The initial cadre for the new battalion was made up of officers and enlisted men transferred from the 758th Tank Battalion. The men of the 761st Tank Battalion were known as the "Black Panthers" based on their unit emblem which showed the snarling head of a black panther.[30] As with the 758th Tank Battalion, the 761st Tank Battalion was initially equipped with M5 light tanks. Likewise, just as the 758th Tank Battalion had suffered mistreatment and even violence in the

Soldiers from Company D, 761st Tank Battalion in the town square of Coburg, Germany, under a statue of Albert of Saxe-Coburg-Gothe, the Prince-Consort of Queen Victoria, on 25 April 1945. (NARA)

nearby town of Alexandria, Louisiana, the men of the 761st Tank Battalion had similar negative experiences.

In March 1943, a few weeks before the first anniversary of the organization of the 761st Tank Battalion, the body of an African American soldier from another unit at Camp Claiborne was discovered severed in half on the nearby railroad tracks. The Army's investigators claimed that the man was drunk and passed out on the train tracks, however, the individual in question was a strict Baptist who did not drink.[31] When this incident became public knowledge of a group of tankers commandeered six tanks and a half-track to attack Alexandra. At the camp gate, the battalion commander, LTC Paul L. Bates, stopped them and convinced the soldiers to let him investigate the situation. After Bates' intervention, no members of the battalion were ever harassed again during visits to Alexandria.[32]

In September 1943, the 761st Tank Battalion traveled to Camp Hood for its final phase of training. While at Camp Hood, the members of the battalion received a surprise when they were redesignated a medium tank battalion and issued M4 "Sherman" tanks.[33] The "Sherman" tank was larger, better armed (75 mm vs. 37 mm main gun), and better armored than the M5 light tank. The size of the battalion also increased—previously the battalion consisted of three lettered companies (Companies A, B, and C), but now the battalion included a fourth lettered company (Company D) in addition to the service and HQ companies. The new Company D retained the M5 tanks and functioned as a reconnaissance element for the battalion. While the combat utility of the light tank remained debatable, its use as a reconnaissance vehicle made sense and arguably increased the combat strength of the battalion. While initially excited about the prospect of training at Camp Hood with their new tanks, what should have only taken a matter of weeks turned into seemingly endless months. After finishing their training, the battalion became "school troops" and remained at Camp Hood to train other units. The battalion's soldiers began to believe they would never actually see combat. However, the seemingly endless simulated combat against tank and tank destroyer battalions meant that the battalion was arguably one of the best trained in the entire Army, which proved important in combat.

In April 1944 around the second anniversary of the formation of the 761st Tank Battalion, a new officer joined the unit who later became famous in his own right—2LT John Roosevelt "Jackie" Robinson. Robinson was drafted in 1942 and initially trained as an enlisted man in the cavalry at Fort Riley. While at Fort Riley, Robinson met and was befriended by the world heavyweight boxing champion, Joe Louis. Louis helped Robinson, who was only one semester short of a bachelor's degree from UCLA, obtain a slot in OCS. After commissioning as a 2nd lieutenant of cavalry in January 1943, Robinson transferred to the Armored Force and, ultimately, to the 761st Tank Battalion.[34]

Robinson and his battalion commander, Bates, hit it off right away. Bates, a Los Angeles native, was an All-American football player at Western Maryland College (now McDaniel College), where he also earned a reserve commission as an infantry officer through the Army Reserve Officers Training Course. The two men connected over their affection for Los Angeles and football and Robinson finally began to enjoy Army life. Robinson even began to consider a career as an Army officer. As a result of an ankle injury he received while playing college football, Robinson had been classified as fit for "limited duty," which meant that he could not deploy overseas. Now, however, he wanted to remain with the 761st Tank Battalion when they deployed to Europe, so he appeared before a medical board at McCloskey General Hospital in Temple, Texas. The board rather confusingly determined that Robinson was still only fit for "limited duty," but was able to serve overseas. This meant that he could deploy to Europe, but not with a combat unit.[35] Unfortunately, while returning from McCloskey, his thoughts of a military career suffered a fatal setback.

On 6 July 1944, Robinson took a seat on a bus next to the wife, Virginia Jones, of one of his battalion's soldiers. Jones was very light-skinned and had become accustomed to sitting anywhere she liked on the bus, rather than the back row of the bus which was reserved for African Americans. The white bus driver was outraged when Robinson took the seat, both because Robinson was sitting in the middle of the bus and since the driver may have believed Robinson was sitting next to a white woman. The bus driver demanded that Robinson move to the back, which Robinson refused to do. Robinson was on good legal grounds because the Army was then in the process of publishing War Department Order Number 97, which barred discrimination on, "buses, trucks or other transportation owned and operated either by the Government or by governmental instrumentality…"[36] When the bus arrived at its destination, the driver immediately summoned the Military Police (MP) to have Robinson arrested.

Initially, the MPs treated Robinson with the respect due to his rank as an officer. They asked him to accompany them to the MP station for further discussion. Unfortunately, at the station, an enlisted man, PFC Ben W. Mucklerath, a trainee at Camp Hood who was waiting for a bus, referred to Robinson as a "nigger," which outraged Robinson. An MP officer arrived, who ignored Robinson and was only concerned with what the white enlisted MPs were saying. Finally, CPT Gerald M. Bear, the commander of Camp Hood's MPs, arrived. As with the previous MP officer, Bear initially ignored Robinson but then ordered him out of the MP station's office while witness statements were taken because Robinson continued to disagree with the statements. Perhaps not surprisingly, the only witness whose statement was not taken was Virginia Jones. Finally, Bear ordered Robinson to be transported to McCloskey General Hospital to test for alcohol. The blood test proved he had no alcohol in his system as he did not drink.[37]

The next morning Robinson's commanding officer, Bates, was informed what had happened. The official version was that Robinson had acted in a "berserk" manner toward both the bus driver and the MPs. When Bates spoke to both Robinson and Virginia Jones he got a completely different version of events, which coupled with the blood test and his knowledge of Robinson, convinced Bates that Robinson was innocent. Therefore, Bates suggested Robinson take some leave to visit his family in California, "… in hopes the incident would 'blow over' in his absence."[38] Unfortunately, things did not "blow over." Upon his return, Robinson discovered that he had been transferred to the 758th Tank Battalion and court-martial proceedings had been initiated. Some confusion exists as to whether Bates refused to court-martial Robinson and that resulted in his transfer or whether Robinson's "limited duty" status resulted in his transfer since his original battalion was preparing to leave for Europe.[39]

Robinson was initially charged with insubordination, disturbing the peace, conduct unbecoming an officer, insulting a civilian woman, and refusing to obey the lawful order of the superior officer.[40] Not unreasonably, Robinson was convinced he would not get a fair trial. He appealed for help to Truman K. Gibson, who felt it was inappropriate for him to become directly involved in the case. Robinson also wrote to the National Association for the Advancement of Colored People (NAACP) to request legal assistance but was informed that the organization's lawyers were stretched too thin to be of assistance. Camp Hood's senior lawyer, the Staff Judge Advocate, determined that the original charges against Robinson were stacked against him. Therefore, the Army dropping all charges that did not directly relate to Robinson's interaction with the MPs. When the court-martial began on 2 August 1944, Robinson only stood charged with conduct unbecoming an officer and refusing to obey the lawful order of a superior officer.

During the court-martial itself, the prosecution and its principal witness, Bear, reiterated the original accusations, but during cross-examination, several inconsistencies in the testimony were revealed. Robinson's defense council, 2LT William A. Cline, was able to prove that Robinson was not treated with the respect he was due as a commissioned officer by the enlisted MPs and Bear. Most crucially, Cline got Mucklerath to admit that Robinson said that if Mucklerath "… called him a nigger again he would break me in two," just after Mucklerath had claimed he'd never used the offending word. After Mucklerath left the stand, a white MP admitted that Mucklerath had used the derogatory word in Robinson's presence.[41] Bates, CPT James R. Lawson, Robinson's former company commander, 2LTs Harold Kingsley and Howard B. Campbell, both of whom were Robinson's fellow platoon leaders, all testified that Robinson was an excellent officer with whom they would like to serve in combat. The court-martial board deliberated quickly before finding Robinson not guilty on both counts. It seems clear that Mucklerath's perjury and the excellent recommendation made by his commander and fellow officers were the deciding factors in the court's judgment. Unfortunately, this whole episode soured Robinson on the Army once and for all. In the time since the original incident on the bus, the 761st Tank Battalion had begun to leave Camp Hood on its way to Europe. With Bates and his original unit gone, Robinson had no desire to take his chances with the rest of the Army. In November 1944, Robinson requested and was granted an honorable discharge on medical grounds and released from the Army.[42]

On 1 August 1944, an advanced detachment of the 761st Tank Battalion left Camp Hood for Camp Kilmer to prepare for the battalion's deployment to the ETO. The battalion was transported on the HMS *Esperanza Bay*, a troopship owned by the British government. After a journey of eleven days, the battalion landed in the United Kingdom on 8 September 1944.[43] On 9 October, they loaded aboard LSTs (landing ship, tank) and made their way across the English Channel.[44] While most members of the battalion felt fear or nervousness about the forthcoming combat, one officer was positively terrified. MAJ Charles Wingo, the battalion executive officer, was convinced that not only would the battalion fail under fire, but he would die in the process. "What in the world is the War Department thinking about? These folks aren't fit for combat."[45]

On the morning of 10 October 1944, the 761st Tank Battalion began to unload their tanks on Omaha Beach. Four months earlier, the beach was the scene of tremendous carnage and bravery during the D-Day invasion. Now, however, it was the busy main shipping point in France for Allied units. The tanks issued to the battalion in the United Kingdom were both a welcome surprise and a tremendous morale booster. The tanks were M4A3E8 "Easy Eights," which had an improved suspension system and, therefore a smoother ride, as well as a high velocity 76-mm main gun.[46] The earlier models of the M4 tank had a low-velocity 75-mm gun which was originally developed as an antipersonnel weapon rather than an antitank weapon. The improved 76-mm gun was equivalent to the main gun on the German Panzer IV, the mainstay of the German tank forces, and could disable or kill most German tanks.

Upon arriving in France, the 761st Tank Battalion was attached to the 26th Infantry Division, a National Guard division from New England known as the "Yankee Division." The 26th Infantry Division had only entered combat on 12 October and was just as inexperienced in actual combat as the 761st Tank Battalion. As with most other infantrymen, division commander MG Willard S. Paul had almost no experience with tanks or tank destroyers. Paul envisioned his attached tank and tank destroyer battalions as providing firepower to aid his infantry formations and gave little or no thought to tank-on-tank warfare. However, Paul's welcome to the battalion was very unexpected. He spoke to the assembled officers and men of the battalion in enthusiastic terms. "You are the first colored tank battalion in this Third Army, and I can tell you I'm proud as hell to have you supporting my division."[47]

The men of the 761st Tank Battalion were cheered by the division commander's enthusiastic welcome, but an even more enthusiastic welcome followed from a more high-ranking source. On 3 November 1944, LTG George S. Patton, the commander of the Third Army, arrived to address the 26th Infantry Division. After addressing the division, Patton asked Bates if he would like him to address the battalion, which Bates welcomed.

> Men you are the first Negro tankers to ever fight in the American army. I would never have asked for you if you weren't good. I don't care what color you are so long as you go up there and killed those Kraut sons of bitches. Everyone has their eyes on you and is expecting great things from you. Most of all, your race is looking forward to you. Don't let them down, and damn you, don't let me down.[48]

While many soldiers had mixed opinions about Patton, the battalion had nothing but good things to say about him after that speech.

On 8 November 1944, the 761st Tank Battalion entered combat for the first time, but not as they assumed they would. As experienced by most other tank battalions, it was broken up and its companies attached to support the 26th Infantry Division's three infantry regiments. CPT David Williams, the commander of Company A, discovered that the situation was even worse for his company. Upon arriving at the 104th Infantry Regiment's HQ, COL Dwight T. Colley, the regimental commander, told Williams to keep two of his platoons with him and send the other platoon to assist the 101st Infantry Regiment.[49] Infantry officers frequently viewed tanks as nothing more than their World War I incarnation—armored machine gun carriers to support slow-moving infantrymen. The other three companies of the battalion were attached to the division's 328th Infantry Regiment under Bates' direct control.

Though it may seem counterintuitive, it was very difficult to lead tanks from inside a tank. Successful tank officers often had to scout on foot before leading their tanks into combat. Bates followed this procedure and was wounded by German machine-gun fire in the lower left thigh on the first day of combat. He initially refused evacuation and ordered his medics to bandage him up so that he could stay with his battalion. However, the wound was so bad that the medics gave him no choice but evacuation. Unfortunately, this left the 761st Tank Battalion's white executive officer, Wingo, in command. Wingo, who had never expressed anything but contempt for the men of the battalion, did not even last a day in command. Only hours after learning that Bates was wounded and evacuated, Wingo abandoned the command post where Bates had left him and retreated to the aid station. Eventually, he was transferred to the 95th General Hospital with a case of "battle fatigue," which had occurred on the first day of battle when he was nowhere near the front line. He later wrote to several officers of the battalion, including Bates, but all considered him a coward and refused to reply.[50]

The first day's combat against the Germans' so-called Siegfried Line was taking a toll on the 761st Tank Battalion and the infantry units it supported. With Bates wounded and Wingo incapacitated, the Army sent a new command team—LTC Hollis A. Hunt and MAJ John F. George. Hunt, a cavalryman who transferred to the Armored Force, was a competent commander, but he never received the loyalty the men reserved for Bates. The 26th Infantry's problems continued when the commander of the 1st Battalion, 104th Infantry Regiment, was relieved of duty after he came unhinged during a German artillery bombardment on the first day. Then, only a few days later, the 104th Infantry Regiment's commander, Colley, was badly wounded by German artillery and evacuated.

On 8 November, Williams' two platoons attacked German positions in the French town of Vic-sur-Seille. The German defenders had blocked the road to force the American tanks into a killing zone. Realizing this, SSG Ruben Rivers, a platoon sergeant who commanded the lead tank of the formation, climbed out of his tank in full view of the enemy and dragged a heavy cable around the roadblock. After attaching the cable, Rivers remounted his tank and removed the obstacle. Williams later lectured Rivers about having endangered himself in such a reckless manner but also recommended him for a Silver Star.[51] Rivers' heroic actions of the first day were not his last. On 16 November, Rivers' tank struck a German Teller mine and a piece of shrapnel cut his leg almost to the bone. After having the wound cleaned and disinfected, he refused a shot of morphine or evacuation. Instead, he took over command of one of the other tanks in his platoon.[52]

In the days that followed, the 761st Tank Battalion and the 26th Infantry Division slowly but consistently overwhelmed German defensive positions. On 18 November, Williams' two platoons supported the 104th Infantry Regiment's assault on the city of Guebling. Rivers' tank was moving around the city when he encountered two German tanks. Outnumbered and outgunned, he and his crew engaged the Germans until they were forced to withdraw. The next day, the company continued its offensive. Williams had four of his tanks, led by Rivers, spread out to destroy German infantry and machine-gun positions, while Williams with the three other tanks approached in column formation. Williams' column quickly came under German artillery fire that disabled the main gun of one of the tanks before all three were forced to retreat. Meanwhile, Rivers' and one other tank spotted several German tanks[53] and tank destroyers. Ordered via radio to withdraw by Williams, Rivers instead advanced with the final message, "I see them. We'll fight them."[54] The tank accompanying Rivers was knocked out and Rivers' tank was hit by two high-explosive shells killing him instantly. For his actions over four days, Williams recommended Rivers for the Medal of Honor and submitted the paperwork despite seeming indifference by Hunt. Afterward, the paperwork disappeared, a phenomenon that happened many times to African Americans during World War II. It was not until 1997 that Williams was present when Rivers' sister and nephew accepted the Medal of Honor for his actions during World War II.

In early December, the 26th Infantry was pulled from the front line and the 761st Tank Battalion was then attached to the newly arrived 87th Infantry Division.[55] Perhaps not surprisingly, the battalion, which was in the line for only one month less than the 26th Infantry Division, received nothing more than a short rest during which they performed much-needed maintenance on their tanks. A serious problem that faced all three African

American tank battalions in the ETO was a lack of trained replacements for the crew members who were killed or seriously injured. Since all enlisted Army training was segregated, the only trained African American tankers were the original members of the three battalions. All replacement crews assigned to the battalions came from the general pool of African American replacements provided to all African American units. This meant that the average African American replacement in the infantry, Armored Force, and other combat arms units had only received the standard Army basic training (at that time sixteen weeks) before use as replacements. When these replacements arrived, therefore, they had to receive all of their technical training as on-the-job training. Yet, the more technical the task, the longer it took for an individual to meet minimum standards. The Army never solved this problem during World War II.

On 16 December 1944, the Germans launched their final offensive on the Western Front, which became known as the Battle of the Bulge. As with the rest of Patton's Third Army, the 761st Tank Battalion rushed into battle to help rescue the besieged 101st Airborne Division at Bastogne. Once again, the battalion found itself divided up to support the infantry regiments of the new infantry division. While the battalion was not directly involved with the liberation of the 101st Airborne Division, they participated in the general Allied counterattack against the Germans. The icy winter conditions made life unbearable inside tanks. While infantrymen often envied tankers who were out of the wind, tankers refer to their tanks as "armored Frigidaires."[56] The conditions also hampered the driving of tanks on the ice and snow lead to almost comical scenes in which huge tanks skidded down roads and into ditches with no way of stopping.

Throughout the winter, the 761st Tank Battalion, along with most other Allied units, slowly slogged their way through horrible weather as they pushed the Germans back. For the battalion, this meant slow attrition as long-serving officers and men were wounded or killed. A bright spot occurred on 17 February 1945 when former commander, Paul Bates, returned to the battalion. After recovering from his wounds suffered in November, Bates was offered command of a white tank battalion or a staff position in an armored division. Had he chosen one of those assignments, he could have undoubtedly expected promotion to colonel within a few months, if due to nothing more than attrition. However, Bates turned down those opportunities to return to *his* battalion.[57]

As the 761st Tank Battalion and the rest of the Allied forces made their way into Germany in the spring of 1945, they encountered a strange mixture of reactions from Germans and German armed forces. Some Germans soldiers and civilians seemed to welcome the end of the war, while others fought to the bitter end. While the hardcore Nazis, like the *Waffen SS*, fought the hardest, the battalion occasionally encountered individual German men and women who chose suicide rather than defeat. At the same time, the battalion began to experience discipline problems, almost exclusively from the replacements who joined the battalion after they arrived in the ETO. Soldiers were court-martialed for rape and even murder, which angered Bates who knew how hard the vast majority of the men in the battalion had worked to be tankers.[58]

In the final weeks of World War II, the 761st Tank Battalion traveled 465 miles in only 36 days.[59] On 7 May 1945, the battalion found itself in Steyr, Austria, as the war officially ended. Like many other units, the battalion did not return to the United States together but rather returned as individuals based on the Army's point system. Despite the transfers of veteran soldiers out of the unit, the battalion remained on active duty until 1 June 1946 when it was finally disbanded. On 24 November 1947, the battalion was reactivated at Fort Knox to serve as a training unit for African American tankers. The desegregated unit was disbanded for a second and final time on 15 March 1955.[60]

The 761st Tank Battalion's combat record was truly impressive. From 31 October 1944 to 26 May 1945, the battalion destroyed or captured 461 wheeled and tracked vehicles, killed 6246 enemy soldiers, and captured another 15,818. During the same period, the battalion lost seventy-one tanks destroyed, as well as three officers and thirty-one enlisted KIA. From members of the battalion, 8 received battlefield commissions, 11 received the Silver Star, 70 received the Bronze Star for valor or achievement, and 296 received the Purple Heart for wounds or death in battle (8 received more than one).[61] The battalion was recommended for the DUC, but the recommendation was denied. It was not until 1978 that President Jimmy Carter retroactively awarded the battalion the PUC for their achievements during World War II.

The third and final African American tank battalion organized during World War II was the 784th Tank Battalion. It was organized on 1 April 1943 as a light tank battalion with a cadre of officers and enlisted men from the 758th and 761st Tank Battalions at Camp Claiborne. Despite having received an initial cadre, the Army was slow in filling the battalion and it was not until January 1944 that the 784th Tank Battalion was finally at full strength.[62]

Correspondent Ted Stanford of the Pittsburgh *Courier* interviewed First Sergeant (FSG) Morris O. Harris of the 784th Tank Battalion. (NARA)

The battalion was transferred to Camp Hood along with the rest of the 5th Tank Group and arrived on 15 September 1943. Only six weeks later, the battalion changed its designation from light to medium with a reception of M4 tanks. Strangely, during the reorganization, all of the battalion's African American officers transferred to the 761st Tank Battalion.[63]

After a year of training and service as "school troops" at Camp Hood, the 784th Tank Battalion left Texas for Camp Shanks, New York, on 3 October 1944. Setting sail aboard the HMS *Moreton Bay* on 31 October, the battalion arrived in Liverpool on 11 November.[64] The battalion spent a month recovering from their voyage and training in Wales until the Battle of the Bulge accelerated their timetable. On 22 December 1944, the battalion boarded LSTs to cross the English Channel and spent Christmas Day in Rouen, France. The battalion was attached to the 104th Infantry Division and its companies were dispersed between the division's three infantry regiments.[65]

The first elements of the 784th Tank Battalion entered combat on 31 December 1944 but saw only limited action in January and almost all of their casualties resulted from frostbite. The battalion was initially used either as reconnaissance or as *de facto* artillery for the infantry regiments to which they were attached.[66] In February, the battalion was attached to the 35th Infantry Division (a National Guard unit with troops from Kansas, Missouri, and Nebraska), and its companies were divided between the three infantry regiments of the division, and Company D and its light tanks were attached to the division's reconnaissance troop.[67]

Operation Grenade, which was to begin on 10 February 1945, was a plan for the U.S. Ninth Army to cross the Roer River and meet up with a Canadian First Army and was intended to be the first major offensive action for the 784th Tank Battalion. However, the Germans destroyed a dam and caused the river to expand from a normal distance of twenty-five yards to three hundred or more yards across. For the next two weeks, the battalion waited on the west side of the river for the water to dissipate and helplessly received artillery fire from Germans on the other side. The battalion finally went on the offensive on 26 February in support of the 35th Infantry Division. German resistance was uncoordinated and, other than the presence of three antitank guns and some land mines, American infantry and tanks quickly overwhelmed the enemy. The retreating Germans left behind a significant amount of equipment and even rations, indicating they were not prepared for the American offensive. During this phase of combat, only one member of the battalion was killed[68] while eleven others were injured to various degrees.[69]

On 1 March 1945, the 784th Tank Battalion (less Company A) was the lead element in a task force formed around the 35th Infantry Division's 320th Infantry Regiment. The goal of the task force was to reach the Rhine River near the town of Drupt, Germany. The battalion's Company A supported the other two infantry regiments (134th and 137th) of the division, which followed the task force in support. The battalion moved so rapidly that they encountered almost no enemy resistance. Likewise, the Germans were unable to destroy any bridges because they were not prepared for the speed of the offensive. By the end of the first day, the battalion reached the Dutch town of Venlo on the border with Germany. The next morning the battalion quickly captured two more towns before being slowed down by a patch of road destroyed by the Germans. The terrain in the Netherlands and that portion of Germany was wet and soft enough that tanks quickly bogged down when they left the roads. Once the road was repaired, the battalion renewed its offensive taking approximately two hundred German prisoners, capturing several antitank and artillery pieces, and ending the day in the German town of Sevelen.[70]

On the third day, 3 March, the 784th Tank Battalion spent most of the day securing Sevelen, and the next day, the battalion performed reconnaissance and searched for intact bridges. On 5 March, the battalion began to experience more resistance from German formations, most particularly the 2nd and 7th *Fallschirmjaeger* (Airborne) Divisions, and the presence of several heavy antitank guns also slowed the battalion's advance. The battalion's after-action report stated that the paratroopers put up greater resistance than any other German forces.[71] For the next few days, the battalion proceeded in a northeasterly direction capturing small German towns against varied resistance. On 10 March, the battalion had reached Ossenberg on the Rhine River just south of their original objective.[72]

For the next two weeks, the 784th Tank Battalion was placed in reserve and allowed to recuperate. On 26 March, the 35th Infantry Division began its offensive across the Rhine River.

> The enemy resistance here showed signs of disorganization, lack of preparation and a readiness to surrender rather than stand and fight. No system of defenses have been prepared or were being prepared except an occasional roadblock, and there was almost complete absence of mines. Antitank defense came mainly from SP guns rather than towed and *Panzerfaust* bazookas.[73]

For the last few days of March 1945, the battalion encountered large numbers of German artillerymen, antiaircraft gunners, and other normally nonfront-line soldiers.

> Numerous prisoners taken by the infantry coordinating with the tanks indicated the beginning of the disintegration of the *Wehrmacht* and its ability to resist our advance further into the heart of Germany.[74]

The month of March had brought the most intense fighting that the battalion had experienced in the war and casualties began to mount. One officer and twenty-three enlisted men were KIA or DOW, while another nine officers and seventy-one enlisted men were WIA.[75]

From 1 to 13 April, the 784th Tank Battalion continued its offensive from the Rhine River to the Ruhr Pocket. While the initial German resistance included the 2nd *Fallschirmjaeger* and the 190th Infantry Divisions, the quality of the units they encountered as they advanced further into Germany worsened. Unusual and sometimes *ad hoc* formations such as the 454th Infantry Replacement Battalion, the 1st Infantry Technical Replacement Battalion, and various *Volksturm*[76] units became more commonplace.[77] From 13 to 31 April, the battalion was out of direct contact with the enemy. In contrast to the previous month, casualties were relatively light with only five enlisted men KIA or DOW, while one officer and nine enlisted men were WIA. Based on the previous month's combat, the first decorations were issued in April as two officers and two enlisted men each received the Silver Star, and five officers and ten enlisted men received the Bronze Star for valor or achievement.[78]

The last few days of the war in early May 1945 found the 784th Tank Battalion occupying German villages and generally mopping up the battle-field. No casualties were reported, but several decorations were received for the combat from March and April. Four officers and three enlisted men received the Silver Star, while another officer received an oak leaf cluster indicating a second award of the Silver Star. Additionally, seven officers and twenty-three enlisted men received the Bronze Star for valor or achievement.[79] During June with the war now officially over in Europe, the battalion spent most of its time conducting maintenance on vehicles and train-ing for a possible deployment to the Pacific. Also in June, the final decorations for the combat from March and April were received. Four officers and three enlisted men received the Silver Star, while another officer received an oak leaf cluster to his Silver Star. Moreover, twelve officers and twenty-eight enlisted men received the Bronze Star for valor or achievement, while one officer and ten enlisted men received an oak leaf cluster for their Bronze Stars.[80]

The 784th Tank Battalion remained in Germany on occupation duty for the rest of the year. On 24 December 1945, the battalion departed from Le Havre, France, aboard the SS *Argentina*, which reached New York on 1 January 1946.[81] The battalion took up quarters at Camp Kilmer, but they were not finally disbanded until 29 April 1946. On 7 July 1947, the battal-ion was redesignated the 84th Tank Battalion and then, eight days later on 15 July 1947, was reactivated at Fort Knox as a training battalion for African American tankers. The by-then desegregated battalion was finally disbanded on 15 March 1955.[82]

Except for the "Tuskegee Airmen," the members of the 758th, 761st, and 784th Tank Battalions did more to dispel racist notions of African American intellectual inferiority and cowardice than anyone else in the Army during World War II. The mechanical nature of tank maintenance and the intricacies of armored warfare made it impossible to argue that African Americans were incapable of performing technical or tactical tasks. Likewise, the excellent performance of these three battalions in combat dispelled the idea that African Americans lacked sufficient valor for success as combat arms soldiers.

Chapter 8

Tank Destroyers

During World War II, in addition to the Armored Force, the U.S. Army created a second new "branch"—Tank Destroyers.[1] Just as with the Armored Force, African Americans were not initially welcomed because of the general white belief that the vehicles and equipment were too technically complicated for African Americans to operate. Likewise, during World War II, solid combat performance on these technically complicated vehicles/equipment and equally complex tactics was crucial to proving African Americans' value in modern warfare and to undermining segregation within the Army.

The Tank Destroyers were perhaps the most misunderstood Army "branch" of the war. It is important to remember how new and innovative tank warfare was at the time. There was no set doctrine for the use of tanks before World War II and, likewise, there was no set antitank doctrine. While it was later taken for granted that tanks fought other tanks, at the time many theorists envisioned tanks as primarily an anti-infantry/anti-emplacement weapon. If that were true, then another weapon was necessary to combat tanks.

Initially, nations fought tanks with towed antitank guns. These towed antitank guns (perhaps the most famous of which was the German 88 mm) were successful at killing tanks but suffered from several deficiencies. First, towed guns required time to set up before engaging their targets. Second, the crew serving these guns was completely vulnerable to enemy fire. Last, the guns were mostly towed by wheeled vehicles which often had difficulty moving anywhere other than roads. To solve these problems, the antitank guns were mounted on tracked vehicles to increase speed, protect the crews, and make cross country travel easier.

In the U.S. Army, the decision to create large numbers of antitank forces resulted from the success of German armor, especially against France in 1940 and the Soviet Union in 1941. For instance, it was not until 23 September 1940 that American infantry regiments finally included an antitank company.[2] Then on 24 June 1941, the Army finally created separate provisional antitank battalions which, like the infantry regimental antitank company, used towed guns as their primary weapon.[3] During the Louisiana GHQ maneuvers in August and September 1941, these antitank battalions were temporarily combined to form the 1st, 2nd, and 3rd Antitank Groups.[4] Then, during the Carolina maneuvers in November 1941, not only were the previous three antitank groups used, but three new *ad hoc* formations were created called Tank Attackers 1, 2, and 3.[5] Both of these maneuvers had a profound effect on several developments within the Army, but most important for this discussion was the decision that the majority of antitank functions needed centralization.

On 3 December 1941, the Army redesignated all antitank battalions as tank destroyer battalions, and they were no longer associated with the infantry or field artillery. Only the infantry's regimental antitank companies remained outside of the tank destroyer battalions. LTC (later MG) Andrew D. Bruce established the Tank Destroyer Tactical and Firing Center at Fort Meade following a directive of 27 November 1941. On 30 January 1942, Bruce was ordered to move it to Camp Hood where it became the Tank Destroyer Center.[6] Initially, the Army intended to use tank destroyers in large formations and they organized tank destroyer groups and brigades. In the end, only one of the two brigades and fourteen of the twenty-four groups saw combat service. In practice, the tank destroyer battalions were usually parceled out to infantry and armored divisions to provide temporary extra firepower on an "as needed" basis.[7]

Initially, the Army organized three types of tank destroyer battalions: light towed, light self-propelled, and heavy self-propelled. However, experiments quickly demonstrated that the 37-mm antitank gun used by the light formations was relatively useless against modern armored vehicles. As a result, development focused on producing a single type of self-propelled tank destroyer armed with a gun of at least 75 mm. The first, and largely expedient, vehicle was the M3, which was a half-track with a 75-mm gun mounted on the back. After using the M3 in North Africa in late 1942 and early 1943, the Army decided that it was woefully inadequate in the tank destroyer role. Therefore, half of the tank destroyer battalions were redesignated as towed and the other half self-propelled. The new self-propelled vehicle, the M10, used a Sherman tank chassis with an open-topped turret mounting a three-inch (75 mm) low-velocity gun. The tank destroyer leadership wanted a completely different vehicle, which was capable of high-speed maneuvering and equipped with a more powerful high-velocity gun. Unfortunately, this vehicle, eventually designated the M18 "Hellcat," would not begin production until mid-1943.

The M-18 could achieve speeds of over fifty miles an hour and weighed less than twenty tons. It had a ground pressure of only 11.9 pounds per square inch, less than twice that of a man (seven pounds per square inch), which ensured that the M-18 could traverse most of the ground that a foot soldier could.[8]

Interestingly, the Army's senior leadership did not think the M18 was necessary and wanted to continue to produce the M10 until a much better vehicle, the M36 "Jackson" which mounted a 90-mm gun, was ready for production. After the Normandy invasion, the M10's inadequacy became apparent to everyone and M18 production was rapidly increased.

Amid all this confusion, the first two African American tank destroyer battalions were organized in December 1941. Ultimately, eleven African American tank destroyer battalions were organized during the war.[9] However, only three (614th, 679th, and 827th Tank Destroyer Battalions) saw combat service, while the rest were broken up and used to form engineer, quartermaster, and other support units.

The 614th Tank Destroyer Battalion was organized on 25 July 1942 at Camp Carson, Colorado, with the initial cadre from the 366th Infantry Regiment. The battalion performed initial training while equipped with the M3 in Colorado before moving to Camp Bowie, Texas, on 18 December 1942. In July 1943, the battalion reorganized with towed three-inch anti-tank guns and became school troops for Camp Hood, which they remained until 20 December. In February and March 1944, the battalion trained in the Louisiana maneuver area at Camp Beauregard before returning to Camp Hood.[10]

On 10 August 1944, the 614th Tank Destroyer Battalion began preparing for deployment to the ETO. Beginning on 8 October 1944, the battalion landed on the French coast at Normandy after a month's stay in the United Kingdom. For two months, the battalion saw the devastation of the French countryside and heard fire in the distance but did no more than fire their guns in support of other units. This situation changed in November when the battalion was attached to the 3rd Cavalry Group near Ober-Perl, Germany. The mission of the 3rd Cavalry and the attached 614th Tank Destroyer Battalion was to protect the left flank of the XX Corps.

In their first real combat, 1st Platoon, Company C, 614th Tank Destroyer Battalion was caught in the open and heavily shelled by enemy artillery. Understandably, the men's initial reaction was to seek shelter rather than worry about their vehicles and equipment. The platoon leader, 1LT Walter S. Smith, and one NCO, SSG Christopher J. Sturkey, exposed themselves to the artillery fire to rally the men and save the platoon from sure destruction. Both men received the Silver Star for their actions that day.[11] In the days that followed, the other companies of the battalion also received their baptisms under fire.

On 7 December 1944, the 614th Tank Destroyer Battalion was attached to the 103rd Infantry Division at Luneville, France. As was common practice with attached armor and tank destroyer battalions, the division commander divided the battalion and attaching the companies to the infantry regiments of his division. Companies A, B, and C were attached to the 410th, 409th, and 411th Infantry Regiments respectively. On 10 December 1944, the first member of the battalion died during a German ME109 fighter strafing run.

CPL Louis Gregory refused to leave his post and was engaging the aircraft with a .50 caliber machinegun when he was killed.

On 14 December 1944, a task force was assembled, commanded by LTC John P. Blackshear, executive officer of the 411th Infantry Regiment, to capture the town of Climbach, France. The task force consisted of one platoon of the 614th Tank Destroyer Battalion, one platoon of tanks from the 14th Armored Division, and one reinforced infantry company from the 411th Infantry.[12] When he heard about the mission, 1LT Charles L. Thomas, commander of Company C, volunteered his 3rd Platoon for the mission. While the Germans were thought largely dispirited, the task force encountered heavy fire from entrenched enemy soldiers in the woods and hills around the town. The tank destroyer platoon was sent in first to provide direct fire on the enemy positions. Unfortunately, the only good position from which to do so was an open field that offered no protection for the guns and largely unarmored vehicles of the towed tank destroyer platoon. The lead vehicle in the column, Thomas' M20 scout car, was immediately hit by enemy fire. Thomas was severely wounded and he and his vehicle were knocked out of action.

> Lieutenant Thomas received multiple gunshot wounds in his chest, legs, and left arm. In spite of the intense pain caused by his wounds, Lieutenant Thomas ordered and directed the dispersion and emplacement of his first two antitank guns. In a few minutes these guns were effectively returning the enemy fire. Realizing that it would be impossible for him to remain in command of the platoon because of his injuries, Lieutenant Thomas then signaled for the platoon commander to join him. Lieutenant Thomas then thoroughly oriented him as to the enemy gun positions, his ammunition status, and the general situation. Although fully cognizant of the probable drastic consequences of not receiving prompt medical attention, Lieutenant Thomas refused evacuation until he felt certain that his junior officer was in full control of the situation. Only then did Lieutenant Thomas allow his evacuation to the rear.[13]

For his actions that day, Thomas received the DSC. In 1997, Thomas' DSC was upgraded to the Medal of Honor.

Despite losing their company commander and under heavy artillery and mortar fire, the soldiers of 3rd Platoon set up their guns and engaged enemy targets. Quickly two of the platoon's four guns were knocked out by direct hits and many soldiers became casualties. German infantrymen then began to converge on the platoon to wipe them out, which forced some tank destroyer personnel to man small arms to defend their guns while the remainder of the platoon continued to man their three-inch guns. During the four hours of this battle, many men exhibited extraordinary courage and four received the Silver Star while another nine received the Bronze Star for Valor.

Some examples of this courage include T/5 Robert W. Harris, who realized that his gun crew were running out of ammunition and braved enemy artillery and small arms fire to bring back a truckload of supplies. When he was stopped and informed by the task force commander that the way forward would almost certainly lead to his death, Harris continued, "... unloaded the truck, uncrated ammunition boxes and valiantly carried the ammunition forward to each gun emplacement."[14]

SGT Dillard L. Booker, one of the Bronze Star recipients, provided a vivid account of that day's fighting.

> The enemy now awakened to the fact that they were being attacked, opened all its guns on the task force, small arms, machine guns, martars [sic], light and heavy artillery fire fell deadly all around us. ... Sgt. Tabron [sic] gun crew was dwindled down in size in matter of minutes, Cpl. Peter Simmons fired on every target until he was hit by direct tank fire. ... Cpl. Sheldon Murph [sic] gunner took his commands coolly as the commander picked the targets, he too fought earnestly until he had to be evacuated do to a lost [sic] of a leg. ... Lucious Riley opened up his fifty Caliber MG Gun raking woods and surrounding territory until the Half Track was hit by direct fire from a Tank Killing him at the Gun.[15]

Three members of the platoon were KIA and one died later in the hospital, while seventeen men were WIA. Three of the platoon's four guns were destroyed as well as two half-tracks, one scout car, and two jeeps.[16]

Almost immediately after the battle, Blackshear proposed the platoon for the DUC which was the highest award available for units rather than individuals.

Despite several casualties, one of which was the company commander, being inflictied [*sic*] in the initial burst of enemy fire, the two antitank guns were immediately put into position and effectively returned the enemy fire. So fierce and accurate was the fire of these two guns that the enemy guns withdrew temporarily to defillade [*sic*] positions, and then attempted to overrun the gun positions with combined armor and infantry attack. ... Despite the fact that one gun crew had been reduced to a lone cannoneer, the remaining gun crews alternated between the use of small arms and their guns as the threat of the close pressing Infantry and the harrassing [*sic*] tank fire became respectively paramount. Undaunted by the failure of tank support mired down too far to the rear to be effective; undismayed by the numerous casualties they were sustaining, which reduced their gun crews to skeleton size and eliminated completely their ammunition chain but inspired by such individual actions as the driver of an ammunition truck who deliber-ately drove his vehicle into the open toward the gun positions until it was mired down, and then personally carried the shells to the guns; this small group of determined fighters held off superior enemy force until foot elements could be deployed to relieve the pressure of the enemy Infantry, and artillery could be registered on the enemy armor. The unflinching determination of this group constituted the most magnificient [*sic*] display of mass heroism I have ever witnessed.[17]

The 3rd Platoon, Company C, 614th Tank Destroyer Battalion, was the first African American unit awarded the citation.[18]

The 614th Tank Destroyer Battalion continued fighting along the Sieg-fried Line as the American forces tried to entire Germany proper. For most of January, the battalion operated in support of the 103rd Infantry Division by providing direct fire on targets, men to perform raids on German positions, and indirect fire in support of the division's artillery. The most significant event of the month occurred on 25 January when the longsuffering 3rd Platoon, Company C, was posted to the town of Schillersdorf, France. At 4:30 a.m., a battalion of German infantrymen (sometimes reported as *Waffen SS*) attacked the town without warning. The American soldiers did not realize they were under attack until the Germans were already in the town itself. Overwhelmingly outnumbered, the platoon fought their way back but then discovered that their platoon leader, 1LT George Mitchell, and eleven enlisted men were left behind and captured by the Germans. Thankfully, all twelve men survived their time in German hands and returned to the battalion soon after the war.[19]

On 5 February 1945, a raiding party consisting of two officers and thirty enlisted men selected from the 1st and 2nd Reconnaissance Platoons of the battalion HQ company of the 614th Tank Destroyer Battalion performed a successful raid against a German position near Bitchholtz, France. While sustaining no casualties themselves, the raiding party captured six prisoners and killed another eight Germans.[20] The operation was carefully planned by 1LT Joseph L. Keeby and was especially important because several prior attempts by other elements of the 103rd Infantry had failed. The raid's success demonstrated to the division's white soldiers what African Americans were capable of. Keeby and four members of the party received the Bronze Star for Valor as a result of their actions.[21]

The rest of February and the early part of March passed uneventfully for the battalion. On 15 March, the Seventh Army, of which the 614th Tank Destroyer Battalion was a part, renewed its general offensive against Germany. As usual, the battalion was spread out in support of various elements of the 103rd Infantry. While Company A fired on German positions in the town of Kindwiller, France, the company commander, CPT Beauregard King, with elements from the company's HQ platoon were given the mission of capturing the town. Soon after entering the town, King was severely wounded by German machinegun fire. Upon seeing him wounded, PFC Thomas L. Kilgo, Jr., the accompanying medic, and SSG Charles L. Parks rushed forward. As Kilgo administered first aid to King, the captain instructed Parks to take command and continue to the capture of the town. "Don't stop for me—finish the job!"[22] The town was quickly captured and all three men received the Silver Star for their actions.[23]

By late March, the 614th Tank Destroyer Battalion had reached the Rhine River and spent most of its time mopping up any remaining elements of German resistance. It was not until 21 April that the battalion renewed its offensive operations this time in the direction of Austria. The battalion's final combat action came on 2 May when the reconnaissance platoons of the battalion were acting as the division reconnaissance element. 1LT Joseph L. Keeby's armored car came under fire near Scharnitz, Austria, and was disabled by a mine. Keeby refused to abandon his disabled vehicle and was killed while firing his .50 caliber machine gun at enemy positions. He posthumously received the Silver Star, which along with his previous awards made him the single most decorated member of the battalion.[24] On 3 May, elements of Company C attached to the 411th Infantry Regiment seized the Brenner Pass and the next day made contact with the 88th Infantry Division from the Fifth Army in Italy.[25] After occupation duty for two months, the battalion was ordered to Marseilles, France, on 19 July. Upon arrival, the battalion was broken up and its men sent to support units. MG Anthony J. McAuliffe, who gained fame during the Battle of the Bulge and then commanded the 103rd Infantry Division, intervened to save the battalion. The battalion was then slated for transport to the Pacific, but when the war against Japan ended, the battalion was sent to Germany on occupation duty. The battalion returned to the United States in early 1946 and was disbanded on 31 January at Camp Kilmer.[26]

The 679th Tank Destroyer Battalion was organized on 26 June 1943 at Camp Hood also as a towed antitank gun unit.[27] Unfortunately, the battalion spent most of its unit lifecycle on stateside training, almost exclusively at Camp Hood. As other African American tank destroyer battalions were disbanded and their personnel used to form noncombat units, the morale of the battalion plummeted. This situation did not improve when men from these disbanded units joined the battalion. Despite this handicap, the officers and men of the 679th continued to train though not always with a great deal of enthusiasm. Much to everyone's surprise on 20 October 1944, the battalion was alerted for overseas service. This remarkable news caused a flurry of activity in the battalion as the men began to take their training more seriously again.

An advanced detachment of the 679th Tank Destroyer Battalion left on 9 December 1944, while the rest of the battalion left for Camp Shanks on 22 December. After spending Christmas and New Year's Day in New York City, the battalion left for Europe aboard the USS *Monticello* (AP-61) on 10 December 1945 and arrived at Le Havre, France, on 21 January. After spending a month at Camp Lucky Strike in Normandy, the battalion moved by train to Marseilles where they boarded a ship for Italy on 1 March.[28] Arriving at Leghorn, Italy, the battalion was attached to the 92nd Infantry Division on 6 March. On 17 March, the battalion moved into combat positions and fired their first shot in anger the next day. The only sustained combat seen by the battalion involved neutralizing the Italian coast artillery guns on the Punta Bianca Peninsula which fired on the now Allied-occupied cities of Massa and Carrara. All 36 of the battalion's three-inch guns were part of this effort with each gun having a specific target and ready to fire within 45 seconds after an opportunity arose. From 14 April to 19 April 1945, the battalion fired 11,066 rounds at these targets effectively neutralizing them.[29] After the war ended in May, the battalion returned to the United States and disbanded on 26 October 1945 at Camp Kilmer.[30]

The final African American tank destroyer battalion to serve in combat was the 827th Tank Destroyer Battalion. Organized as a heavy self-propelled unit equipped with the M3 on 24 April 1942 at Camp Forrest, Tennessee, the battalion received its initial cadre of ten officers and seventy-seven enlisted men from the 4th Cavalry Brigade at Fort Riley. The battalion was transferred to Camp Hood on 4 September, where it was assigned to the Advanced Unit Training Center and performed 12 weeks of tactical training. In December 1942, the battalion was designated a School Troop Battalion of the Tank Destroyer Training Center. Throughout early 1943 while still serving as a "school battalion," the battalion was frequently called upon to provide cadres for other newly activated units, most particularly the 649th Tank Destroyer Battalion.[31]

On 4 June 1943, the 827th Tank Destroyer Battalion was reorganized as a towed antitank gun unit, but then less than seven weeks later on 20 July, the battalion was again reorganized this time as a self-propelled antitank battalion equipped with the M10. The battalion then began a six-week refresher course under this third organization. On 30 September, the battalion, which had previously always rated at least "satisfactory" or a higher, received its first "unsatisfactory" rating. LTC Herschel D. Baker, who had only become commander of the battalion on 25 August, blamed the poor rating on both inadequate training that the battalion's young officers had received at the tank destroyer school and on the failure of the former battalion commander to eliminate inefficient officers and NCOs. In a November report, Baker provided three other reasons for the battalion's poor rating.

a. Changes in type of unit from self-propelled M-3s to towed three-inch to self-propelled M-10s.

b. Use of the Battalion as school troops from 2 January 1943 to 21 July 1943.

c. Shortages of equipment in supply branches. According to the best information available, the battalion has never been properly equipped with either organization or individual equipment.[32]

While at first glance Baker might be seen as trying to cover for his own failures, his short time in command (thirty-five days) before the first negative rating and the previous positive ratings seemed to portend serious problems within the battalion.

On 2 October, the 827th Tank Destroyer Battalion transferred to the Desert Training Center in California where they spent the next month in the field performing exercises alongside the 93rd Infantry Division. The battalion was then alerted on 31 December 1943 to prepare for overseas movement and, surprisingly, almost one hundred officers and men were transferred out of the battalion, while twenty-six officers and ninety-seven men transferred in. Though all of the enlisted men were properly trained, some of the new officers were trained as field artillerymen, which further added to the confusion over roles, missions, and skills. In February 1944, the alert was called off and the battalion moved to Fort Huachuca.[33] The battalion reorganized for the fourth and final time with a new T/O and a new vehicle—the M18—on 27 July 1944.[34]

By August 1944, the 827th Tank Destroyer Battalion had failed five Army Ground Forces battalion tests and, before leaving for Europe, the battalion's commanding and executive officers were replaced. From its activation in April 1942 until it arrived in Europe, the battalion was commanded by eight different officers (not counting temporary command by the executive officer or other company-grade officers). The new executive officer believed that the battalion was, "railroaded through the training tests," and not prepared for combat.[35] Despite having spent two-and-a-half years in stateside training, the frequent leadership turnover and reorganization undermined unit efficiency. As a result of all the turnover, the battalion never formed a strong cadre of officers or NCOs. The battalion's African American company-grade officers were expected to motivate their men beyond any reasonable standard. When these officers were deemed to have failed, they were removed and replaced by white officers, most of whom were Southerners and/or had previously served with now disbanded African American tank destroyer units. Unsurprisingly, these white officers were no more successful in motivating the men of the battalion than their African American predecessors. In September 1944, preparations for overseas movement were disrupted by two courts-martial, one involving an ax murder and the other a shooting. Both cases demonstrated a significant lack of discipline within the unit.[36]

The 827th Tank Destroyer Battalion arrived in Marseilles, France, on 13 November 1944. After a month of recuperation and maintenance, the battalion performed a five-day march in December over icy roads to join the Seventh Army. So many accidents and breakdowns occurred that, when the battalion arrived in Sarrebourg, many of its vehicles immediately went in for significant repairs. After this bad start, things only get worse. On 20 December 1944, the battalion was attached to the 12th Armored Division and placed on the front line the next day. Though the battalion saw no action, it experienced problems with discipline as men frequently left their vehicles unguarded to gather firewood and built fires—in direct violation of standing orders.[37]

On 6 January 1945, the 827th Tank Destroyer Battalion was ordered to join the 79th Infantry Division, but before they could move out, three major incidents occurred. In one company, an officer and an enlisted man shot each other while, in another company, a disgruntled soldier attacked the first sergeant. The first sergeant, while defending himself, accidentally shot a different enlisted man by accident. In yet another company, the company commander reported that approximately 75 percent of his men were missing or drunk.[38]

Between 8 and 20 January, after finally joining the 79th Infantry, the battalion's companies performed at varying levels—some extremely well and others very poorly. Among the positive actions were: on 9 January, Company B destroyed eleven German tanks and one half-track; on 10 January, Company B destroyed three German Mark IV tanks and killed nineteen Germans soldiers; on 11 January, one platoon of Company B destroyed four German Mark IV tanks while suffering no damage; on 12 January, Company A knocked out two German Mark IV tanks; and on 17 January, Company A knocked out two German tanks at a range of fourteen hundred yards.[39] Most of the negative incidents centered on the refusal of members of the battalion to engage the enemy and/or their tendency to "disappear" during combat or during movements unless officers or NCOs were present. Since officers were closely involved in even routine activities, their casualties were disproportionately high. In less than a month (8–20 January), two of the battalion's officers were KIA and eight WIA.[40] One telling incident took place on 13 January, when German artillery set fire to a truck containing ammunition and fuses. When ordered to unload a truck to prevent an explosion, the African American soldiers refused to comply. Instead, CPT Douglas H. Sullivan, a white officer, jumped on the truck and began to unload it by himself before several white infantrymen assisted him. Sullivan received the Bronze Star for Valor as a result of his actions.[41]

The Army pulled the 827th Tank Destroyer Battalion off the frontline on 20 January and launched an investigation by the VI Corps' IG. Despite the excellent performance of some soldiers, the battalion had serious problems and every officer of the battalion (white and African American) expressed some doubts about their men's abilities and courage. After four days of investigation, the IG had two primary recommendations. First, withdraw the battalion from the front, retrain it, and then return it to combat. Second, court-martial men who refused to engage the enemy. MG Edward H. Brooks, commander of the VI Corps, and his superior, LTG Alexander M. Patch, commander of the Seventh Army, recommended disbanding the battalion, but LTG Jacob L. Devers, commander of the 6th Army Group, refused. The IG had only questioned officers, not NCOs and enlisted men, and Devers wanted their opinions as well. A new investigation questioned a dozen NCOs and enlisted men and found them competent in their basic tasks, but eleven of the twelve did not want to go back into combat with the battalion.[42] With no way to determine the competence of the unit, the battalion's equipment was turned over to other tank destroyer units and the battalion itself was used by the 6th Army Group for casual duties. After the war ended, the battalion was listed as a surplus unit and returned to the United States where it was disbanded on 2 December 1945 at Camp Patrick Henry.[43]

The problems of the 827th Tank Destroyer Battalion were mostly the result of poor training, discipline, and leadership. The frequent changes in organization, equipment, and officers were the breeding ground for those problems. Despite all of the battalion's difficulties, however, several subunits performed well in combat. Arguably, if fair-minded white and well-prepared African American officers had led the battalion, it might have performed in combat more like 614th Tank Destroyer Battalion, which accomplished far more while possessing inferior organization and equipment.

The combat record of African American tank destroyer battalions was more complicated than their Armored Force comrades. Though also only fielding three battalions in combat, one battalion saw negligible combat and another failed rather miserably. Nevertheless, the superb performance of the 614th Tank Destroyer Battalion prevented any blanket condemnations of African American tank destroyer battalions. If anything, the problems of the 827th Tank Destroyer Battalion highlighted the inherent failings of segregation—poor white leadership, discriminatory promotion, and person-nel policies, and the tendency to blame all problems on African American rank-and-file while white-washing any mistakes of white leadership.

Section V

Sea Services and
Technical Knowledge

Chapter 9

U.S. Navy

At the beginning of World War II, African American sailors were only allowed to serve in U.S. Navy kitchens. Ironically, from the time of the Civil War until World War I, almost all ratings (career specialties) within the Navy were open to African Americans. Then in 1919, the Navy completely barred African Americans from enlisting. The complete moratorium on African American enlistment remained in place until 1933 when new President Franklin D. Roosevelt allowed African Americans to enlist, but only as mess attendants. The expansion of African American career opportunities in the Navy during World War II helped to undermine racist stereotypes regarding African American intellectual abilities.

The first African American Navy hero of World War II was Doris "Dorie" Miller. Miller, a Texas native, enlisted at age 20, on 16 September 1939, as a Mess Attendant, 3rd Class. He chose the Navy because he wanted to travel the world and learn a trade (cooking) useful in civilian life. Miller's first assignment was the USS *Pyro* (AE-1), an ammunition ship, which was followed on 2 January 1940, by the USS *West Virginia* (BB-48), a battleship.[1] On 7 December 1941, Miller was onboard the *West Virginia* in Pearl Harbor, Hawaii, when the Japanese attacked. When general quarters was sounded, he headed for his battle station, an antiaircraft position, only to find it destroyed. Miller then went up to the main deck, where he helped wounded sailors until ordered to the ship's bridge to aid mortally wounded CAPT Mervyn S. Bennion. After moving the captain to a safer position, Miller manned a .50 caliber antiaircraft gun until he ran out of ammunition and the order was put out to abandon ship. Sometimes credited with shooting down one or more Japanese aircraft, no evidence exists that he did so.[2] The *West Virginia* was so badly damaged on 7 December that severe flooding below decks caused the ship to slowly sink to the bottom of Pearl Harbor. Thankfully, the ship's human losses were quite light, only 130 killed and 52 wounded out of a crew of 1,541 men. For his courage, Miller was awarded the Navy Cross, the Navy's second-highest decoration for valor, but for African Americans, he was the first, and perhaps the greatest, hero of World War II.

Only a little more than a week after the Japanese attack, Miller was reassigned to the armored cruiser USS *Indianapolis* (CA-35). In November 1942, he returned to the United States and began a war bond tour. Then in June 1943, Miller volunteered for sea duty and was assigned to the newly constructed escort carrier USS *Liscome Bay* (CVE-56). At 5:10 a.m. on 24 November, while the *Liscome Bay* was supporting Operation Galvanic, the attack on Makin and Tarawa Atolls in the Gilbert Islands, a torpedo from the Japanese submarine *I-175* struck near the rear of the carrier. Unfortunately, the ship's bomb magazine detonated soon thereafter and the ship sank within only a few minutes. Miller was among the 646 sailors who died in the sinking.

Though the Navy later honored Miller with the naming a Knox-class frigate and a Gerald Ford-class aircraft carrier, Miller's position as an icon of the Civil Rights movement was far more important. While he was still alive, many African Americans questioned why someone who had proved himself in combat was still relegated to the ship's kitchens. After his death, Miller became a martyr for the cause of Civil Rights—good enough to decorate for valor and to die for his country, but not good enough to serve freely alongside white sailors.

Doubtless, Miller influenced Roosevelt's decision to open all Navy ratings to African Americans, which became official policy on 1 June 1942.[3]

This decision was followed only a few months later by the announcement that only seventeen-year-olds could voluntarily enlistment and all other males were subject to the Selective Service System starting on 1 January 1943. By 1 February 1943, of the 26,909 African Americans in the Navy, more than two-thirds were mess attendants (18,227), while the rest were rated for general service (6,662) or served in naval construction battalions (NCBs, better known as "Seabees") (2,020).[4]

Beginning in October 1942, the Navy created segregated NCBs to utilize African American sailors away from the kitchens, but also to keep them off of ships. NCBs performed the Navy's overseas construction work, including building airfields, bridges, canals, defensive positions, docks, housing, roads, storage facilities, and wharves, as well as unloading supplies and equipment. They were also frequently called upon to fight alongside U.S. Army or U.S. Marine Corps units or to protect themselves from Japanese attacks, which resulted in one of their mottos: "We build, we fight."

Ultimately, African American sailors filled the ranks of two NCBs and fifteen Special NCBs, all of which had white officers and chief petty officers (CPOs).[5] More than 12,500 African Americans served in these NCBs during World War II. African American sailors assigned to the two "regular" NCBs received instruction in a wide variety of duties, while those assigned to the special NCBs were only used for manual labor. Since most of their work took place close to the front lines, the two "regular" NCBs also received combat training in small arms and small unit tactics. The Special NCBs were created because the Navy lacked stevedores to unload ships in combat zones. By the end of the war, forty-one of these battalions were organized, of which fifteen were manned by African Americans.[6] The modern Navy includes Navy Cargo Handling Battalions, which are considered the descendants of these World War II units.

The Navy's Bureau of Yards and Docks (BuDocks) was given the responsibility for recruiting and organizing the African American NCBs. Unfortunately, the commander of BuDocks, Rear Admiral Ben Moreell decided to use only white Southern officers and CPOs because of "their ability and knowledge in handling" African Americans. Moreell's decision was particularly surprising because he was both Jewish and grew up in St. Louis rather than the Deep South. The 34th NCB was organized on 24 October 1942 and, after specialized training, spent twenty months constructing facilities in the Pacific before returning to the United States in October 1944. In January 1943, the 80th NCB, a second African American "regular" NCB, was organized and deployed to Trinidad in the Caribbean in July of that year.[7]

While both of the African American "regular" NCBs performed well while overseas, they both suffered from racism and discrimination at the hands of their white officers and CPOs. These problems in the 34th NCB did not come to a head until after the unit returned to the United States. Not only did the battalion commander refuse to promote any African Americans to the rank of CPO, but he also even refused to allow African American petty officers[8] to lead working parties. In response to these incidents, the African American sailors of the battalion performed a hunger strike on 2–3 March 1945 during which they continued to perform their regular duties but refused to eat. As a result, BuDocks launched an investigation that ended with the removal of the battalion's commanding officer, executive officer, and approximately 20 percent of the remaining officers and CPOs. The replacement officers were almost exclusively Northerners who were screened first for their racial attitudes. One of the first actions by the new battalion commander, a New Yorker, was to make sure that qualified African American sailors were promoted to CPO.[9]

The situation with the 80th NCB came to a head more quickly. When the African American sailors complained about discrimination during transport to and while stationed at Trinidad, the battalion commander decided to court-martial nineteen sailors in September 1943 on the charge of seditious behavior. These men then contacted the NAACP and ultimately a Navy review board honorably discharged all but five of the sailors in question. In July 1944, BuDocks removed all of the battalion's white officers and CPOs and replaced them with Northerners. Both battalions deployed a second time under new leadership and experienced no racial incidents.[10]

Despite never intending them for combat duty, several of the Special NCBs did find themselves under fire. The 17th Special NCB landed on Peleliu on 15 September 1944 alongside the 7th Marine Regiment. The marines soon found they did not have sufficient numbers to both man their lines and evacuate their wounded. African American sailors of the 17th Special NCB volunteered, alongside African American marines of the 11th Marine Depot Company and the 7th Marine Ammunition Company, to occupy the line alongside the white marines, man heavy weapons which had lost their crews, and carry wounded marines to rear evacuation areas. The performance of the 17th Special NCB, as well as the African American marines, was noted by MG William H. Rupertus, commander of the 1st Marine Division, who wrote almost identical letters to all three units' commanders.

> The Negro race can well be proud of the work performed by the [unit] as they have demonstrated in every respect that they appreciate the privilege of wearing a Marine uniform and serving with Marines in combat. Please convey to your command these sentiments and inform them that in the eyes of the entire Division they have earned a 'Well Done'.[11]

Interestingly, late in the war, several of the Special NCBs began adding white and African American sailors without any regard to segregation, which made them the Navy's first fully integrated units of the 20th century.[12]

Despite the Navy's best efforts to keep African Americans on land, pressure continued from the African American press and public to allow them to serve on ships in a capacity other than mess attendants. Finally, the Navy decided to conduct an "experiment" to determine whether African Americans were capable of performing more than menial tasks. The ship used was the USS *Mason* (DE-529). The first captain of the ship was Lieutenant Commander (LCDR) William M. Blackford, who had previously captained the USS *Phoebe* (AMc-57), a minesweeper working in the Aleutian Islands for a year and a half. Blackford, who grew up in Seattle, Washington, and came on active duty from the Naval Reserve in January 1941 while he was working on a PhD in chemistry at the University of Virginia.[13] The Navy did not choose Blackford because he had any particular attitude toward African Americans, rather he was available, had already commanded a ship, and was

On 27 May 1942, Admiral Chester W. Nimitz, Commander in Chief, Pacific Fleet, decorated Steward's Mate 3rd Class Doris Miller with the Navy Cross at Pearl Harbor, Hawaii. (NARA)

willing to accept the assignment. Ultimately his success rested merely on his treating his sailors with respect. Ironically, the Navy did not know that his great-grandmother, Mary Berkeley Minor Blackford, was an abolitionist from Virginia who supported the Union during the Civil War.[14]

Men of the U.S. Navy's 34th Construction Battalion (better known as the Seabees) disembark from their landing craft during assault training in December 1942. (NARA)

The USS *Mason* was commissioned on 20 March 1944 and her first real test was a shakedown cruise in April, during which the ship itself, as well as the crew's ability to man their stations and work together as a team, were tested. Night and day, exercises were performed, including dropping depth charges, gunnery, refueling, and towing. While the *Mason* and her crew performed well during the cruise, the Navy's Bureau of Personnel report on the ship included more discussion of the ship's cleanliness, or lack thereof, than her actual performance.[15] The *Mason* then embarked on her first convoy cruise, which was largely uneventful except for the crew's reception in Northern Ireland. It came as quite a shock when the local white populace treated the African American sailors as equals. For many members of the crew, this represented the first time they were ever treated courteously by white people and it had a profound effect on them.[16] On her return trip to America, the *Mason* was assigned to a hunter/killer group searching for German U-boats. While there were some possible sightings and depth charges were dropped, no submarines were captured or sunk.

In October 1944, the USS *Mason*'s second voyage to the United Kingdom was also her most difficult. The ship was part of Convoy NY-119, in which four destroyer escorts shepherded a convoy of Army tugboats and barges. The convoy leader, Commander Alfred L. Lind, described this cruise as the "battle of the barges." Over thirty days, the convoy traveled 3,539 miles at an average speed of only 4.74 miles per hour. While the conditions at sea were difficult for the first twenty days, ten-foot waves and twenty-mile-per-hour winds, the last ten days of the voyage included wind gusts of up 290 miles per hour and waves between forty and fifty feet high. Some of the barges in question were originally used to ferry railroad cars across New York Harbor—these wooden structures were 250 to 360 feet long and 45 feet wide. The storm sunk three tugboats, eight steel car floats, and five wooden cargo barges as well as took the lives of nineteen Americans. Lind decided to send as many small craft as possible ahead of the main force to prevent greater loss of life. These small crafts were sent under the protection of the *Mason*. Once the *Mason* reached the safety of Falmouth harbor on the west coast of England, they remained for only two hours. While at the sea, the ship's deck split when two beams in one compartment collapsed and the seam holding the deck together broke. After repairing the deck, the *Mason* rejoined the convoy and assisting twelve other ships to port. Then the *Mason* sailed to the coast of France to salvage damaged barges until the end of the month.[17] Both Blackford and Lind recommended the *Mason* and her crew for commendations for their efforts during the convoy, but none ever materialized. Surprisingly, the *Mason*'s crew did not know about these recommendations until fifty years after the fact when they were interviewed by a researcher who produced an oral history of the ship.

After the USS *Mason* returned to the United States in late 1944, tensions began to surface between the African American crew and the ship's white CPOs. The CPOs, especially the chief radioman, clearly did not like their assignment and often actively attempted to prevent the African American sailors from properly performing their jobs. Things came to a head during a meeting between Blackford and the CPOs, during which they produced a long list of demands. The next day, in response to their demands, Blackford transferred all of the CPOs from the ship to the receiving station in New York

In February 1944, twelve members of the "Golden Thirteen," who were the first African Americans commissioned in the U.S. Navy: (*left to right* front row) Ensigns George Clinton Cooper, Graham Edward Martin, Jesse Walter Arbor, John Walter Reagan, Reginald Ernest Goodwin; (*left to right* back row) Dennis D. Nelson II, Phillip George Barnes, Samuel Edward Barnes, Dalton Louis Baugh, James Edward Hair, Frank Ellis Sublett, and Warrant Officer Charles Byrd Lear. Not pictured: Ensign W. Sylvester White). (NARA)

to await further orders. In essence, Blackford fired them all. In the weeks that followed, the ship's qualified African American sailors began to receive more promotions though none were promoted to CPO before the war ended.[18]

The USS *Mason* participated in three more convoys across the Atlantic in February, March, and April 1945. On 12 June 1945, Blackford was promoted to commander and transferred to Recruit Training Center Great Lakes (now known as Great Lakes Naval Training Station). The ship's next captain, LCDR Norman Meyer, was a member of the U.S. Naval Academy

African American sailors at the Boston Navy Yard look at their newly commissioned ship, the USS *Mason* (DE-529), which was the first Navy vessel to have an African American crew. (NARA)

Class of 1935, who left the Navy two years after graduation because of poor eyesight. After the attack on Pearl Harbor, he was recalled to active duty and served as a staff officer ashore for almost the entire war. Perhaps unsurprisingly, Meyer only received command of the *Mason* after the war in Europe had ended. He took a negative view of the crew and his assignment almost immediately. Meyer wrongly believed that the majority of his crew were illiterate and that he had inherited a ship with a poor record. As late as an interview he conducted in July 1990, he wrongly referred to Blackford as a "drunken slob" and the *Mason* as a "terrible ship." Ironically, it was Meyer who was responsible for the most embarrassing incident involving the ship, when he accidentally rammed the USS *Spangenburg* while pulling into New York harbor.[19] After only three months on board, he left the *Mason* on 20 September 1945 and she was decommissioned a month later.

On 12 April 2003, the Navy commissioned a new Arleigh Burke-class destroyer, the USS *Mason* (DDG-87), in honor of the contributions of the African American sailors on the World War II ship.

The only other African American crewed Navy vessel was the patrol craft USS *PC 1264*. The *PC 1264* was smaller (only 300 tons as opposed to 1,100) and had a smaller crew (only 63 as opposed to 156) than the USS *Mason* but was actually in service longer. A total of 369 patrol craft, popularly known as "subchasers," were launched during World War II. They were designed for simple operation and were almost exclusively crewed by reservists and draftees with minimal sea experience. These vessels were used for a wide range of tasks during the war, including bombarding landing areas, escorting convoys, hunting submarines, leading landing craft onto invasion beaches, and sinking small enemy ships and boats. The design was easy to produce in smaller yards and the subchasers were used in all theatres.[20]

The *PC 1264*'s captain was Lieutenant Eric Purdon who, like Blackford, was chosen because he was available, had already commanded another "subchaser," and was willing to volunteer. Purdon later stated that he volunteered because the assignment offered two things he wanted—a command and a challenge.[21] The ship's other officers were also volunteers but, except for the executive officer who was a jazz aficionado and had African American friends, none had any particular attitudes toward African Americans. It is interesting to note that all of the officers were Northerners or Californians.[22]

After commissioning at the Brooklyn Navy Yard on 25 April 1944, the *PC 1264* served for 22 months of largely uneventful duty.[23] The ship spent her entire career patrolling along the east coast of the United States and in the Caribbean, as well as escorting convoys to Cuba and Key West. During the first week of November 1944, the white senior petty officers transferred off the ship, and thereafter all enlisted personnel on the ship were African American.[24] Other than a single sonar contact, which resulted in dropping depth charges, the closest the crew came to combat was during stays in Southern ports. The ship was preparing for duty in the Pacific when the war ended and, on 17 September 1945, Purdon relinquished command and the ship was decommissioned on 7 February 1946.[25]

The absence of African American commissioned officers in the Navy became an issue during World War II. The Navy had never in its history had African American commissioned officers and it was only as a result of pressure from both the African American community and First Lady Eleanor Roosevelt that the situation changed. Starting in January 1944, a group of sixteen African American enlisted men began officer training at Camp Robert Smalls, Recruit Training Center Great Lakes. The majority of the group who were ultimately commissioned[26], known collectively as the "Golden Thirteen," were college graduates and, eventually, three possessed master's degrees, one a doctorate, and one a law degree. In March 1944, twelve were commissioned as ensigns[27] and another was appointed a warrant officer.[28] Additionally, in the summer of 1944, thirteen other African Americans, all civilians with special professional qualifications, were trained alongside similarly qualified whites and commissioned as staff officers in the Medical, Chaplain, Civil Engineer, and Supply Corps.[29]

None of the "Golden Thirteen" saw combat during the war and the majority served in logistics, but several had interesting service histories. Jesse W. Arbor served on Guam not long after the island's liberation. Phillip G. Barnes and Reginald E. Goodwin both served as logistics support officers on Saipan, while Samuel E. Barnes did the same on Okinawa. James E. Hair commanded the tugboat USS *Cahto* (YTB-215) in New York harbor before serving aboard the USS *Mason*. Unfortunately, Charles Lear committed suicide soon after discharge, apparently because he wanted to stay in the Navy and could not find a job in civilian life. Graham E. Martin served on the USS *YP-131*, an 83-foot patrol boat built in 1929 and originally named the SS *Sobre Las Olas*. Dennis D. Nelson was the only member of the group to remain in the Navy after the war and retired as a lieutenant commander in 1963. John W. Reagan also served on the USS *Cahto* and then in logistics support on Guam and Okinawa. Frank E. Sublett, Jr., served on the USS *YO-106*, a 174-foot fuel tanker built in 1944. William S. White served as a public relations officer first at Camp Robert Smalls and then in Washington, DC.[30]

The same year that the "Golden Thirteen" were commissioned another African American was commissioned in the Navy by a different route. Samuel L. Gravely, Jr., was the first African American to take part in the

In September 1944, during the invasion of Peleliu, this group of African American Seabees acted as stretcher bearers for the 7th Marines. (NARA)

Navy's V-12 program[31], which trained naval and marine officers through civilian universities. On 14 December 1944, he was commissioned as an ensign and served on the USS *PC-1264* before discharge in 1946. Recalled to active duty in 1949, Gravely first worked as a naval recruiter to encourage more African Americans to enlist in the then-desegregated Navy. During the Korean War, Gravely served as a communications officer on the battleship USS *Iowa* (BB-61) and then on the heavy cruiser USS *Toledo* (CA-133).

In 1961, Gravely became the first African American to command a Navy warship, the destroyer USS *Theodore E. Chandler* (DD-717). Then, in 1962, he became the first African American to graduate from the Naval War College, before taking command of the destroyer escort USS *Falgout* (DE-324). In 1966, Gravely became the first African American to command a warship in combat when he led the destroyer USS *Taussig* (DD-746) off the coast of Vietnam. In 1967, he became the Navy's first African American captain and commanded the guided-missile frigate

USS *Jouett* (DLG-29). Then in 1971, Gravely become the Navy's first African American flag officer when he was promoted to rear admiral and commanded Cruiser-Destroyer Group 2. He commanded the Third Fleet in Hawaii from 1976 to 1978, then the Defense Communications Agency until his retirement as a vice admiral in 1980.[32]

While they were not combat troops, one of the most dangerous duties performed by African American sailors during World War II involved the loading and unloading of munitions from ships. One of the busiest port facilities for munitions was located at Port Chicago, California, thirty-five miles north of San Francisco. By 1944, the pier at Port Chicago was capable of the loading of two ships simultaneously. Most of this work was done by African American sailors and neither they nor their white officers received any special training in the loading and unloading of munitions. Different work crews loaded ships around the clock and they often competed to see who could load the most in an eight-hour shift. Since the competition increased the loading speed, the officers encouraged it.[33]

On the evening of 17 July 1944, sailors loaded two merchant ships, the Victory ship SS *Quinault Victory* (MC-115) and the Liberty ship SS *E.A. Bryan* (MC-2761), with a combination of aerial bombs, antiaircraft ammunition, high explosives, and smokeless powder. Additional munitions sat on sixteen railroad cars on the pier and a total of 320 men were on the pier or the ships as cargo handlers and crewmen that night. At 10:18 p.m., an enormous explosion erupted from the pier and a few seconds later another explosion erupted as the contents of the *E.A. Bryan* detonated. The explosions were so massive that the seismic shock wave was felt as far away as Boulder City, Nevada. The *E.A. Bryan*, the pier, and several nearby buildings completely disintegrated, while the *Quinault Victory* spun in the air and crashed into the bay five hundred feet away. The 320 men (202 of whom were African Americans) died instantly, while another 390 were wounded to varying degrees. Debris from the explosion traveled as far as two miles and damage was even discovered forty-eight miles away in San Francisco.[34]

As a result of the explosion, since the existing U.S. Coast Guard instructions on safe ship loading were violated, the Navy instituted new rules on munitions handling and formalized training with required certification.

Soon after the explosion, the surviving sailors at Port Chicago were put to work at another facility at the Mare Island Naval Station twenty-five miles northeast of San Francisco in Vallejo, California, again loading munitions. These sailors were understandably disturbed by the idea of working with munitions again. On 9 August 1944, 258 African American sailors refused direct orders to load munitions. After two days spent on a barge as prisoners, the sailors were given another chance to go back to work. A total of 208 sailors volunteered to back to work, but instead, they remained prisoners and were now interrogated to determine the identity of the mutiny's "ringleaders." The fifty sailors who refused to work were considered the "ringleaders," which was largely true though a small number of these men simply ran afoul of their officers.[35]

On 31 August, President Franklin D. Roosevelt was informed of this situation by Secretary of the Navy James V. Forrestal. Roosevelt recommended only minor sentences for the 208 sailors who volunteered to go back to work because "… they were activated by mass fear and … this was understandable."[36] As a result, these sailors all received summary court-martials and were sentenced to forfeiture of pay for three months. The fifty "ringleaders" received general court-martials on the charge of mutiny, which carried a possible death sentence. None of the sailors were given a death sentence, but ten men received fifteen years in prison, twenty-four men received twelve years, eleven men received ten years in prison, and the youngest five men received eight years in prison.[37]

After the end of the war in September 1945, the Navy reduced the sentences of each of the fifty "ringleaders" by one year, while the next month a recommendation was made for further reductions in the sentences.[38] On 6 January 1946, all but one of the sailors were paroled and returned to active duty in the Navy. The one sailor who was not paroled already had a bad disciplinary record, while other sailors had no problems other than the "mutiny." For several months these men served throughout the Pacific, some onboard ships and some on islands. Finally, the men were given general discharges "under honorable conditions." By the 1990s, only a few of the fifty sailors remained alive and, though they were urged to apply for presidential pardons, most refused because they had done nothing wrong and did not need a pardon. Finally, one of the survivors, Freddie Meeks, agreed to apply to President Bill Clinton for a pardon, which was granted 23 December 1999.[39]

During World War II, the Navy underwent a substantial change. When the war began, African American sailors were found only in kitchens and no African Americans had ever served as commissioned officers. By the end of the war, these strict structures had been weakened. African American sailors were serving in ratings other than mass attendants and more than sixty African Americans served as commissioned and warrant officers. Unfortunately, the traditional nature of the institution meant that, like the Army, direct intervention by the president was required to complete the process of integration.

Chapter 10

U.S. Coast Guard

While African Americans served in the U.S. Coast Guard almost from the beginning of the service, it was not until 1831 that "free persons of color" were officially allowed to enlist.[1] Like the U.S. Navy, after World War I the Coast Guard stopped recruiting African Americans to serve in capacities other than mess stewards until March 1942, with a few small exceptions. A small group of African Americans crewed the lifesaving station at Pea Island, North Carolina, and a small number of African Americans crewed lighthouses in the Mississippi River basin. All of these coast guardsmen were previously members of the U.S. Lighthouse Service, which was absorbed by the Coast Guard in 1939.[2] The small size of the Coast Guard allowed change to proceed more quickly than in a larger organization and the World War II experience of the service demonstrated the effectiveness and efficiency inherent in racial integration.

The history of the U.S. Coast Guard began on 4 August 1790, when the first Secretary of the Treasury, Alexander Hamilton, established the U.S. Revenue Cutter Service (USRCS). The Coast Guard was ultimately a combination of five predecessors: the USRCS; the Lifesaving Service (created in 1878 and merged with the USRCS in 1915 with the new service then taking the name "Coast Guard"); the U.S. Lighthouse Service (created in 1789; absorbed in 1939); and the Bureau of Navigation and Steamboat Inspection (itself a merger of two separate agencies organized in 1884 and 1838 respectively; absorbed by the Coast Guard in 1942).

Ironically, the Coast Guard has never technically been a military service. As part of the Department of the Treasury, the duties and responsibilities of the Coast Guard centered more on safety aboard private and commercial vessels as well as preventing the smuggling of either contraband items or to prevent paying duties and customs taxes.[3] In 1915, a new statute allowed for the president to direct the Coast Guard to operate as part of the U.S. Navy during wartime. During both World War I and World War II, the Coast Guard passed to the control of the Secretary of the Navy.[4] While the Coast Guard served under the Department of the Navy, Secretary of the Navy Frank Knox made it clear that the Navy's operational control of Coast Guard ships, planes, and stations occurred only when they were assigned to U.S. Navy commands, which allowed the Coast Guard a significant level of autonomy, especially stateside.

Soon after America entered World War II, the Coast Guard Commandant, Rear Admiral Russel R. Waesche, planned to expand the number of African Americans in his service. Before this decision, African Americans had made up only 1.6 percent of the Coast Guard, almost all in the steward's branch. On 24 February 1942, he designated eighteen Coast Guard vessels, mostly buoy tenders and patrol boats, exclusively for African American crews. During World War II, all African American coast guardsmen were trained at the Manhattan Beach Training Station in New York City. Given the small size of the Coast Guard, segregated training facilities were not established. African American recruits were organized into separate training companies for meals and housing but were otherwise trained alongside white recruits. The majority of those who completed the training were assigned to shore duty, which included jobs such as boatswains, carpenters, coxswains, electricians, labor details, pharmacists, radiomen, security, storekeepers, and yeomen. Others served as part of horse and dog patrols on American beaches to prevent enemy infiltration along the coast.[5] The African American coast guardsmen who were selected for sea duty were grouped so that they could assume all but the petty officer (noncommissioned officers) and commissioned officer positions on the ship or boat to which they were assigned. The initial plan was not to enlist any further African Americans until the first group was assigned for long enough to prove themselves. However, the pace of the war changed this decision.[6]

On 1 January 1943, voluntary enlistment in the armed services was suspended and American men became subject to the Selective Service System. While the Coast Guard received a relatively small number of draftees, roughly 10 percent of those draftees were African American. Ideally, the Coast Guard would have preferred to place all African Americans in the steward's branch, but the branch could accommodate fewer than half of them. All other African American draftees were assigned to shore duties, but their number was too small to create segregated units. This left the Coast Guard in a situation where they had too many African Americans for the preexisting establishment, but not enough African Americans to organize them into separate units. Some level of integration was required, but the question remained how much and where.[7]

Another issue also made integration more likely. Since all African Americans who were not stewards were assigned to shore duty, the Coast Guard had a manpower problem. Over time it became more difficult to rotate white coast guardsmen to shore duties without transferring African Americans to sea duty—therefore necessitating some level of integration. In June 1943, Lieutenant Carlton Skinner, an officer assigned to the Coast Guard's HQ, proposed integrating the crew of a single ship as an experiment. Skinner emphasized in his proposal that he was not attempting an "… experiment in social democracy," but rather "… an efficient use of manpower to help win a war."[8] Commandant Waesche agreed to the proposal, promoted Skinner to lieutenant commander, and gave him command of the weather ship USS *Sea Cloud* (IX-99) in November 1943.

The USS *Sea Cloud* experiment of integration only lasted a year (November 1943 to November 1944), during which no racial incidents occurred and the integrated crew proved just as efficient as any other in the Coast Guard. Ultimately, the ship's integrated crew of 22 officers and 175 enlisted men included four African American officers and 50 African American enlisted men. The *Sea Cloud* served on weather stations off the coasts of Greenland,

Newfoundland, and France as part of Task Force 24. The most exciting incident of the ship's yearlong duty occurred on 10 June 1944 when it made night-time sonar contact with a submarine off the Azores Islands. For eight hours, the *Sea Cloud* dropped depth charges and fired antisubmarine weapons before losing contact with the submarine. The following day, based on the information provided by the *Sea Cloud*, a hunter-killer group led by the escort carrier USS *Croatan* (CVE-25) sank the German submarine U-490, a Type XIV "*Milchkuh*" supply vessel. Since the *Sea Cloud* had the initial sonar contact, she was given credit for assisting with the sinking of the submarine. During its year of service in the North Atlantic, the ship passed two fleet inspections with no deficiencies and was rated "excellent" or "very good" in every department.[9]

The only racial incidents that occurred were in port at the Boston Navy Yard. The ship's African American sailors quickly learned never to travel to and from the ship alone, especially at night. Skinner even forced the Navy Yard's officers' club to integrate by appearing with a group of white and African American officers. As a result of the presence of Skinner and the white officers, the African American officers were not refused service. Skinner did this for four days in a row, then on the fifth day the African American officers appeared at the club by themselves and they were treated like any other officers.[10]

After the USS *Sea Cloud* was decommissioned, Skinner was next given command of the USS *Hoquiam* (PF-5), a *Tacoma*-class frigate, on 8 March 1945. This ship had a crew of 12 officers and 178 enlisted men. Skinner arrived with two African American officers and thirty enlisted men who had previously served on the *Sea Cloud* and ultimately 49 percent of the crew were African American.[11] The *Hoquiam* spent the remainder of World War II operating out of Adak in the Aleutian Islands, escorting Lend-Lease shipping throughout Alaska that was ultimately bound for the Soviet Union.[12] Despite the success of both of Skinner's ships, they did not lead to full integration of the Coast Guard during World War II. Skinner later blamed this initial outcome on a lack of publicity.

I have wondered if I should not have evangelized for my theories, put on a campaign for their general adoption. I did not, first because I was too busy as a commanding officer making them work, and second because of my basic belief that this kind of thing should happen naturally and should not be in the spotlight.[13]

Skinner's conclusions about integration were simple. If African Americans were provided with the same opportunities as whites, they almost always seized those opportunities and performed at the same level.[14]

During this same period, the Coast Guard commissioned its first three African American officers. The first African American Coast Guard officer was Joseph C. Jenkins[15], who was commissioned an ensign in April 1943, almost a year before any African Americans were commissioned in the Navy.[16] Jenkins, who earned a degree in civil engineering from the University of Michigan in 1937, enlisted in the Coast Guard in 1942. He was promoted to chief petty officer after only one month of service and only a few months later advanced to the rank of warrant officer—the first African American warrant officer in Coast Guard history. Jenkins then became an instructor at the Manhattan Beach Training Station. In April 1943, he completed the Coast Guard officer training course, then conducted at the U.S. Coast Guard Academy in New London, Connecticut, and was commissioned an ensign. In November 1943, Jenkins was promoted to lieutenant junior grade (LTJG) and assigned to the USS *Sea Cloud*, where he served as the ship's navigation officer. After the *Sea Cloud* was decommissioned, he served aboard the USS *Hoquiam* in Alaska. Jenkin's military career did not end with World War II. After the war, he served in the Michigan Army National Guard as an engineer captain.[17]

The second African American Coast Guard officer was Clarence Samuels, who originally joined the Coast Guard in 1920. Despite the restrictions imposed on African Americans in the Coast Guard, he spent most of his service outside the steward's branch. In 1928, Samuels became the first African American to command a Coast Guard vessel[18] when, while only a petty officer, he assumed command of Patrol Boat *AB-15*, which operated out of Savannah, Georgia. In 1930, he reported to the Pea Island Coast Guard Station in North Carolina, which was the only lifeboat station in the country manned exclusively by African Americans. In 1939, Samuels was promoted to Chief Photographer's Mate, which was an amazing achievement

First two African American U.S. Coast Guard commissioned officers
(*right to left*) LTJG Clarence Samuels and ENS Joseph C. Jenkins aboard
the Coast Guard cutter USS *Sea Cloud* in the North Atlantic. (NARA)

considering how few African Americans served both in the Coast Guard and
outside the steward's branch. Three years later, he was appointed a warrant
officer as well as an instructor and the Director of Visual Signaling at the
Manhattan Beach Training Station. When all qualified instructors at Manhattan

Beach were declared eligible for commissions, Samuels, based on his long years of service rather than education, was commissioned and quickly became a lieutenant junior grade in August 1943. He served aboard the USS *Sea Cloud* as the damage control officer for several months, before assuming command in July 1944 of the lightship *Frying Pan* (LV-115), which served on the Frying Pan Shoals, off Cape Fear in North Carolina. Samuels was promoted to full lieutenant in September 1944 and assumed command of the *Mesquite*-class seagoing buoy tender USCGC *Sweetgum* (WLB-309) in August 1945. In June 1946, like many other temporarily commissioned officers in the armed forces, he was demoted back to the permanent grade of Chief Photographer's Mate and retired from the Coast Guard in September 1947.[19]

The third African American Coast Guard officer was Harvey C. Russell, Jr, who was the son of the president of Western Kentucky Industrial College (which no longer exists) and completed his degree at the Kentucky State College for Negroes (now Kentucky State University). Russell enlisted in the Coast Guard in December 1942 and served as a signal instructor at the Manhattan Beach Training Station. After all qualified instructors at Manhattan Beach were declared eligible for commissions, he became an ensign in February 1944.[20] After service as the training officer aboard the USS *Sea Cloud* and promotion to lieutenant junior grade, he later served aboard the USS *Hoquiam*. In October 1945, Russell's final assignment was command of the Coast Guard-crewed U.S. Army-owned tanker *TY-45*, despite an entirely white crew. After the war, he was a successful business executive with several companies and eventually a vice president with the Pepsi-Cola Company.[21]

Arguably the most famous African American to serve in the Coast Guard during World War II was Alex Haley. Alexander P. Haley enlisted in the Coast Guard in May 1939 after completing two years at the *Elizabeth City State Colored Normal School* (*now* Elizabeth City State University) in North Carolina. Unsurprisingly, he was forced to enlist as a mess attendant because no other positions were open to African Americans at the time. In his free time, the well-educated Haley ghost-wrote letters for other coast guardsmen, which at times earned him more money each month than his normal pay.[22]

In May 1943, Haley was transferred to the Coast Guard-crewed cargo vessel USS *Murzim* (AK-95) and served in the Pacific for most of the remainder of World War II. During this time, he also began to write articles that he submitted to civilian publications. His first article to appear in print was entitled "In the Pacific" and appeared in the February 1944 issue of *Coast Guard Magazine*. The article described life aboard the *Murzim*, which then transported cargo to and from ports in the South Pacific. Beginning in October 1944, the *Murzim* principally carried ammunition in support of the liberation of the Philippines, which was an especially dangerous mission in a combat zone. An example of this danger was when, on 27 November 1944, one of the cargo ship's 20-mm antiaircraft guns shot down an attacking Japanese airplane.[23]

Toward the end of the war, Haley was transferred to the Coast Guard's Personnel Separation Center, where he edited their official publication, *Outpost*. After the war, while serving in New York City, he was a reporter, then assistant editor, and finally the editor of the Coast Guard publication *Helmsman*. Amazingly, during all of these assignments, Haley was still a member of the steward's branch. Not until June 1949 was his rating finally changed to Journalist, 1st Class. Then in December 1949, Haley became the first member of the Coast Guard to receive the rating Chief Journalist's Mate. While still serving in New York, he was an assistant to the head of Coast Guard public relations until his retirement after twenty years of service in June 1959.[24] Haley became world-famous later when he coauthored the *Autobiography of Malcolm X* and wrote the bestselling book *Roots*.

By the end of World War II, approximately five thousand African Americans had served in the Coast Guard. Of these, 965 served as petty officers or warrant officers, which represents close to 20 percent of all African Americans who served.[25] Nevertheless, African Americans never represented more than 2.1 percent of the service's wartime strength, which was substantially lower than the other armed forces. Part of the reason for this lower percentage was that the Coast Guard only participated in the Selective Service System for a little more than a year—all of 1943 and early 1944. Therefore, except for that period, all members of the service were volunteers. The Coast Guard's relatively smoother path toward integration correlated to its small size and generally practical attitude to problem-solving.

Section VI

Officers, Pilots, and Skilled Experts

Chapter 11

Air Corps/Air Forces

As a result of the efforts of veterans, their families, and historians, African Americans who served in the Army Air Corps/Air Forces during World War II have received more attention than any other African American veterans of the war. These African American members of the Air Corps/Air Forces were known collectively as the "Tuskegee Airmen," a nickname acquired as a result of their training site at Tuskegee Army Airfield near the campus of the Tuskegee Institute (now Tuskegee University) in Alabama. The "Tuskegee Airmen" were seen as one of the many "experiments" involving African Americans during the war, because these men were both officers and pilots. While the Army had plenty of experience with African American enlisted men and NCOs, there were very few African American officers and, as demonstrated by the post-World War I officer selection boards, many senior Army officers did not believe that African Americans had the necessary intellectual and leadership capabilities to serve as officers. Furthermore, many whites did not believe that African Americans possessed the requisite intelligence and/or hand-eye coordination to become pilots. The ultimate success of the "Tuskegee Airmen" was a major blow to racist ideologies about African American intellectual, leadership, and physical abilities.

The first African American officer accepted for pilot training was Benjamin O. Davis, Jr. Davis, the son of BG Benjamin O. Davis, Sr., was also the first African American admitted to the U.S. Military Academy (USMA) in the 20th century. In 1932, after having attended Western Reserve University (now Case Western Reserve University) in Cleveland for a year and the University of Chicago for two years[1], Davis received an appointment to USMA from Republican U.S. Congressman Oscar S. De Priest of Chicago, who was then the only African American in either the House of Representatives or the Senate. As with most of the 19th century African American cadets at the USMA, Davis endured four years of "silencing," during which no other cadet spoke to him unless required to do so. Despite four years of loneliness during which he had no roommate and even ate alone, he seems to have earned the respect of his fellow cadets as evidenced by the caption below his picture in the USMA 1936 yearbook, *The Howitzer*. "The courage, tenacity, and intelligence with which he conquered a problem incomparably more difficult than Plebe year won for him the sincere admiration of his classmates, and his single-minded [*sic*] determination to continue in his chosen career cannot fail to inspire respect wherever fortune may lead him."[2] Davis graduated 35th out of 276 cadets in his class, which put him ahead of his classmates and future U.S. Army Chiefs of Staff Creighton W. Abrams, Jr., and William C. Westmoreland.

Davis wanted to become a pilot in the Air Corps, but since the Army remained segregated and there were no African American units in the Air Corps, he was instead commissioned as a 2nd lieutenant of infantry. Davis was assigned to the 24th Infantry Regiment at Fort Benning, which was a professional disappointment for him. Unsurprisingly, Davis confronted racial prejudice and segregation as soon as he arrived in Georgia. "Silenced" at USMA for four years, he was now likewise "silenced" by white Army officers, who refused to interact with him unless it was required by their duties. During his initial year at Fort Benning, Davis had few duties and believed the African American soldiers of the 24th Infantry Regiment were little more than laborers performing maintenance and other duties on the post. To his surprise, he was selected to attend the Infantry School after only one year on active duty, a year earlier than most white officers. After completing the one-year course,

African American U.S. Army Air Corps cadets report to LTC
Benjamin O. Davis, Jr., the commander of 99th Fighter Squadron
at Tuskegee Field, Alabama. Davis, the fourth African American to
graduate from the U.S. Military Academy, was also the first African
American to be rated as an Army pilot. (NARA)

Davis discovered that he was assigned as the professor of military science at
the Tuskegee Institute—a position his father held several times.[3]

   After a year at the Tuskegee Institute, Davis was promoted to 1st lieutenant and a year later, in 1940, he was promoted to captain. The second
promotion was more rapid than usual, but Davis himself credited its rapidity
to the increase in the Army's size after the start of the nation's first peacetime draft that same year.[4] During the two and half years that he spent at
the Tuskegee Institute, Davis' talents were significantly underutilized. From
September to May the entirety of his duties consisted of delivering three

In May 1943, the commander and staff officers (*left to right*) LTC
Benjamin O. Davis, Jr., commanding officer; CPT Hayden C. Johnson,
squadron adjutant; CPT E. Jones; and LTs William R. Thompson;
Hervert E. Carter; Erwin B. Lawrence, Squadron Operations
Officer; and George R. Currie of the 99th Fighter Squadron near Fez,
French Morocco. (NARA)

forty-five-minute lectures per week. During the summers, he had no duties
whatsoever. Experiencing the same frustration that his father had endured
for decades, the future seemed bleak. Many friends, relatives, and prominent
African Americans suggested that perhaps Davis was wasting his talents in
the Army. Some of them suggested that he leave the Army with the proposal
that perhaps a career in the law might afford him more opportunities both
professionally and personally. Thankfully, however, an occurrence in his
father's career also provided him with an opportunity.[5]

In 1940, when Davis' father was promoted to brigadier general, he
requested his son serve as his *aide-de-camp*. Rescued from the Tuskegee,
Davis arrived at Fort Riley in February 1941. Since he was denied the use

of all white facilities on the post, Kansas did not appear any more welcoming than Georgia or Alabama. Then an even more surprising opportunity presented itself—Davis was informed that he was accepted for pilot training. President Roosevelt ordered the creation of a segregated African American air corps unit—the 99th Pursuit Squadron, which was activated on 22 March 1941.[6] The first class of African American aviation cadets at Tuskegee Army Airfield consisted of Davis and twelve other men, eight of whom failed the course. Along with Davis, 2LTs Lemuel R. Custis, Charles H. DeBow, Jr., George S. Roberts, and Mac Ross completed flight training and received their pilot's wings on 7 March 1942.[7]

In May 1942, Davis received two sets of orders in quick succession promoting him to major and then lieutenant colonel, and, in August, he became commander of the newly renamed 99th Fighter Squadron. Also, in August, the squadron finally had a sufficient number of pilots, and, in September, the Army Air Forces[8] declared the unit ready for combat. The question now was where to send the 99th Fighter Squadron. Originally, the squadron was scheduled to deploy to Liberia in Africa, but following the successful invasion of North Africa in November 1942, this deployment was deemed unnecessary.[9] The next suggestion was to send the squadron to the China Burma India (CBI) Theater, but the leadership in the CBI vetoed this idea. Finally, the decision was made to deploy the squadron to North Africa and the move began in April 1943. Unfortunately for Davis and the 99th Fighter Squadron, the North African Campaign formally ended on 13 May 1943 before they entered combat.

On 13 October 1942, while the 99th Fighter Squadron was awaiting their combat assignment, the Army Air Forces activated the 332nd Fighter Group at Tuskegee with the 99th, 100th, 301st, and 302nd Fighter Squadrons. Even after the 99th Fighter Squadron deployed to North Africa, the influx of officers, cadets, and enlisted men at Tuskegee caused a hopelessly overcrowded situation. The attitude of the white community in Tuskegee made this situation at the airfield even worse. The Jim Crow system of segregation which reigned in Alabama caused great resentment among the African Americans at the airfield, most particularly with the officers, many of whom were from the North and had never experienced such overt racism. Therefore, on 26 March 1943, the Army Air Forces moved the remainder of the group to Selfridge Field, Michigan, which both relieved the overcrowding and lessened the racial issues.

One of the other problems that contributed to the cramped facilities at Tuskegee was an excess of nonflying personnel. After the declaration of war against Germany and Japan in December 1941, the Army Air Forces stopped discharging individuals who had flunked out of pilot training. These individuals became privates and were retained at Tuskegee because unlike white failed aviation cadets, who were simply reassigned to other aviation programs (principally as bombardiers, navigators, and aerial gunners), there was no other place for them. By September 1943, most of the over two hundred failed aviation cadets were still at Tuskegee and suffered from very low morale as they spent their days working in kitchens and performing grounds-keeping duties. Also, an average of seven African American OCS graduates arrived each month at Tuskegee. By November 1943, Tuskegee reported an excess of ninety officers, most of whom were lieutenants who were not pilots or otherwise trained as aircrew. For the rest of the Army, Tuskegee Army Airfield became a dumping ground for unwanted African American officers. Interestingly, not all the pilots who graduated from Tuskegee were American. On 28 July 1943, Raymond Cassagnol, an officer in the Haitian Army Air Corps, became the first non-American to graduate from pilot training at Tuskegee.[10]

In December 1942, LTC Noel F. Parrish, who served as the director of training at Tuskegee, became commanding officer of the post. He was supportive of African Americans almost since his arrival at Tuskegee as a captain in June 1941 and, as commander, created a positive atmosphere on the post. Though deeply respected by his African American subordinates, Parrish was, oddly enough, a Southerner and before his assignment at Tuskegee, not involved in or particularly interested in Civil Rights issues. Despite this, he refused a combat reassignment during that war which would have almost guaranteed him an overseas command and undoubtedly aided his career. Parrish was an example of a decent person who did the right thing when the circumstances arose. An example of Parrish's attitude toward African Americans was that Tuskegee's service club, which functioned as an officer's club, was open to all officers, but Parrish was the only white officer to join.[11]

In October 1944, 2LT Andrew D. Marshall, a pilot in the 332nd
Fighter Group, was shot down by flak during a strafing mission over
Greece. Greek partisans hid him until he could be evacuated. Marshall
discusses his adventures with an American pilot from the 51st Troop
Carrier Wing. (NARA)

On 12 April 1943, the 332nd Fighter Group began to move from
Selfridge Field to Oscoda Army Airfield, which was also located in
Michigan, only to move back to Selfridge Field in July. In the meantime,
an incident occurred at Selfridge Field that served as a reminder of the
insidious nature of racism within the Army. After midnight on 5 May
1943, COL William T. Colman, the commander of Selfridge Field, called
for a car to transport him from the officers' club to his home. Colman,
who was drunk, was incensed that his driver was an African American—
PFC Willie McRae. Colman then drew a privately owned, nonissue pistol
and shot McRae twice. LTC Sam W. Westbrook, the commander of the
332nd Fighter Group, arrested Colman and relieved him of his command in

preparation for a court-martial. Colman's court-martial, which took place from 6 to 15 September 1943, found him guilty of being drunk and disorderly, conduct unbecoming an officer, and careless discharge of a pistol. Though he was not found guilty of the more serious charge of assault with a deadly weapon, Colman was reduced in rank from colonel to captain and then, on 3 November 1943, a review board recommended his discharge, which was approved by the Secretary of War on 30 November 1943.[12]

In June 1943, the 99th Fighter Squadron entered combat for the first time with a patrol over the Mediterranean. On 2 July, a flight of P-40 "Warhawk" fighters from the squadron was escorting B-25 "Mitchell" bombers on a raid against targets in Sicily when they encountered German FW-190 fighters. In the ensuing combat, 1LT Charles B. Hall[13] became the first African American pilot to shoot down enemy aircraft in World War II.[14] In late July, the 99th Fighter Squadron redeployed from North Africa to Licata, Sicily, and continued to conduct routine operations over Italy and the Mediterranean Sea throughout the summer and fall. On 17 October 1943, the squadron began to move from Sicily to the Italian peninsula. During this time, the squadron was active enough that, on 22 December 1943, 1LT James Wiley became the first pilot of the 99th Fighter Squadron to complete fifty missions.[15]

Throughout this early period of combat, the 99th Fighter Squadron's missions tended to focus more on ground attack rather than air-to-air combat. These mission assignments were the result of serious doubts within the Army Air Forces' hierarchy about the abilities of African American pilots. As a result of these types of missions, the squadron's pilots were not having the opportunity to frequently engage German aircraft, shoot them down, and amass "kills"—the *sine qua non* of fighter pilots. Despite these support missions, the squadron was criticized by COL William Momyer[16], the commander of the 33rd Fighter Group, to which the squadron was attached.

Air discipline has not been completely satisfactory. The ability to work and fight as a team has not yet been acquired. Their formation flying has been very satisfactory until jumped by enemy aircraft, when the squadron seems to disintegrate. This has repeatedly been brought to the attention of the Squadron, but attempts to correct this deficiency so far have been unfruitful. ... The unit has shown a lack of aggressive spirit that is necessary for a well-organized fighter squadron. ... Based on the performance of the 99th Fighter Squadron to date, it is my opinion that they are not of the fighting caliber of any squadron in this Group. They have failed to display the aggressiveness and desire for combat that are necessary to a firstclass [*sic*] fighting organization. It may be expected that we will get less work and less operational time out of the 99th Fighter Squadron than any squadron in this Group.[17]

Despite these rather specific allegations, Momyer provided no specific dates or otherwise verifying information to support his comments. MG Edwin J. House, commander of the XII Tactical Air Command and the 33rd Fighter Group's immediate superior, agreed with Momyer's assessment and even added to it.

On many discussions held with officers of all professions, including medical, the consensus of opinion seems to be that the negro [*sic*] type has not the proper reflexes to make a first-class fighter pilot. ... I believe it would be much better to assign the 99th to the Northwest African Coastal Air Force, equip it with P-39's and make the present P-40's available to this Command as replacements for the active operations still to come in this theater. It is recommended that if and when a colored group is formed in the United States, it be retained for either the eastern or western defense zone and a white fighter group be released for movement overseas.[18]

These recommendations went up the chain of command and were also endorsed by MG John K. Cannon (commander of the Northwest African Tactical Air Force), LTG Carl Spaatz (commander of 12th Air Force), and GEN Henry H. Arnold, the commander of the U.S. Army Air Forces. The final decision regarding the future of the 99th Fighter Squadron was in the hands of Chief of Staff Marshall. However, he decided that before any decision he wanted a further investigation. Marshall directed the Army's G-3

Members of the ground crew (*left to right*) TSG Charles K. Haynes, SSG James A. Sheppard, and MSG Frank Bradley of the 332nd Fighter Group in Italy place a wing tank on a P-51 Mustang. (NARA)

(Operations and Training) to carry out an objective study of the squadron's combat performance.

In September 1943, Davis was recalled from Sicily to assume command of the 332nd Fighter Group in Michigan. Upon his return to the United States, he was called upon to defend the 99th Fighter Squadron against the allegations lodged by Momyer and House. Davis testified before the McCloy Committee (officially known as the Committee on Negro Troop Policies), which was chaired by Assistant Secretary of War John J. McCloy and included both Judge William H. Hastie, a civilian advisor to the Secretary of War Henry L. Stimson on African American issues, and BG Davis. LTC Davis testified:

> The squadron was handicapped in that no one in the squadron had had combat experience. There was a lack of confidence due to this lack. There is no question as to the quality of training. In the first missions

there were mistakes. ... After that confidence picked up and became part of the squadron. ... If there was a lack of aggressive spirit, it was at first; later we had it. ... The report is a surprise to me... The squadron operated at a disadvantage due to having only 26 pilots as compared to from 30 to 35 in other squadrons. The reason for this was that the standards set up for replacements—four per month—didn't come through. We were in combat two months before we received replacements.[19]

Davis also argued that any initial problems encountered by the squadron were almost identical to those encountered by any inexperienced white fighter squadron upon first entering combat.[20]

The final report of the G-3, entitled "Operations of the 99th Fighter Squadron Compared With Other P-40 Squadrons in the Mediterranean Theater of Operations," examined the squadron's operations over eight months. The report found no quantitative difference between the 99th Fighter Squadron and white P-40 fighter squadrons assigned to the same theater and missions.[21] While this report alone should have been enough to silence the squadron's critics, the events of 27–28 January 1944 were the final and the best defense of the squadron. On those two days, pilots of the squadron, now under the command a MAJ George S. Roberts[22], shot down 13 German fighters in aerial combat over the beaches of Anzio, Italy.[23] Interestingly, CPT Charles B. Hall, the first African American pilot to achieve an aerial victory of the war, shot down two more enemy aircraft on 28 January and became the first African American pilot to earn the Distinguished Flying Cross (DFC) in World War II.[24]

On 8 October 1943, Davis assumed command of the 332nd Fighter Group, and that same month the three stateside squadrons of the group began flying P-39 "Airacobras" rather than the P-40 for which they had originally trained. The P-39 was an aircraft that was not well received in the United States and other Western nations. Problems with the aircraft's supercharger meant that it could not fly at high altitudes and, therefore, was used almost exclusively at low altitudes and most often in ground support missions. Also, the aircraft did not have a traditional sliding canopy but was equipped with side-facing doors that made evacuating the aircraft in a crisis difficult.

Another criticism was that the engine was located behind the pilot, which meant that in a crash-landing situation the pilot might be crushed to death by the engine if it were to break free of its mountings. Lastly, the odd layout of the fuselage meant there was no room for fuel storage and the fuel tanks were located in the wings which made them more vulnerable to enemy fire, possessed less fuel capacity, and had a shorter range than most other American fighters. The decision to transition the group from the P-40, an air-to-air platform, to the P-39, a mainly ground-attack platform, reflected the continued contempt exhibited toward African American pilots by the leadership of the Army Air Forces.

On 22 December 1943, the 332nd Fighter Group began its move overseas—first by train to Virginia. The group then sailed for Europe on 3 January 1944 aboard four ships, SS *William Few*, SS *John M. Morehead*, SS *Clark Mills*, and SS *Thomas B. Robertson*, and arrived in Italy between 1 and 3 February 1944.[25] While the group was sailing overseas, a racial incident occurred involving African American pilots back at Selfridge Field. The 553rd Fighter Squadron was activated at Selfridge Field on 1 November 1943 to supervise supplementary training for African American replacement pilots. The squadron was commanded by a white officer, LTC Charles A. Gayle, but its pilots were African American and included both recent flight school graduates from Tuskegee and veteran combat pilots from the 99th Fighter Squadron who were transferred home to act as instructors (which was also done with white pilots). From 1 to 5 January 1944, several pilots from the 553rd Fighter Squadron attempted to enter the officers' club at Selfridge Field. On each of the five nights they tried to enter the club, they were stopped either by Gayle or the post commander, COL William L. Boyd. Since a superior officer ordered them out, they complied with the orders. However, those orders were in direct violation of a War Department Regulation 210-10, Paragraph 19c.

> ... no officer clubs, messes, or similar organization of officers will be permitted by the post commander to occupy any part of any public building ... unless such club, mess, or other organization extends to all officers on the post the right to full membership ...[26]

After long missions, fighters often returned to base with only a few minutes' worth of fuel in their tanks. The officers' club of the 332nd Fighter Group was given the name, "The Three Minute Egg Club," in honor of those pilots who got back just in time. Pictured (*left to right*): 1LTs Clarence A. Dart and Wilson D. Eagelson, and 2LT William N. Olsbrook. (NARA)

Additionally, the airfield was located in Michigan, a Northern state that had no segregation laws. Though Gayle and Boyd decided to close the club on 6 January rather than deal with any further controversy, both officers were later relieved. Strangely, when the club was reopened, it remained segregated. The issue of African American access to officers' clubs reappeared later.

On 15 January 1944, the 477th Bombardment Group was activated at Selfridge Field. The group, which was composed of the 616th–619th Bombardment Squadrons, was equipped with B-25 bombers. The men of the group were the first African Americans trained as both multiengine aircraft and bomber pilots. Just six days later, on 21 January 1944, COL Robert R.

Selway, Jr., became the group commander.[27] In early May 1944, the group was transferred to Godman Field, Kentucky, as a result of racial tensions at Selfridge and in nearby Detroit, which had even experienced race riots. The situation at Godman was an improvement because the African American pilots were able to use a post's officers' club, and white officers, if they chose not to mingle with their African American counterparts, used the officers' club at nearby Fort Knox. While this still resulted in segregation, it was voluntary rather than statutory.

On 15 February 1944, the 301st Fighter Squadron became operational and started flying combat missions in Italy. Within only a few days, the other two squadrons of the 332nd Fighter Group, the 100th and 302nd Fighter Squadrons were also flying combat missions. Unfortunately, after re-equipping with P-39 aircraft before they left the United States, they were initially restricted to convoy escort, harbor patrol, and other patrol missions. In early March 1944, Davis met with LTG Ira C. Eaker, the commander of the Mediterranean Allied Air Force, a combined American and British organization that included numerous fighter and bomber units. Eaker wanted the group to transition from patrol duties to flying fighter escort for the B-17 "Flying Fortress" and B-24 "Liberator" bombers of the 15th Air Force. This mission change also required the replacement of the group's P-39s with the P-47 "Thunderbolt" fighter.[28] Davis jumped at the opportunity to change the missions and the aircraft his group was flying since it represented a real chance for the group to finally prove itself.[29]

In the middle of April 1944, several experienced pilots from the 99th Fighter Squadron rotated back to the United States. Having served in combat for a year and participated in a sufficient number of missions, they generally transferred to the 477th Bombardment Group or instructor pilot positions at Tuskegee. The aircraft transition process of the 332nd Fighter Group began in late April with the arrival of the first P-47s. On 29 May 1944, Davis was promoted to full colonel and the group flew its first bomber escort mission in support of B-17s from the 5th Bombardment Wing on 8 June.[30] These escort missions represented the opportunity for the "Tuskegee Airmen" to finally win their greatest fame. The very next day on 9 June, 35 fighters of the 301st and 302nd Fighter Squadrons took off on a mission to support five bomber wings flying missions on targets near Munich, Germany. The number of fighters assigned to the mission was wholly inadequate as they were supposed to be supporting more than one hundred bombers. When the formation reached northern Italy they came under attack from German fighters and during the ensuing dogfights four "Tuskegee Airmen" shot down a total of five German aircraft. The mission was so successful that Davis was awarded the DFC because he "... so skillfully disposed his squadrons that despite the large number of enemy fighters, the bomber formation suffered only a few losses."[31] Even though the 332nd Fighter Group had only transitioned from P-39 to P-47 in April, they were astonished when they discovered in late June that they would transition to the P-51 "Mustang." The P-51 was generally recognized as the best American fighter of World War II, and quite possibly the best of any nation in the entire war.

One of the visible symbols of the "Tuskegee Airmen," which also became a nickname, was the red tails of their aircraft. As with so many things regarding the "Tuskegee Airmen," there is some myth regarding their "red tails." The myth is that Davis ordered the painting of the aircraft tails in the distinct red color to instill unit *esprit décor* among his pilots. However, this myth does not stand up to historical scrutiny. In actuality, in June 1944 after the 332nd Fighter Group began performing their escort missions they were mandated to paint their aircraft tails to distinguish their group from other groups flying with the bombers. All of the fighter groups that were flying bomber escort had painted their tails with distinctive colors and/or patterns. Some examples of these distinctive colors and/or patterns were the 31st Fighter Group had red stripes on their tails, the 52nd Fighter Group had yellow tails, and the 322nd Fighter Group had black and yellow checkerboard painted tails.[32] No record exists as to why each fighter group chose the color or pattern they chose. Perhaps, the grain of truth in the myth was that Davis did indeed choose the color red, but the decision to paint the tails in the first place was mandated by higher command.

Despite the presence of the 332nd Fighter Group in Italy for six months, it was only on 28 June 1944 that the 99th Fighter Squadron finally received orders to join the group both administratively and physically.[33] In coordination with the move, the squadron also transitioned from the P-40 to the P-51.

On 4 July 1944, the entire group flew its first mission in P-51 fighters. From that date forward, the majority of the group's missions involved escorting bombers. Interestingly, the group was the largest fighter group in Europe, with four squadrons rather than the three squadrons of other groups. Tragedy struck the group on 10 July 1944, when CPT Mac Ross, one of the first five African American pilots to graduate from flight training at Tuskegee Army Airfield and then serving as the group's S-3 (Operations) officer, was killed in a crash during a routine transition flight. The very next day, CPT Leon C. Roberts, the 99th Fighter Squadron's S-3 officer was also killed in a crash during a routine transition flight.[34] The deaths of experienced pilots in noncombat situations demonstrated both the inherent danger of all military flying and the substantial differences in transitioning to new aircraft.

On 12 July 1944, forty-four fighters from the 100th, 301st, and 302nd Fighter Squadrons escorted bombers from the 49th Bomb Wing against Nimes, France. During the actual bomb run, the bombers were attacked by twenty-eight German fighters. During the ensuing dogfights, 1LT Joseph D. Elsberry shot down three enemy fighters for which he earned the DFC. This feat also represented the first aerial victory of a "Tuskegee Airmen" since they had transitioned to the P-51.[35] Less than a week later, on 18 July, sixty-six fighters representing all four squadrons of the group flew a mission to support the 5th Bomb Wing. The wing first came under attack from German fighters in northern Italy, but the "Tuskegee Airmen" provided excellent support and shot down nine enemy aircraft. By the time the bombers reached their target area over Memmingen, Germany, only thirty-six of the group's fighters remained to support them as the other fighters were tasked to other missions, damaged in route, experienced mechanical difficulties, or escorted damaged American aircraft back to base. Over the target area, German fighter aircraft engaged the bombers, and dogfights ensued during which another three Germans were shot down. During that day, 2LT Clarence D. Lester shot down three enemy aircraft and 1LT Jack D. Holsclaw shot down two.[36]

Back at the Tuskegee Army Airfield in August 1944, African American officers demanded service in a restaurant designated for white officers. When they were refused service, they produced the War Department orders that prohibited the denial of service in recreational facilities and post exchanges to any otherwise authorized personnel. Tuskegee's post commander, now-COL Parrish[37], was notified of the protest and supported the demands of the African American officers. From this point forward, Tuskegee Army Airfield was effectively the first fully integrated U.S. Army post—though most white officers responded to this new policy by eating and socializing almost exclusively off the post.

After transitioning to the P-51 and assuming the bomber escort missions, some portion of the 332nd Fighter Group flew almost daily and the different missions included bomber escort, close air support, or fighter sweeps (sending out aircraft to engage any enemy fighters they come across). While the bomber escort missions seemed straightforward, they could be quite complicated. For instance, since the bombers and fighters took off from different airfields, it was often difficult to meet up in the air. One unit of aircraft might arrive before or after the other reached the agreed-upon rendezvous coordinates. Since fuel was a consideration, aircraft could only linger in one place for so long before having to continue the mission. On 6 March 1945, the Army Air Forces decided to disband the 302nd Fighter Squadron and transfer its personnel to the three other squadrons of the group. The decision was based on the fact that no other fighter group had four squadrons and the action in no way harmed the combat performance of the group.[38]

Over time a myth grew up surrounding the 332nd Fighter Group that they had "never lost a bomber" on escort missions during World War II. For decades, the "never lost a bomber" myth was widely believed by the American public, especially in the African American community. Unfortunately, it was a myth and at least twenty-seven of the bombers under escort from the group were lost to enemy fighters.[39] The "never lost a bomber" myth appears to have begun with an article written by famed African American journalist Roi Ottley. The article, entitled "Dark Angels of Doom" appeared in *Liberty* magazine on 10 March 1945, and stated that the 332nd Fighter Group had not lost a single bomber in more than one hundred escort missions.[40] Why Ottley made the claim is difficult to determine. Whether he believed it true or knowingly lied to inflate the reputation of the "Tuskegee Airmen" will never be known since Ottley died in 1960, long before the myth was exposed. After Ottley's article, the myth continued to grow. Just two weeks later, the *Chicago Defender* newspaper stated that the group had flown two hundred missions without losing a single bomber. Even the War Department believed the "never lost a bomber" myth. On 21 June 1945, War Department announced that Davis was taking command of the 477th Bombardment Group and included the statement, "… Davis' group had completed 200 missions … without losing a single bomber to the enemy fighters."[41] Even Davis, himself, who was on most of the missions, repeated the myth in his autobiography.[42]

The myth remained the accepted and "official" truth until 2003. In that year William Holton, an African American World War II U.S. Navy veteran and the official historian of the Tuskegee Airmen, Inc., veterans' organization, encountered a fellow World War II veteran who argued that the "never lost a bomber" idea was unbelievable. Holton decided to do some serious primary research to confirm what he believed was the truth. To his surprise, Holton discovered that he and the "Tuskegee Airmen" themselves were incorrect. The Tuskegee Airmen, Inc., refused to accept Holton's initial assessment and instead appointed a research committee to explore the question more thoroughly. At almost the same time that these events were occurring, a historian (Dr. Daniel L. Haulman) at the Air Force Historical Research Agency, Maxwell Air Force Base, came to the same conclusion as Holton while researching the "Tuskegee Airmen." Haulman and Holton later met and compared their research, which established that the "never lost a bomber" idea was false.[43] The Tuskegee Airmen, Inc., research committee visited the Air Force Historical Research Agency in 2007 and, after a thorough examination of the primary source documents, agreed with the original conclusions advanced by Haulman and Holton— "never lost a bomber" was a myth. However, it was not until 31 July 2010, at the Tuskegee Airmen, Inc., national convention in San Antonio, Texas, that the organization officially accepted the research of Holton, Haulman, and their research committee.[44]

Unfortunately, many "Tuskegee Airmen" veterans, their descendants, and the African American community, in general, saw the historical research of Haulman, Holton, and others as an attack on the valor and competence of the "Tuskegee Airmen." This was most certainly not the case. Those involved were attempting to get to the truth of a historical argument. Likewise, this line of questioning was not somehow an example of covert racism. Holton was African American as were the other members of the official research committee. Lastly, there was no intention to imply that the veterans were intentionally lying to the public for decades. Since the myth began during World War II and memory dulls with age, the veterans assuredly believed what they were saying was true. As for historians repeating the myth, this phenomenon is well known. Historians often rely on older works or "common knowledge" to create the initial outlines for their work. If something is deemed "common knowledge," they are more likely to reiterate the "fact" rather than trying to track down its origins.

On 12 October 1944, sixty-eight fighters from all four squadrons of the 332nd Fighter Group were sent on a mission to strafe ground targets in an area that ranged from Budapest, Hungary, to Bratislava, Slovakia. During their ground attacks, the "Tuskegee Airmen" destroyed dozens of railroad cars, motor vehicles, river barges, locomotives, and aircraft on airfields. The only air to air combat of the mission resulted in an amazing feat. Three He-111 medium bombers escorted by seven Me-109 fighters suddenly appeared on the horizon and, in the ensuing dogfight, 1LT Lee A. Archer shot down three of the Me-109s. Archer's victory total was now four and the "Tuskegee Airmen" shot down nine of the ten German aircraft that day.[45]

After World War II, another myth about the "Tuskegee Airmen" arose regarding Archer and two other African American pilots. This myth surrounds the fact that none of the "Tuskegee Airmen" achieved the status of "ace," which is the act of shooting down five enemy aircraft in aerial combat. The status of an "ace" among fighter pilots is highly coveted and arguably the dream of anyone who trains to fly a fighter aircraft. After World War II, a myth began to circulate in the African American community that the white leadership of the Army Air Forces intentionally prevented any African Americans from becoming an "ace." This myth was repeated quite literally dozens of times by "Tuskegee Airmen" in interviews and books about the group.

The problem with the myth is that aerial victories in World War II were recorded within the squadron and group to which the pilot was attached. The higher commands merely confirmed the victory totals reported to them by the groups and there was no opportunity for white superior officers to change the numbers.[46] The aerial victory totals of the "Tuskegee Airmen" were available from the original reports submitted by the 99th Fighter Squadron and later the 332nd Fighter Group. These reports reveal a total of 112 aerial victories from the first on 2 July 1943 by 1LT Charles B. Hall to the last four victories on the same day—26 April 1945—by three different airmen.[47] Ultimately, three African American pilots claimed four aerial victories throughout their service in World War II—1LT Lee A. Archer[48], CPT Joseph D. Elsberry[49], and CPT Edward L. Toppins[50].[51]

Rather than any kind of conspiracy, most likely no "Tuskegee Airmen" became an "ace" because of the types of missions they were assigned and when they entered the air campaign in Europe. Though the first aerial victory was recorded on 2 July 1943, it was almost six months until another happened on 27 January 1944. The victories achieved in January and February 1944 were almost exclusively achieved while in support of the Anzio beachhead. No further victories were achieved until the summer of 1944. This early gap was mostly the result of the type of missions flown by the "Tuskegee Airmen" in their initial deployment, mostly ground attack which provided very few opportunities for air-to-air combat. With the arrival of the rest of the 332nd Fighter Group, more and more aerial victories were achieved in the summer and fall of 1944. There is another gap in aerial victories from the fall of 1944 to the spring of 1945. This later gap was most likely the result of the Allies having achieved almost complete air supremacy. The final victories of the "Tuskegee Airmen" achieved in March and April 1945 were almost all achieved in aerial combat over Germany itself and represented the last gasp of the German Luftwaffe.[52]

On 24 March 1945, the 332nd Fighter Group flew its longest mission of World War II when it was selected to escort bombers to Berlin, Germany. A total of fifty-nine fighters from the three remaining squadrons of the group escorted bombers from the 5th Bombardment Wing. As they approached the target, approximately twenty-five German fighters attacked the formation. These fighters included both Me-262 jets and rocket-powered Me-163s. The jets and rockets were faster than the American P-51s, but not as agile. In the ensuing dogfight, three "Tuskegee Airmen" shot down German jets—a first for the group. The mission was such a success that the 332nd Fighter Group earned the DUC. Just one week later on 31 March, forty-seven fighters from all three squadrons launched a fighter sweep/strafing mission against targets in Munich and the surrounding area of Bavaria. German fighters rose to challenge the American airmen and what ensued was the most successful day for the group in terms of aerial victories with thirteen enemy aircraft destroyed.[53]

While the 332nd Fighter Group continued its heroic efforts in skies over Europe in the fall of 1944 and spring of 1945, the 477th Bombardment Group continued its arduous climb toward combat readiness. There was a consistent shortage of trained African American personnel to complete the group. Unlike the 332nd Fighter Group, the 477th Bombardment Group required not only pilots, but also navigators, bombardiers, radio operators, flight engineers, and aerial gunners. However, the refusal by the leadership of the Army Air Forces to open more training facilities for African Americans meant that all African American airmen were trained at Tuskegee, which simply did not have enough capacity to meet the demands of the new group. On 5 March 1945, the 477th Bombardment Group moved from Godman Field, Kentucky, to Freemen Field, Indiana.[54] While the situation at Godman Field was generally positive, the facilities were too small to support all four squadrons of the group at one time. As a result of the overcrowding, the 618th Bombardment Squadron had previously moved to Atterbury Army Airfield, Indiana.

Unfortunately, the racial climate at Freemen Field became more and more volatile as the white leadership tried to enforce segregation. While Indiana was a Northern state which did not have legal segregation, the state was generally recognized as the most racist state in the North and had the largest Ku Klux Klan membership of any state in the country during the 1920s. The ultimate result of the efforts to enforce segregation was a series of incidents at the segregated officers' club at Freeman Field. On 5 April 1945, thirty-six African American officers of the 118th Army Air Forces Base Unit, who were then training as replacements for the 477th Bombardment Group, attempted to enter the officers' club. When they were ordered to leave, three officers, 2LTs Roger C. Terry, Marsden A. Thomson, and Shirley R. Clinton, ignored the order and pushed their way inside.[55] The next day, 6 April, 25 more African American officers attempted to enter the club and they, along with the officers from the previous day, were arrested on the charge of disobeying the direct order of a superior officer.[56] On 7 April, the Freeman Field JAG advised Colonel Robert R. Selway, commander of both Freeman Field and the group, to drop the charges against all the African American officers except the three who had pushed their way into the club.[57]

On 9 April 1945, Selway issued Base Regulation 85-2, ordering personnel to use not only two separate officers' clubs, but also separate recreational buildings, mess buildings, and officers' quarters. Since this order contradicted War Department policy, 101 African American officers (roughly 25 percent of those assigned to the post) refused to sign the new regulation and were arrested.[58] Selway wanted to get support for his actions, so he contacted MG Frank O. Hunter, his superior and the commander of the 1st Air Force, who agreed with him. However, Hunter wanted to make sure that he was doing the right thing legally, so he asked the chief JAG of the Army Air Forces, BG L. H. Hendrick, for his opinion. Hendrick argued that the African American officers' use of Regulation 210-10 was not valid. Hunter requested that opinion in writing, which Hendrick gave him.

Paragraph 19, AR 210-10, 20 December 1940, is not interpreted as a requirement that all officers on a base be permitted the use of all clubs. It is the view of this officer that this regulation was designed to insure every officer the right to membership in an officers' club; but does not prohibit a reasonable division of club facilities where circumstances make such division necessary or desirable from a practical, disciplinary, or morale standpoint. It should also be noted that this paragraph imposes a restriction upon post commanders restricting the use of public buildings ... but does not extend a right to the individual officers ...[59]

On 23 April 1945, Army Chief of Staff Marshall personally intervened and ordered the release of the African American officers who refused to sign Base Regulation 85-2. Hunter was furious but the most he could do was have Selway issue written reprimands to the officers who refused to sign the regulation.[60] On 2 July 1945, a court-martial trial began for two of the three African American officers who had "shoved" their way into the officers' club. Thomson and Clinton were found not guilty, largely because they had not come into physical contact with anyone.[61] On the next day, 3 July 1945, a court-martial trial began for the third officer, Terry[62], who was convicted primarily because he had made physical contact with a superior officer. He was fined $150, reduced in rank to private, and dishonorably discharged.[63]

On 8 June 1945, at least in part as a result of the April incident (which many people called the "Freeman Field Mutiny"), Davis was transferred from command of the 332nd Fighter Group to take over the 477th Bombardment Group. When he officially assumed command of the group on 21 June, all white personnel in the group were transferred to other organizations. This decision continued the longstanding Army policy of never placing African Americans in leadership positions over white servicemen. The very next day, the War Department disbanded the 616th and 619th Bombardment Squadrons and redesignated the group as the 477th Composite Group.[64] On 27 July 1945, the 99th Fighter Squadron was disbanded in Italy and then reactivated as part of the 477th Composite Group.[65] The group was preparing for deployment in the Pacific Theater when the war ended on 2 September 1945.

Throughout World War II, a total of 992 pilots graduated from flight training at Tuskegee Army Airfield. Of these 685 were trained as single-engine fighter pilots, 245 were trained as twin-engine bomber pilots, 51 were trained as liaison pilots, and a final 11 were trained as service pilots. An additional nine African American liaison pilots were trained at

Fort Sill, which was (and still is) the home of the Field Artillery School and where field artillery spotter pilots were then trained. After entering combat, the "Tuskegee Airmen" completed 1491 combat missions. The pilots of the four squadrons of the 332nd Fighter Group were awarded a total of ninety-six DFCs for their achievements in the air and the individual squadrons and/or group were awarded three DUCs.[66] By the end of the war, the "Tuskegee Airmen" had thoroughly disproved all of the racial stereotypes regrading African American leadership and physical/intellectual abilities.

Section VII

Conclusions

Chapter 12

Post–World War II

When World War II ended in September 1945, the African American community was finally able to take stock in its contributions. Almost one million African Americans served in the U.S. armed forces during the war. However, these individuals did not all serve at the same time as people were killed or discharged for wounds, family issues, and other causes, and new servicemen were continually drafted. As a result, the high point of African American service was September 1944 when 701,678 African Americans were on active duty. For African American commissioned officers, the high point came at the end of the war in September 1945, when there were 5,718 on active duty.[1] Among the line officers (i.e., not including chaplains, lawyers, doctors, etc.), this number included only 49 field grade officers (three colonels, 13 lieutenant colonels, and 33 majors) or less than 1 percent, while the remainder were company-grade officers.[2] While African Americans had made great advances in the armed forces, they were still commonly relegated to the lower ranks (even among officers) and their service was generally not appreciated by white Americans, who continued to view them in a subservient role. Several post-war events/decisions were necessary to complete the process of integration and recognition of African Americans in the armed forces.

In the summer of 1945, the War Department Special Staff solicited the views of senior U.S. Army officers regarding the performance of African American troops and their future role in the post-war Army. The opinions and recommendations were divided between the Army Service Forces (ASF), Army Air Forces (AAF), and Army Ground Forces (AGF). In the ASF, which included support personnel and possessed a disproportionate number of African American soldiers, it was recommended African Americans only train for units that did not, "... require technical skill, such as dump truck companies, port companies, quartermaster service companies, and other labor type units."[3] Likewise, the military occupational specialties for which African Americans were recommended included, "... painters, cooks, bakers, orderlies, truck drivers, ammunition handlers, stevedores, freight handlers, and others of low-skilled requirements, and not be trained in such military occupational specialties as armor's, machinists, topographical specialists, and others of similar nature requiring high technical skills."[4] The ASF further recommended that extreme care was needed in the selection of officers for duty with African American troops and limiting these African American support units to company-size.

The AAF, on the other hand, stated that in the training of pilots, navigators, and bombardiers, the training time required for African Americans was the same as whites and the proficiency attained by these graduates also compared to whites. Furthermore, the training time in technical schools was the same for African Americans and whites, and the proficiency attained by African American technical school graduates was also the same as whites. Nevertheless, the AAF also argued that the training time for African American units was considerably longer than white units and that the proficiency of African American units, specifically those requiring technical knowledge, was below that of white units. This rather confusing set of assertions seemed to imply that as individuals African Americans performed well, but as units, they did not. The AAF comments ended by arguing for assigning African American units only to localities where there were large civilian African American populations that allowed adequate off-post recreational opportunities. Lastly, it was essential that African Americans, "... be treated and considered as individuals and not as a group."[5]

The AGF began by reiterating the already tired mantra that the Army was not in a position to act as an agent of social change in America and should, therefore, abide by the social constructs of American society. Surprisingly, the AGF then advocated for a compromise between total segregation and total integration. As already suggested by more than one Army study during the Interwar Period, the AGF recommended attaching smaller African American units to larger white formations. These African American units were recommended as no larger than battalion-size and this was no doubt also influenced by the success of the volunteer infantry replacement program in World War II. Furthermore, the AGF argued that the same standards should apply to the utilization of all individuals in the armed forces, regardless of race.

> That the same standards should apply to the assignment, promotion, and the provision of living and recreation facilities, and for awards to individuals of all racial groups. ... That the opportunities for developing officers and noncommissioned officers, both in time of peace and war, be equally available to members of all races. ... That insofar as capable officers can be developed, the organizations composed of Negro enlisted men should the officered by members of that race.[6]

The AGF further recommended that African Americans serve not only in the Regular Army but also in the National Guard and Reserve.

The next significant discussion of African American service in the Army came from a board of general officers under the leadership of LTG Alvan C. Gillem, Jr., commander of the XIII Corps and U.S. Ninth Army during World War II.[7] From October 1945 to April 1946, the Board for Utilization of Negro Manpower, commonly known as the "Gillem Board," interviewed dozens of witnesses and reviewed numerous reports and recommendations. The conclusions of this board formed the basis of the Army's post-war policy regarding African Americans and remained in effect until the Korean War.

The Gillem Board's final report began by discussing the lessons of World War II regarding African American military service. In evaluating the combat performance of African Americans, the board argued that African Americans, "… definitely contributed to the success attained by our military forces."[8] After that statement, they discussed the significant disadvantages under which African Americans worked. The board heavily criticized the Army for its woeful unpreparedness for the massive influx of African American personnel despite prewar decisions which decided that 10 percent of all future draftees would be African Americans. "The initial lack of plans for the organization and utilization of a wide variety of combat units was reflected in the frequent reorganization, regrouping, and shifting from one type of training to another."[9] Unfortunately, the board, based largely on the combat experience of the 92nd Infantry Division, argued that African Americans were least successful in combat units that required close contact with the enemy (i.e., infantry), while they were more successful further from the enemy (i.e., artillery). The board then unfairly laid the blame for the poor performance of African American infantry at the feet of African American company-grade officers and NCOs.

The Gillem Board provided a list of twenty-seven conclusions. Among these conclusions, the board emphasized that in the future the Army needed to make greater and more efficient use of African American manpower. The board argued that the peacetime Regular Army needed to increase the number of African American soldiers, and most particularly officers, to the same proportion they represented in American Society—10 percent. As with the AAF, the board recommended stationing African American soldiers only in parts of the country that did not have an unfavorable attitude toward them. Based on the success of the volunteer infantry replacement program in World War II, they recommended using smaller African American combat units in coordination with similar white formations. Lastly, African American officers needed to have the same rights, privileges, and promotion opportunities as white officers.[10]

In addition to these suggestions, the Gillem Board also included eighteen recommendations for policy changes. The majority of these recommendations mirrored the conclusions of the report. Three of the eighteen recommendations specifically addressed the topic of African American commissioned officers, while consistently negatively critiquing the quality of those officers during World War II. The board also argued for the creation of so-called composite units with African American and white subunits to replace traditional segregated African American units in the combat arms.[11]

While the Gillem Board did not radically alter the Army's policy regarding African Americans in the immediate post-war era, other branches of the armed forces came to different conclusions. On 27 February 1946, the U.S. Navy Bureau of Personnel issued the circular letter "Negro Naval Personnel, Abolishment of All Restrictions Governing Types of Assignment for Which Eligible," which effectively desegregated the Navy.

> Effective immediately all restrictions governing the types of assignments for which Negro naval personnel are eligible are lifted. Henceforth they shall be eligible for all types of assignments in all ratings in all activities and all ships of the naval surface.[12]

Despite the official policy change, however, Navy recruiters tended to only enlist African Americans as mess attendants and the number of African American sailors in other specialties remained very small. Although the U.S. Marine Corps was part of the Department of the Navy, the Navy's personnel decisions did not affect the marines. In October 1945, the Marine Corps reduced the African American strength from seventeen thousand to twenty-eight hundred. At the same time, the Marine Corps decided to maintain the segregation of those African Americans.[13]

While the "Tuskegee Airmen" were still part of the Army, the AAF increasingly operated as a semiautonomous organization. On 8 October 1945, the stateside 477th Composite Group was reduced to only two squadrons—the 99th Fighter Squadron and the 617th Bomber Squadron. Meanwhile, the 332nd Fighter Group returned to the United States on 17 October 1945 and along with its two remaining squadrons was disbanded on 19 October.[14] On 30 June 1946, Tuskegee Army Airfield began the process of closing down. Thereafter, new African American pilots who received flight training did so at predominantly white AAF flight schools.[15] On 1 July 1947, the 477th Composite Group and 617th Bomber Squadron were disbanded and the 99th Fighter Squadron was reassigned to the newly reactivated

332nd Fighter Group along with the reactivated 100th and 301st Fighter Squadrons at Lockbourne Army Airfield, Ohio.[16] The U.S. Air Force then became an independent branch of the armed forces on 18 September 1947. On 26 April 1948, GEN Carl A. Spaatz, the first Chief of Staff of the independent Air Force, announced that he intended to desegregate his branch as soon as possible.[17]

On 26 July 1948, President Harry S. Truman ended racial segregation in the armed forces with Executive Order 9981. The order stated in part, "… there shall be equality of treatment and opportunity for all persons in the armed forces without regard to race, color, religion or national origin."[18] As part of the desegregation process, the president established a seven-person advisory committee, officially known as the President's Committee on Equality of Treatment and Opportunity in the Armed Forces. This committee became known as the "Fahy Committee" in honor of its chairman, Charles Fahy, a naval aviator in World War I and the U.S. Solicitor General during World War II. The Fahy Committee's task was to monitor the progress of desegregation. Essentially, their job was to prevent the armed forces from dragging their feet.

While some might argue that Truman's decision represented pandering to a voting bloc, the situation was radically different in 1948. At that time, whites in the South voted almost exclusively for the Democratic Party. While the shift in party allegiance among African Americans from the Republicans to the Democrats was then ongoing, African American voting in the South was negligible because of voter suppression. Therefore, Truman risked the 1948 presidential election on this issue which invariably lost him white votes in the South and, at the same time gained, very few African American votes. Truman's decision was possibly motivated by the assault on SGT Isaac Woodard. On 12 February 1946, Woodard, who only hours earlier was discharged from the Army after serving in the Pacific, was dragged off a greyhound bus in Batesburg, South Carolina, for asking the driver to allow him to use the restroom. Using the trumped-up charge of drunk and disorderly, Woodard was arrested and then so severely beaten while in jail that he was blinded in both eyes and suffered partial amnesia. The local police chief, who administered the beating, was eventually tried but found not guilty.[19] Truman was deeply disturbed when he read about the incident and frequently used it as an example of the problem with the South.

> The main difficulty with the south is that they are living 80 years behind the times and the sooner they come out of it the better it will be for the country and themselves. I am not asking for social equality, because no such thing exists, but I am asking for equality of opportunity for all human beings and, as long as I stay here, I am going to continue that fight. ... When a mayor and city marshal can take a negro [sic] sergeant off a bus in South Carolina, beat him up and put out one of his eyes, and nothing is done about it by the state authorities, something is radically wrong with the system. ... I am going to try to remedy it and if that ends up in my failure to be reelected, that failure will be in a good cause.[20]

Arguably, part of Truman's motivation also rested on a threat by A. Phillip Randolph, the president of the Brotherhood of Sleeping Car Porters, and other African American leaders to boycott the new military draft enacted into law on 24 June 1948.[21]

Unsurprisingly, the executive order met with opposition throughout most of the armed forces. U.S. Army Chief of Staff GEN Omar N. Bradley, who was born and raised in rural Missouri, brought out the tired trope that Army was unable to desegregate while parts of the nation remained deseg-regated. The Army's resistance was so substantial that, on 27 April 1949, Truman demanded the resignation of Kenneth C. Royall, the last Secretary of War and the first Secretary of the Army, for resistance to the execu-tive order. The Army's general attitude toward the executive order was to point out that nowhere in its wording did it explicitly prohibit segrega-tion, a tactic also used by the Marine Corps. In September 1949, Secretary of Defense Louis A. Johnson agreed to a compromise with the Army and allowed them to temporarily maintain a quota on the number of segregated units in the Regular Army.

The Navy had officially opened all specialties to African Americans in February 1946. The same policy change also forbade any ship or unit from having more than 10 percent African American strength. On paper, therefore, the Navy was completely desegregated. In reality, as late as 1949, 65 percent of African Americans in the Navy still served as mess attendants. While the percentage of African Americans in the Steward's Branch continued to drop, in 1958 African Americans were still 23 percent of Navy mess attendants.[22] Between the end of World War II and the beginning of the Korean War, the percentage of African Americans in the Navy decreased almost every year.[23] The situation among African American commissioned officers was especially bleak. From a wartime high of sixty, the number plummeted to only three— Samuel L. Gravely, Jr., Dennis D. Nelson II, and John W. Lee, the last of whom was also a product of the V-12 program and was the first African American granted a regular commission in 1947. The situation seemed unlikely to rapidly improve since between 1946 and 1948 the Navy commissioned only sixteen African Americans from OCS and fourteen from Navy ROTC.[24] Ironically, of the six racial categories[25] then recorded by the Navy, the only group that significantly increased during this time were Filipinos. One positive event for the Navy occurred in the summer of 1945 when Wesley A. Brown became only the sixth African American midshipmen admitted to the U.S. Naval Academy. While the first five African American midshipmen failed to graduate, Brown became the first African American graduate of the Academy and retired from the Navy in 1969 as a lieutenant commander in the Civil Engineer Corps.[26]

The Air Force was the first of the armed forces to fully comply with Truman's executive order. On 1 July 1949, the Air Force disbanded the last segregated African American units.[27] However, according to the guidelines established by the Department of Defense any unit containing 49 percent or more African Americans was still considered segregated. According to that standard, the Air Force still had 106 segregated units. By May 1950, again according to the Department of Defense standard, only twenty-four segregated units remained and 82 percent of African Americans served in completely integrated units.[28]

Ultimately, the process of desegregating the U.S. armed forces was drastically sped up by the Korean War. For the Army and Marine Corps, both of whom were heavily engaged in ground combat operations on the Korean peninsula, available manpower became the most important factor. Given the choice between African Americans and nothing, both services chose African Americans. This process first began unofficially as African American replacements were assigned to otherwise white units. Likewise, back in the United States, Army basic training was integrated because segregation proved too inefficient, expensive, and time-consuming.

On 17 May 1951, GEN Matthew B. Ridgway, the commander of U.S. Far East Command and United Nations Forces in Korea, requested permission to disband the 24th Infantry Regiment and integrate African Americans into all Army units under his command. Only six days later, the Army approved Ridgway's request but ordered him not to integrate the 40th and 45th Infantry Divisions of the California and Oklahoma National Guard for fear of upsetting the state governments.[29] Interestingly, a higher percentage of African American volunteers served in combat arms than African American draftees, though the most overrepresented branches among both draftees and volunteers remained Transportation (34.7 percent) and Quartermaster (20.7 percent).[30] On 1 July 1954, Secretary of Defense Charles E. Wilson announced that the Army was completely desegregated.[31] Perhaps unsurprisingly, segregation in the National Guard and Army Reserve in the South continued until 1962 when Secretary of Defense Robert S. McNamara ordered the identification and integration of those units.[32] The Marine Corps completed desegregation by December 1951 but allowed commanders of individual units in the Marine Corps Reserve the right to accept or reject all prospective members.[33] By the end of the Korean War, African Americans made up 6 percent of the Marine Corps.[34]

Another cabinet secretary of the Kennedy Administration also helped to complete integration, but this time in the U.S. Coast Guard. Though the Coast Guard itself was already integrated, Democrat President John F. Kennedy was disturbed when an all-white contingent of U.S. Coast Guard Academy (USCGA) cadets paraded at his inauguration. The Secretary of the Treasury, Douglas Dillon, under whose branch the Coast Guard was then located, discovered that no African American had ever graduated from the USCGA even though African Americans served as Coast Guard officers since World War II. Only one African American cadet (Javis L. Wright, Jr., in 1951) had ever been admitted to the USCGA, but he was forced to resign after two years due to serious health problems. After Kennedy and Dillon's pressure, in 1962, African American Merle J. Smith, Jr., was admitted as a cadet to the USCGA. Smith, the son of an Army colonel who had grown up in Germany and Japan, among other places, was well prepared for the rigors that awaited him. In 1966, he became the first African American to graduate from the USCGA.[35]

The path to African American integration of the U.S. armed forces was long and arduous. Though African Americans served the United States in combat since the American Revolution, full integration was not finally achieved until 1954. While not the only explanation for the final success of integration, the experience of African American combat units in World War II undoubtedly hastened the integration process. The willingness of these men to so often volunteer for dangerous assignments, most particularly the example of the Army's volunteer infantry replacements, finally destroyed the myth of African American cowardice. The valor and accomplishments of these African Americans proved that they were capable of serving as equals with whites if they were given the proper training, leadership, and opportunities. While it took another war to finish the process, undoubtedly without the World War II experience the process might have taken decades longer.

Endnotes

Notes for Chapter 1

1. U.S. Army Center of Military History, accessed 24 May 2019, https://www.army.mil/africanamericans/timeline.html.
2. Digital History, accessed 5 April 2019, http://www.digitalhistory. uh.edu/active_learning/explorations/revolution/dunsmore.cfm.
3. Gail Buckley, *American Patriots: The Story of Blacks in the Military from the Revolution to Desert Storm* (New York: Random House, 2001), 15–16.
4. Douglas R. Egerton, *Death or Liberty: African Americans and Revolutionary America* (Oxford, UK: Oxford University Press, 2009), 65–68.
5. Buckley, 14.
6. Bernard C. Nalty, *Strength for the Fight: A History of Black Americans in the Military* (New York: Free Press, 1986), 17–18.
7. Buckley, 26–27.
8. Nalty, 14.
9. Buckley 24–25.
10. Ibid., 35.
11. *Militia Act of 1792*, Section 1, 8 May 1792.
12. Henry I. Shaw, Jr., and Ralph W. Donnelly, *Blacks in the Marine Corps* (Washington, DC: Marine Corps History and Museums Division, 1975), ix.
13. Buckley, 46.
14. Ibid., 47–48.
15. Ibid., 49–52.
16. Nalty, 27–28.
17. William A. Dobak, *Freedom by the Sword: The U.S. Colored Troops, 1862–1867* (Washington, DC: U.S. Army Center of Military History, 2011), 91.
18. Ibid., 91–92.
19. In order to differentiate between the two regiments historians generally refer to them as the 1st Louisiana Native Guard (CSA) and the 1st Louisiana Native Guard (USA).
20. Dobak, 100–101.
21. These included the four regiments of Louisiana Native Guards, two marching bands, one regiment of cavalry, twenty-two regiments of infantry, five regiments of engineers, and one regiment of heavy artillery.

22. *Militia Act of 1862*, Sections 12–15, 17 July 1862.

23. *Emancipation Proclamation*, 22 September 1862.

24. Dobak, 238.

25. Ibid., 32–43.

26. Ibid., 44–45.

27. Ibid., 53.

28. Congressional Medal of Honor Society, accessed 7 May 2021, https://www.cmohs.org/recipients/christian-a-fleetwood.

29. Dobak, 22.

30. Ibid., 206–207.

31. John Cimprich, *Fort Pillow: A Civil War Massacre, and Public Memory* (Baton Rouge: Louisiana State University Press, 2005), 70–86.

32. Ibid., 129.

33. Earl J. Hess, *Into the Crater: The Mine Attack at Petersburg* (Columbia: University of South Carolina Press, 2010), 199.

34. Ibid., 190–199.

35. American Battlefield Trust, accessed 7 May 2021, https://www.battlefields.org/learn/articles/calamity-crater.

36. Paul Stillwell, ed., *Golden Thirteen: Recollections of the First Black Naval Officers* (Annapolis, MD: U.S. Naval Institute Press, 1993), xv.

37. Dobak, 474–475.

38. John K. Mahon and Romana Danysh, *Infantry, Part I: Regular Army* (Washington, DC: U.S. Army Center of Military History, 1972), 32.

39. U.S. Army Center of Military History, accessed 29 March 2019, https://history.army.mil/moh/indianwars.html.

40. Nalty, 54.

41. Charles M. Robinson, *Fall of a Black Army Officer: Racism and the Myth of Henry O. Flipper* (Norman: University of Oklahoma Press, 2008), 32.

42. Willard B. Gatewood, Jr., "John Hanks Alexander of Arkansas: Second African American Graduate of West Point." *Arkansas Historical Quarterly* 41 (Summer 1982): 103–115, 128.

43. Brian G. Shellum, *Black Officer in a Buffalo Soldier Regiment: The Military Career of Charles Young* (Lincoln: University of Nebraska Press, 2010), 70–92.

44. These 12 units were the 7th–10th United States Volunteer Infantry Regiments, 3rd Alabama Volunteer Infantry Regiment, 8th Illinois Volunteer Infantry Regiment, Companies A and B, 1st Indiana Volunteer Infantry Regiment, 23rd Kansas Volunteer Infantry Regiment,

Company L, 6th Massachusetts Volunteer Infantry Regiment, 3rd North Carolina Volunteer Infantry Regiment, 9th Ohio Volunteer Infantry Regiment, and 6th Virginia Volunteer Infantry Regiment. Nalty, 63–77.

45. It is interesting to note that Dominguez is listed as white in all of the accounts of the incident despite his obvious Latino heritage. In many other cases in 1906, he would not have been considered white simply because of his surname.

46. Garna L. Christian, *Black Soldiers in Jim Crow Texas, 1899–1917* (College Station: Texas A&M University Press, 1995), 73.

47. Ibid., 79–80.

48. See: John D. Weaver, *Brownsville Raid: The Story of America's "Black Dreyfus Affair"* (New York: W.W. Norton, 1970).

49. John D. Weaver, *Senator and the Sharecropper's Son: Exoneration of the Brownsville Soldiers* (College Station, TX: Texas A&M University Press, 1997), xviii.

50. Gerold W. Patton, W*ar and Race: The Black Officer in the American Military, 1915–1941* (Westport, CT: Greenwood Press, 1981), 54–72.

51. Arthur E. Barbeau and Florette Henri, *Unknown Soldiers: African-American Troops in World War I* (New York: Da Capo Press, 1996), 83.

52. Ibid., 84.

53. Ibid., 83.

54. Ibid., 84.

55. Ibid., 152.

56. Chad L. Williams, *Torchbearers of Democracy: African American Soldiers in the World War I Era* (Chapel Hill: University of North Carolina Press, 2010), 140.

57. Barbeau and Henri, 151; and Williams, 138–140.

58. Barbeau and Henri, 155.

59. Williams, 138–139.

60. Ibid., 141–142.

61. American Battlefield Monuments Commission, *American Armies and Battlefields in Europe: A History, Guide, and Reference Book* (Washington, DC: Government Printing Office, 1938), 515.

62. Barbeau and Henri, 137.

63. Ibid., 158.

64. Ibid., 160.

65. Ibid., 160.

66. Ibid., 160.

67. Frank E. Roberts, *American Foreign Legion: Black Soldiers of the 93rd in World War I* (Annapolis, MD: Naval Institute Press, 2004), 1–2.

68. Jeffrey T. Sammons and John H. Morrow, Jr., *Harlem's Rattlers and the Great War: The Undaunted 369th Regiment and the African American Quest for Equality* (Lawrence: University Press of Kansas, 2014), 94–99.

69. Ibid., 201.

70. Ibid., 200–202, 214.

71. Congressional Medal of Honor Society, accessed 3 September 2020, https://www.cmohs.org/recipients/henry-johnson.

72. Roberts, 198–200.

73. Ibid., 195–197.

74. Congressional Medal of Honor Society, accessed 3 September 2020, https://www.cmohs.org/recipients/freddie-stowers.

75. Interestingly, one of the Navy crewmen aboard the USS *Leviathan* was future actor Humphrey Bogart.

76. William W. Giffin, "Mobilization of Black Militiamen in World War I: Ohio's Ninth Battalion," *Historian* 40:4 (August 1978), 701.

77. The 1st Separate Battalion from the District of Columbia was redesignated as the 1st Battalion, 372nd Infantry, while the 9th Separate Battalion from Ohio was redesignated as the 2nd Battalion, 372nd Infantry. The 1st Separate Company from Maryland was redesignated as Company I, 3rd Battalion, 372nd Infantry. Separate Company G from Tennessee was redesignated as Company K, 3rd Battalion, 372nd Infantry. Company L, 6th Infantry Regiment from Massachusetts was redesignated as Company L, 3rd Battalion, 372nd Infantry. The 1st Separate Company from Connecticut was redesignated as Company M, 3rd Battalion, 372nd Infantry. Roberts, 36–41.

78. The Wilmington Massacre of 1898 was an attack and *coup d'état* by two thousand whites against the city of Wilmington, NC, planned by the state's Democrat Party, that overthrew the legitimately elected local Republican government. In addition to physically expelling white and African American leaders and destroying their private property, between sixty and three hundred people (mostly African Americans) were also killed. See: David Zucchino, *Wilmington's Lie: The Murderous Coup of 1898 and the Rise of White Supremacy* (New York: Atlantic Monthly Press, 2020).

79. During World War I, this nickname was softened to "Black Jack."

80. Sammons and Morrow, 397–398.

81. Robert V. Haynes, *Night of Violence: The Houston Riot of 1917* (Baton Rouge, LA: Louisiana State University Press, 1976), 140.

82. Ibid., 166.

83. Frederick B. Wiener, "Seamy Side of the World War I Court-Martial Controversy," *Military Law Review* 123 (Winter 1989), 121.

84. Haynes, 254–296.

85. During most of the wars in American history prior to World War I, volunteer and militia formations were the dominant manpower source, since the Regular Army was historically so small. Though a draft existed during the Civil War, World War I was the first American conflict in which most American soldiers were drafted. The National Army was a combination of the Regular Army, National Guard, and divisions filled with draftees.

86. Patton, 135.

87. Ibid., 136.

88. Ibid.

89. Lieutenant Colonel John E. Green served from 1901 until 1929 when he retired because he was dissatisfied with the poor career opportunities offered since World War I. For example, he spent the entire period from 1920 to 1929 as a professor of military science and tactics at Wilberforce University. Brian G. Shellum, *African American Officers in Liberia: A Pestiferous Rotation, 1910–1942* (Lincoln, NE: Potomac Books, 2018), 215–216.

90. Marvin E. Fletcher, *America's First Black General: Benjamin O. Davis, Sr., 1880–1970* (Lawrence: University Press of Kansas, 1989), 84.

91. Ibid., 158–159.

92. Alexander M. Bielakowski, *From Horses to Horsepower: The Mechanization and Demise of the U.S. Cavalry, 1916–1950* (Oxford, UK: Fonthill, 2019), 36.

93. By comparison, the Army's budget in 2019 was $182 billion.

94. These averages are based on statistics provided in Robert K. Griffith, Jr., *Men Wanted for the U.S. Army: America's Experience with an All-Volunteer Army Between the World Wars* (Westport, CT: Greenwood Press, 1982).

95. Griffith, 233.

96. Ibid., 239.

97. Christopher R. Gabel, *U.S. Army GHQ Maneuvers of 1941* (Washington, DC: U.S. Army Center for Military History, 1992), 8.

98. Ulysses Lee, *United States Army in World War II: Special Studies—Employment of Negro Troops* (Washington, DC: U.S. Army Center of Military History, 1966), 32.

99. Ibid., 32–33.

100. Ibid., 33.

101. Ibid., 34.

102. Ibid.

103. Ibid., 37–39.

104. Ibid., 244.

105. After December 1942, President Franklin D. Roosevelt ordered that the U.S. armed forces no long accept volunteers and all American men were thereafter subject to Selective Service System, commonly known as the draft. Roosevelt's decision was made because too many men with important civilian skills were volunteering for combat duty, which wasted those skills. With the draft, men with important civilian skills were deferred from service for the duration of the war.

106. Lee, 42–44.

107. Ibid., 46.

108. Larry I. Bland, ed., *Papers of George Catlett Marshall*, Volume 2: "We Cannot Delay" July 1, 1939—December 6, 1941 (Baltimore, MD: Johns Hopkins University Press, 1986), 338–339.

109. Lee, 111.

110. Ibid., 134.

111. Ibid., 415.

112. Morris J. MacGregor, Jr., *Integration of the Armed Forces, 1940–1965* (Washington, DC: U.S. Army Center for Military History, 1989), 48.

113. Ibid., 51.

114. Ibid..

115. National Archives and Records Association, accessed 5 April 2019, https://www.archives.gov/historical-docs/todays-doc/?dod-date=625.

Notes for Chapter 2

1. Shelby L. Stanton, *World War II Order of Battle* (New York: Galahad Books, 1984), 387.

2. Ulysses Lee, *United States Army in World War II: Special Studies—Employment of Negro Troops* (Washington, DC: U.S. Army Center of Military History, 1966), 199.

3. Stanton, 252.

4. Hondon B. Hargrove, *Buffalo Soldiers in Italy: Black Americans in World War II* (Jefferson, NC: McFarland Publishers, 1985), 5.

5. Michael E. Lynch, *Edward M. Almond and the U.S. Army: From the 92nd Infantry Division to the X Corps* (Lexington, KY: University Press of Kentucky, 2019), 62.

6. In typical U.S. Army fashion, however, Almond was not actually fired. Instead, he was appointed the commandant of the Army War College as his final assignment on active duty.

7. David Halberstam, *Coldest Winter: America and the Korean War* (New York: Hyperion, 2007), 439.

8. Truman K. Gibson, Jr., *Knocking Down Barriers: My Fight for Black America* (Evanston, IL: Northwestern University Press, 2005), 157.

9. Lee, 589.

10. This was not the 8th Illinois Infantry Regiment, which served in World War I as the 370th Infantry Regiment, but a brand-new draftee infantry regiment raised early in World War II.

11. Hargrove, 5.

12. Lynch, 72–74.

13. Ibid., 98–99.

14. Hargrove, 9.

15. Lynch, 93.

16. Lee, 334.

17. Lynch, 91.

18. Ibid., 97.

19. "Analytical Study of the Mentality and Capabilities of Enlisted Men of 92nd Infantry Division"; Records of the Adjutant General's Office; Record Group 407; E427; Box 13620; National Archives and Records Administration, College Park, Maryland.

20. "Analysis of Defective Personnel with Combat Units"; Records of the Adjutant General's Office; Record Group 407; E427; Box 13620; National Archives and Records Administration, College Park, Maryland.

21. "Analysis of Defective Personnel with Combat Units."

22. "Removal of Unqualified Commissioned Personnel"; Records of the Adjutant General's Office; Record Group 407; E427; Box 13620; National Archives and Records Administration, College Park, Maryland.

23. "Removal of Unqualified Commissioned Personnel."

24. "Removal of Unqualified Commissioned Personnel."

25. "Removal of Unqualified Commissioned Personnel."

26. "Removal of Unqualified Commissioned Personnel."

27. "92nd Infantry Division Narrative with Maps"; Records of the Adjutant General's Office; Record Group 407; E427; Box 13620; National Archives and Records Administration, College Park, Maryland.

28. "History, 370th Infantry Regiment"; Records of the Adjutant General's Office; Record Group 407; E427; Box 13620; National Archives and Records Administration, College Park, Maryland.

29. Hargrove, 24.

30. Ibid., 26–27.

31. "92nd Infantry Division Narrative with Maps."

32. Hargrove, 27–30.

33. "92nd Infantry Division Narrative with Maps."

34. Lee, 558.

35. Edward W. Brooke, *Bridging the Divide: My Life* (New Brunswick, NJ: Rutgers University Press, 2007), 26.

36. Lynch, 113–114.

37. Congressional Medal of Honor Society, accessed 28 October 2019, http://www.cmohs.org/recipient-detail/2744/fox-john-r.php.

38. Lee, 566.

39. Mark W. Clark, *Calculated Risk* (New York: Harper, 1950), 413.

40. Ibid., 414.

41. Lucian K. Truscott, Jr., *Command Missions: A Personal Story* (New York: Dutton, 1954), 455.

42. Ibid., 474.

43. Ibid., 475.

44. Rick Atkinson, *Day of Battle: The War in Sicily and Italy, 1943–1944* (New York: Henry Holt, 2007), 383.

45. Hargrove, 80.

46. Lee, 570.

47. Joe Wilson, Jr., *758th Tank Battalion in World War II: The U.S. Army's First All African American Tank Unit* (Jefferson, NC: McFarland Publishers, 2018), 103.

48. Lee, 571.

49. "History, 365th Infantry Regiment, 1 October 1944 to 15 August 1945"; Records of the Adjutant General's Office; Record Group 407; E427; Box 13673; National Archives and Records Administration, College Park, Maryland.

50. Lynch, 128.

51. Ibid., 127.
52. Hargrove, 130.
53. Lee, 573.
54. Lynch, 133.
55. Hargrove, 128.
56. Ibid., 146.
57. Gibson, *Knocking Down Barriers*, 170.
58. Larry I. Bland, ed., *Papers of George Catlett Marshall*, Volume 5: "Finest Soldier," January 1, 1945-January 7, 1947 (Baltimore, MD: Johns Hopkins University Press, 2003), 49–50.
59. Bland, 50.
60. "History, 371st Infantry Regiment"; Records of the Adjutant General's Office; Record Group 407; E427; Box 13687; National Archives and Records Administration, College Park, Maryland.
61. Hargrove, 147–148.
62. Lee, 575.
63. Ibid., 574.
64. Lynch, 144.
65. Stanton, 498, 502, and 510.
66. Truman K. Gibson, Jr., "Report on Visit to 92nd Division (Negroes Troops)," Records of the Adjutant General's Office; Record Group 407; E427; Box 13620; National Archives and Records Administration, College Park, Maryland.
67. Gibson, "Report on Visit to 92nd Division (Negroes Troops)."
68. Gibson, "Report on Visit to 92nd Division (Negroes Troops)."
69. "Extracts from Mr. Gibson's Comments to the Press"; 27 March 1945; Records of the Adjutant General's Office; Record Group 407; E427; Box 13620; National Archives and Records Administration, College Park, Maryland.
70. Marcus H. Ray, Letter to Truman K. Gibson, Jr., 14 May 1945, Records of the Adjutant General's Office; Record Group 407; E427; Box 13620; National Archives and Records Administration, College Park, Maryland.
71. Lee, 577–579.
72. "Notes on Mr. Gibson's Report"; Records of the Adjutant General's Office; Record Group 407; E427; Box 13620; National Archives and Records Administration, College Park, Maryland.
73. "Notes on Mr. Gibson's Report."
74. "Notes on Mr. Gibson's Report."

75. Truman K. Gibson, Jr., "Report of Visit to Mediterranean and European Theaters of Operation," Records of the Adjutant General's Office; Record Group 407; E427; Box 13620; National Archives and Records Administration, College Park, Maryland.

76. Gibson, "Report of Visit to Mediterranean and European Theaters of Operation."

77. Vernon J. Baker, *Lasting Valor* (Columbus, MS: Genesis Press, 1997), 199.

78. Ibid., 166–177.

79. Lee, 382.

80. Ibid., 581, 584.

81. Lynch, 147.

82. Lee, 584.

83. Lynch, 152.

84. Hans W. Holmer, "Final Report of Colonel H. W. Holmer, Engineer Member, Army Ground Forces Board, Mediterranean Theater of Operations"; Records of the Adjutant General's Office; Record Group 407; E427; Box 13620; National Archives and Records Administration, College Park, Maryland.

85. Paul N. Starlings, "Final Report of Colonel Paul N. Starlings, President and Infantry Member, Army Ground Forces Board, Mediterranean Theater of Operations"; Records of the Adjutant General's Office; Record Group 407; E427; Box 13620; National Archives and Records Administration, College Park, Maryland.

86. "92nd Infantry Division Narrative with Maps."

87. Paul Goodman, *Fragment of Victory in Italy: The 92nd Infantry Division in World War II* (Nashville, TN: Battery Press, 1993), 202.

88. Lynch, 294–295.

89. Leonard R. Boyd, Frederick A. Harris, Charles H. Winkler, and Oliver E. Allen. *93rd Infantry Division: Summary of Operations in World War II*, March 1946, 1–4, Records of the Adjutant General's Office; Record Group 407; E427; Box 13696; National Archives and Records Administration, College Park, Maryland.

90. Larry I. Bland, ed., *Papers of George Catlett Marshall*, Volume 4: "Aggressive and Determined Leadership," June 1, 1943—December 31, 1944 (Baltimore, MD: Johns Hopkins University Press, 1996), 355.

91. The USS *West Point* had originally been commissioned as the SS *America*, a luxury passenger liner. The ship is perhaps most famous for having among her crew two German agents, Franz Joseph Stigler and

Erwin Wilheim Siegler, who used their positions to provide intelligence to Germany about the Panama Canal prior to the German declaration of war against America. See: Peter Duffy, *Double Agent: The First Hero of World War II and How the FBI Outwitted and Destroyed a Nazi Spy Ring* (New York: Scribner, 2015).

92. Boyd, Harris, Winkler, and Allen. *93rd Infantry Division: Summary of Operations in World War II*, 4.

93. Ibid., 5–6.

94. *After action report, 25th Infantry Regiment, 93rd Infantry Division, January 1944-September 1945*, 4, Records of the Adjutant General's Office; Record Group 407; E427; Box 13712; National Archives and Records Administration, College Park, Maryland.

95. Boyd, Harris, Winkler, and Allen. *93rd Infantry Division: Summary of Operations in World War II*, 10.

96. Lee, 513–514.

97. Ibid., 530.

98. During World War II, the U.S. Army created a series of enlisted ranks designed to give higher pay to soldiers with technical skills who were not in leadership positions. The new ranks were Technician 5th Grade (equivalent to a corporal), Technician 4th Grade (equivalent to a three-stripe, or buck sergeant), and Technician 3rd Grade (equivalent to a staff sergeant). While these technicians were officially not supposed to possess command authority, in practice units generally treated them the same as the equivalent noncommissioned rank. The technician ranks were abolished in 1948, but reappeared later in a different form in 1955.

99. Boyd, Harris, Winkler, and Allen. *93rd Infantry Division: Summary of Operations in World War II*, 44.

100. Stanton, 167–168.

101. Ibid., 204.

102. Lee, 475.

103. Ibid., 475–476.

104. Gibson, *Knocking Down Barriers*, 133–134.

105. Ibid., 136–137.

106. Ibid., 139.

107. Lee, 502.

108. Ibid., 504.

109. Ibid., 504.

110. Stanton, 204.

111. "History of 367th Infantry Battalion (Separate)," 3, Records of the Adjutant General's Office; Record Group 407; E427; Box 21090; National Archives and Records Administration, College Park, Maryland.

112. Stanton, 252.

113. "History of 367th Infantry Battalion (Separate)," 7.

114. Stanton, 271.

115. Ibid., 252.

116. The 372nd Infantry Regiment consisted of: HQ Company (District of Columbia); Service Company (Maryland); 1st Battalion (New Jersey); 2nd Battalion (Ohio); and 3rd Battalion (Massachusetts). Steven E. Clay, *U.S. Army Order of Battle, 1919–1941.*, Volume 1: The Arms: Major Commands and Infantry Organizations (Fort Leavenworth, KS: Combat Studies Institute Press, 2010), 484.

117. Lee, 200.

118. Stanton, 254.

119. Bradley Biggs, *Triple Nickles: America's First All-Black Paratroop Unit* (Hamden, CT: Archon Books, 1986), 7.

120. Ibid., 36.

121. James H. Porter, "Historical Narrative 555th Parachute Infantry Battalion," Records of the Adjutant General's Office; Record Group 407; E427; Box 21106; National Archives and Records Administration, College Park, Maryland.

122. Biggs, 55–57.

123. Ibid., 68.

124. Porter, "Historical Narrative 555th Parachute Infantry Battalion."

125. Lee, 688.

126. Ibid., 689.

127. Alfred D. Chandler, Jr., *Papers of Dwight D. Eisenhower*, Volume IV: The War Year (Baltimore, MD: Johns Hopkins University, 1970), 2409.

128. Lee, 693, 695.

129. Ibid., 693.

130. Ibid., 695–696.

131. Congressional Medal of Honor Society, accessed 19 December 2019, https://www.cmohs.org/recipients/willy-f-james-jr.

132. Research Branch, Information and Education Division, HQ, ETO, "Utilization of Negro Infantry Platoons in White Companies" (June 1945), 2; Records of the Office of the Chief of Military History; Record Group 319; Box 509; National Archives and Records Administration, College Park, Maryland.

133. Research Branch, "Utilization of Negro Infantry Platoons in White Companies," 3.

134. Research Branch, "Utilization of Negro Infantry Platoons in White Companies," 5.

135. Research Branch, "Utilization of Negro Infantry Platoons in White Companies," 6.

136. Research Branch, "Utilization of Negro Infantry Platoons in White Companies," 10.

137. E. W. McGregor, "Report on Negro Troops"; 20 June 1945; Records of the Office of the Chief of Military History; Record Group 319; Box 509; National Archives and Records Administration, College Park, Maryland.

138. F. J. Murdoch, "Report on Negro Troops"; 20 June 1945; Records of the Office of the Chief of Military History; Record Group 319; Box 509; National Archives and Records Administration, College Park, Maryland.

139. John R. Achor, "Report on Negro Troops"; 21 June 1945; Records of the Office of the Chief of Military History; Record Group 319; Box 509; National Archives and Records Administration, College Park, Maryland.

140. Benjamin O. Davis, Sr., "Visit to Colored Infantry Rifle Platoons, First United States Army"; 25 April 1945; Records of Headquarters, European Theater of Operations, United States Army; Record Group 498; SA 290; National Archives and Records Administration, College Park, Maryland.

141. Lee, 699.

142. The German *Panzerfaust* was a single use, recoilless antitank weapon that was arguably one of the most effective antitank weapons of World War II. The *Panzerfaust* was particularly deadly at ranges at or under hundred yards where it could penetrate 200 mm (almost eight inches) of armor. Ian V. Hogg, *Encyclopedia of Infantry Weapons of World War II* (London: Saturn Books, 1977), 152.

143. Congressional Medal of Honor Society, accessed 7 May 2021, https://www.cmohs.org/recipients/edward-a-carter-jr.

144. James R. Lankford, "Battling Segregation and the Nazis: The Origins and Combat History of CCR Rifle Company, 14th Armored Division," *Army History* No. 63 (Winter 2007): 27.

145. Ibid., 30.

146. Ibid., 31.

147. Ibid., 38.
148. Benjamin O. Davis, Sr., "Special Visit to Camp Herbert Tarreyton, Near La Havre, France"; 16 August 1945; Records of Headquarters, European Theater of Operations, United States Army; Record Group 498; SA 290; National Archives and Records Administration, College Park, Maryland.
149. Davis, "Special Visit to Camp Herbert Tarreyton, Near La Havre, France."
150. Lee, 704.

Notes for Chapter 3

1. However, Latinos with European complexions and features were allowed to join the Marine Corps. Pedro A. Del Valle, who graduated from the U.S. Naval Academy in 1915, is believed to be the first Latino commissioned officer in the Marine Corps and was a colonel at the outbreak of World War II. Michael A. Ridge, Jr., "Del Valle, Pedro A.," in Volume 1, Alexander M. Bielakowski, ed., *Encyclopedia of Ethnic and Racial Minorities in the U.S. Military* (Santa Barbara, CA: ABC-CLIO, 2013), 155–157.
2. Henry I. Shaw, Jr., and Ralph W. Donnelly, *Blacks in the Marine Corps* (Washington, DC: Marine Corps History and Museums Division, 1975), ix.
3. The first African American Marine officer was commissioned on 10 November 1945. Frederick C. Branch, a veteran of the 51st Defense Battalion, was commissioned a 2nd lieutenant in the Marine Corps Reserve and almost immediately discharged from active duty. Bernard C. Nalty, *Right to Fight: African American Marines in World War II* (Washington, DC: Marine Corps Historical Center, 19950, 27.
4. David J. Ulbrich, *Preparing for Victory: Thomas Holcomb and the Making of the Modern Marine Corps, 1936–1943* (Annapolis, MD: Naval Institute Press, 2011), 119.
5. Ibid., 119
6. Ibid., 121.
7. General Board Study of the Enlistment of Men of the Colored Race in Other than Messman Branch, No. 421 (Serial No. 204), Enclosure (A), 1. Archives Branch, Alfred M. Gray Research Center, Marine Corps University, Quantico, Virginia.
8. General Board Study of the Enlistment of Men of the Colored Race in Other than Messman Branch, 9.

9. Ulbrich, 120.

10. Phillip H. Torrey, Director, Marine Corps Reserve, Enlistment of Colored Personnel in the Marine Corps, 25 May 1942. Archives Branch, Alfred M. Gray Research Center, Marine Corps University, Quantico, Virginia.

11. Ronald K. Culp, *First Black United States Marines: The Men of Montford Point, 1942–1946* (Jefferson, NC: McFarland, 2007), 36.

12. Keller E. Rockey, Director, Division of Plans and Policies, Enlistment of colored personnel in the Marine Corps Reserve, 29 October 1942. Archives Branch, Alfred M. Gray Research Center, Marine Corps University, Quantico, Virginia.

13. Memorandum for the Director, Division of Plans and Policies, Colored Personnel, 26 December 1942. Archives Branch, Alfred M. Gray Research Center, Marine Corps University, Quantico, Virginia.

14. Culp, 62.

15. Johnson continued to serve in the Marine Corps after World War II and retired in 1955. Two years after his death in 1972, Montford Point Camp was renamed Camp Gilbert H. Johnson.

16. Letter, Charles F. B. Price to Keller E. Rockey, 24 April 1943. Archives Branch, Alfred M. Gray Research Center, Marine Corps University, Quantico, Virginia.

17. Thomas Holcomb, Letter of Instruction No. 421, 14 May 1943. Archives Branch, Alfred M. Gray Research Center, Marine Corps University, Quantico, Virginia.

18. Culp, 90–96.

19. Nalty, 28.

20. Culp, 82.

21. Nalty, 14–17, 26.

22. Ibid., 17–18.

23. By the end of the war, the Marine Corps organized twelve ammunition and fifty-one depot companies. Nalty, 28.

24. Nalty, 20–21.

25. Culp, 150.

26. Ibid., 157–158.

27. Gordon L. Rottman, *U.S. Marine Corps World War II Order of Battle: Ground and Air Units in the Pacific War, 1939–1945* (Westport, CT: Greenwood Press, 2002), 157.

28. Culp, 163–164.

29. Nalty, 22.

30. Culp, 181–185.
31. Ibid., 184.
32. Rottman, 348.
33. Culp, 201.
34. Ibid., 201–202.
35. Nalty, 23.
36. Ibid., 24.
37. Ibid., 25.
38. Ibid., 28.

Notes for Chapter 4

1. The 77th, 79th, and 159th Field Artillery Battalions were assigned to the 2nd Cavalry Division. The 597th, 598th, 599th, and 600th Field Artillery Battalions assigned to the 92nd Infantry Division. The 593rd, 594th, 595th, and 596th Field Artillery Battalions assigned to the 93rd Infantry Division. Shelby L. Stanton, *World War II Order of Battle* (New York: Galahad Books, 1984), 73, 166–168.

2. The 353rd Field Artillery Battalion was redesignated the 1697th Engineer Combat Battalion. The 732nd Field Artillery Battalion was redesignated the 1695th Engineer Combat Battalion. The 795th Field Artillery Battalion if was redesignated the 1700th Engineer Combat Battalion. The 930th Field Artillery Battalion was redesignated the 1699th Engineer Combat Battalion. The 931st Field Artillery Battalion was redesignated the 1698th Engineer Combat Battalion. The 993rd Field Artillery Battalion was redesignated the 1696th Engineer Combat Battalion. Stanton, 409, 418, 420, 422, 424.

3. The 333rd, 349th, 350th, 351st, 578th, 686th, 777th, 969th, 971st, 973rd, and 999th Field Artillery Battalions. Stanton, 408, 414, 417, 420, 423, 424.

4. At various times, the brigade included the 1st Battalion, 228th Field Artillery Regiment, 173rd, 193rd, 349th, 350th, 351st, and 353rd Field Artillery Regiments, the 60th and 64th Ordnance Companies, as well as oddly the 846th Tank Destroyer Battalion. George H. Paine, History of the 46th Field Artillery Brigade, 10 February 1941–16 September 1943, Records of the Adjutant General's Office; Record Group 407; E427; Box 20537; National Archives and Records Administration, College Park, Maryland.

5. Department of the Army, Lineage and Honors, Headquarters and Headquarters Battery, 46th Artillery Group. Fort Leslie McNair, Washington: DC, U.S. Army Center of Military History.

6. Stanton, 387.

7. Ulysses Lee, *United States Army in World War II: Special Studies— Employment of Negro Troops* (Washington, DC: U.S. Army Center of Military History, 1966), 199.

8. James A. Sawicki, *Field Artillery Battalions of the U.S. Army*, Volume 2 (Dumfries, VA: Centaur Publications, 1978), 1128–1129.

9. Department of the Army, Lineage and Honors, 333rd Field Artillery. Fort Leslie McNair, Washington: DC, U.S. Army Center of Military History.

10. Stanton, 408, 423.

11. The murdered soldiers were SSG Thomas J. Forte; Technician 4th Grade (T/4) William E. Pritchett; T/4 James A. Stewart; CPL Mager Bradley; T/5 Robert L. Green; PFC George Davis; PFC James L. Leatherwood; PFC George W. Moten; PFC Due W. Turner; PVT (Medic) Curtis Adams; and PVT Nathaniel Moss. See Denise George and Robert Child, *Lost Eleven: The Forgotten Story of Black American Soldiers Brutally Massacred in World War II* (New York: Caliber, 2017).

12. Lee, 650.

13. Ibid., 651.

14. Ibid., 652.

15. Ibid., 656–657.

16. Stanton, 408, 423.

17. Department of the Army, Lineage and Honors, 333rd Field Artillery. Fort Leslie McNair, Washington: DC, U.S. Army Center of Military History.

18. Department of the Army, Lineage and Honors, 72nd Field Artillery Brigade. Fort Leslie McNair, Washington: DC, U.S. Army Center of Military History.

19. John W. Russey, History of the 349th Field Artillery Group, 7 August 1945, Records of the Adjutant General's Office; Record Group 407; E427; Box 20794; National Archives and Records Administration, College Park, Maryland.

20. Lee, 657.

21. Stanton, 361, 408, 417.

22. Truman K. Gibson, Jr., *Knocking Down Barriers: My Fight for Black America* (Evanston, IL: Northwestern University Press, 2005), 111.

23. Stanton, 361, 408, 423.
24. Lee, 657.
25. Stanton, 408.
26. Ibid., 362, 408, 424.
27. Ibid., 366, 414, 424.
28. Lee, 647.
29. Ibid., 652.
30. Ibid., 653.
31. Sawicki, 841.
32. Lee, 655.
33. L. C. Coleman, Jr., Historical Records and Histories of Organizations, 7 October 1946, Records of the Adjutant General's Office; Record Group 407; E427; Box 20400; National Archives and Records Administration, College Park, Maryland.
34. Stanton, 415.
35. Frederick A. Harris, Unit Operations History, 10 September 1945, Records of the Adjutant General's Office; Record Group 407; E427; Box 13707; National Archives and Records Administration, College Park, Maryland.
36. Stanton, 415.
37. Ibid.
38. Lee, 477–478.
39. Truman K. Gibson, Jr., *Knocking Down Barriers: My Fight for Black America* (Evanston, IL: Northwestern University Press, 2005), 129–130.
40. Ibid., 97.
41. "92nd Infantry Division Narrative with Maps"; Records of the Adjutant General's Office; Record Group 407; E427; Box 13620; National Archives and Records Administration, College Park, Maryland.
42. "History, 370th Infantry Regiment"; Records of the Adjutant General's Office; Record Group 407; E427; Box 13620; National Archives and Records Administration, College Park, Maryland.
43. Lee, 539.
44. Ibid., 567.
45. Stanton, 415.
46. L. G. Witmer, Unit History, 24 January 1945, Records of the Adjutant General's Office; Record Group 407; E427; Box 20200; Stack Area 270; National Archives and Records Administration, College Park, Maryland.

47. Emiel W. Owens, *Blood on German Snow: An African American Artilleryman in World War II and Beyond* (College Station: Texas A&M University Press, 2006), 60.

48. Owens, 74.

49. Lee, 658.

Notes for Chapter 5

1. Ulysses Lee, *United States Army in World War II: Special Studies— Employment of Negro Troops* (Washington, DC: U.S. Army Center of Military History, 1966), 122, 129, 160.

2. Mark A. Berhow, ed., *American Seacoast Defenses: A Reference Guide* (Bel Air, MD: CDSG Press, 1999), 418.

3. Berhow, 418.

4. Steven E. Clay, *U.S. Army Order of Battle, 1919–1941*, Volume 2: The Arms: Cavalry, Field Artillery, and Coast Artillery, 1919–1941 (Fort Leavenworth, KS: Combat Studies Institute Press, 2010), 1052.

5. Ibid., 1056, 1068–1069.

6. Lee, 121–122.

7. Clay, 483.

8. Shelby L. Stanton, *World War II Order of Battle* (New York: Galahad Books, 1984), 472.

9. Ibid., 496, 509.

10. Clay, 1081.

11. Stanton, 460.

12. Ibid., 450.

13. Ibid., 485.

14. Ibid., 505.

15. Ibid., 463.

16. Ibid., 443.

17. Ibid., 485.

18. Ibid., 510.

19. Ibid., 464.

20. Ibid., 444.

21. Ibid., 496, 510.

22. Ibid., 445, 465.

23. Ibid., 486, 495, 509.

24. Ibid., 466.

25. Ibid., 486, 495, 509.

26. Ibid., 466.

27. Ibid., 486.

28. Ibid., 490, 491, 506.

29. Ibid., 448, 476.

30. Ibid., 490, 491, 506.

31. The 318th Antiaircraft Artillery Balloon Battalion (Very Low Altitude), 319th Antiaircraft Artillery Balloon Battalion, 321st Antiaircraft Artillery Balloon Battalion, 361st Antiaircraft Artillery Balloon Searchlight Battalion, 458th, 790th, 819th, and 846th Antiaircraft Artillery Automatic Weapons Battalions never left the United States, while the 394th, 395th, 450th, 466th, 477th, 484th, 492nd, and 493rd Antiaircraft Artillery Automatic Weapons Battalions saw overseas assignments. Stanton, 494–509.

32. Stanton, 494.

33. James R. Shock, *U.S. Army Barrage Balloon Program* (Bennington, VT: Merriam Press, 2006), 68–69, 74.

34. David Reynolds, *Rich Relations: The American Occupation of Britain, 1942–1945* (New York: Random House, 1995), 216–324.

35. Linda Hervieux, *Forgotten: The Untold Story of D-Day's Black Heroes, At Home and At War* (New York: Harper, 2015), 155.

36. Jonathan Gawne, *Spearheading D-Day: American Special Units in Normandy* (Paris, France: Histoire and Collections, 2011), 191–192.

37. Gawne, 193.

38. Shock, 76.

39. "Unit History, 320th Antiaircraft Balloon Battalion, Very Low Altitude"; 6; Records of the Adjutant General's Office; Record Group 407; Entry 427; World War II Operations Reports; CABN-312-CABN-320; National Archives and Records Administration, College Park, Maryland.

40. CPL Stith Brooks, CPL Henry J. Harris, and PFC James L. Simmons.

41. "Unit History, 320th Antiaircraft Balloon Battalion, Very Low Altitude"; 9.

42. Hervieux, 239.

43. "Unit History, 320th Antiaircraft Balloon Battalion, Very Low Altitude"; 7.

44. Stanton, 499.

45. Andrew N. Winfree, *"Fire It": The African American Artilleryman in World War II (ETO)—A Chronology* (Victoria, Canada: Trafford, 2006), 311–314.

46. Winfree, 315, 327.
47. T/5 Zeno H. Ellis, SSG William Campbell, PFC Willie Jackson, PFC Edward I. Swindell, and PVT Samuel Jackson received the Silver Star, while 1LT Herbert D. Cisco received the Bronze Star for Valor. Winfree, 314–326.
48. Lee, 659–660.
49. Winfree, 327–333.
50. Stanton, 499.

Notes for Chapter 6

1. Steven E. Clay, *U.S. Army Order of Battle, 1919–1941*, Volume 2: The Arms: Cavalry, Field Artillery, and Coast Artillery, 1919–1941 (Fort Leavenworth, KS: Combat Studies Institute Press, 2010), 570.
2. Historical Data File, U.S. Military Academy Cavalry Squadron. Fort Leslie McNair, Washington, DC: U.S. Army Center of Military History.
3. Clay, 622.
4. Ibid.
5. Ibid., 570.
6. Shelby L. Stanton, *World War II Order of Battle* (New York: Galahad Books, 1984), 73.
7. Ibid., 305, 314.
8. Stanton, 73.
9. Johnson served as an officer in the 1st Infantry Division during World War I but, during the Interwar Period, he served in the National Guard while pursuing a civilian career. In 1940, Johnson was recalled to active duty and commanded the 112th Cavalry Regiment (Texas National Guard), then the 2nd Cavalry Brigade, 1st Cavalry Division, before he took command of the new reactivated 2nd Cavalry Division. Clay, 597, 634.
10. Stanton, 73.
11. C. N. Elliot, "Disbandment and Organization of Units," 22 February 1944. HQ, Mediterranean Base Section, U.S. Army. Records of the Adjutant General's Office, Record Group 407; E427; Box 18078; National Archives and Records Administration, College Park, Maryland.
12. C. N. Elliot, "Inactivation and Organization of Units," 29 March 1944. HQ, Mediterranean Base Section, U.S. Army. Records of the Adjutant General's Office, Record Group 407; E427; Box 18078; National Archives and Records Administration, College Park, Maryland.

13. "Unit history, 92nd Cavalry Reconnaissance Troop"; Records of the Adjutant General's Office, Record Group 407; E427; Box 13666; National Archives and Records Administration, College Park, Maryland.

14. "Unit history, 92nd Cavalry Reconnaissance Troop."

15. "Unit history, 92nd Cavalry Reconnaissance Troop."

16. "Unit history, 92nd Cavalry Reconnaissance Troop."

17. "Unit history, 92nd Cavalry Reconnaissance Troop."

18. "Unit history, 92nd Cavalry Reconnaissance Troop."

19. "Operations of a Cavalry Reconnaissance Troop (Mechz) of an Infantry Division," 92nd Cavalry Reconnaissance Troop. Records of the Adjutant General's Office, Record Group 407; E427; Box 13666; National Archives and Records Administration, College Park, Maryland.

20. "Operations of a Cavalry Reconnaissance Troop (Mechz) of an Infantry Division."

21. "Operations of a Cavalry Reconnaissance Troop (Mechz) of an Infantry Division."

22. "Operations of a Cavalry Reconnaissance Troop (Mechz) of an Infantry Division."

23. It is very likely that while Steinman uses the term "mules," he is most likely talking about donkeys. Mules are an artificial species created by cross breeding donkeys with horses. Mules are relatively rare as compared to both horses and donkeys because they are sterile and can only exist through human intervention.

24. Ulysses Lee, *United States Army in World War II: Special Studies— Employment of Negro Troops* (Washington, DC: U.S. Army Center of Military History, 1966), 568.

25. "Operations of a Cavalry Reconnaissance Troop (Mechz) of an Infantry Division."

26. Lee, 514.

27. Leonard R. Boyd, Frederick A. Harris, Charles H. Winkler, and Oliver E. Allen. *93rd Infantry Division: Summary of Operations in World War II*, March 1946, 19–20, Records of the Adjutant General's Office; Record Group 407; E427; Box 13696; National Archives and Records Administration, College Park, Maryland.

28. 93rd Cavalry Reconnaissance Troop (Mechanized), Unit Operations History (Overseas), 3; Records of the Adjutant General's Office; Record Group 407; Box 13705; National Archives and Records Administration, College Park, Maryland.

29. 93rd Cavalry Reconnaissance Troop (Mechanized), Unit Operations History (Overseas), 4.

30. 93rd Cavalry Reconnaissance Troop (Mechanized), Unit Operations History (Overseas), 5–7.

31. 93rd Cavalry Reconnaissance Troop (Mechanized), Unit Operations History (Overseas), 10.

32. Historical Data File, U.S. Military Academy Cavalry Squadron.

Notes for Chapter 7

1. *National Defense Act, Approved June 3, 1913, As Amended by Act Approved June 4, 1920* (Washington, DC: Government Printing Office, 1920).

2. The 7th Cavalry Brigade was activated in 1933 and consisted of the 1st and 13th Cavalry Regiments as well as artillery and other supporting units.

3. The Provisional Tank Brigade (66th and 67th Infantry Regiments— Light and Medium Tanks, respectively) were organized especially for the maneuvers.

4. Mildred H. Gillie, *Forging the Thunderbolt: A History of the Development of the Armored Force* (Harrisburg, PA: Military Service Publishing Company, 1947), 162–163.

5. Ibid., 163–164.

6. During World War II, American tankers were not yet part of a separate branch (which required congressional legislation and did not actually happen until 1950), but rather existed as part of the "Armored Force" in order to avoid legal issues.

7. Gillie, 166–168.

8. Joe Wilson, Jr., *758th Tank Battalion in World War II: The U.S. Army's First All African American Tank Unit* (Jefferson, NC: McFarland Publishers, 2018), 28.

9. Ibid., 28.

10. Ibid., 36–39.

11. Gina M. DiNicolo, *Black Panthers: The 761st Tank Battalion and Patton's Drive on Germany* (Alexandria, VA: St. John's Press, 2016), 36–37.

12. "'Neither riches or poverty, neither creed or race …'—The Story of Pvt. Robert H. Brooks." Kentucky National Guard, accessed 15 August 2019, https://kentuckyguard.dodlive.mil/2014/02/14/neither-riches-or-poverty-neither-creed-or-race-the-story-of-pvt-robert-h-brooks/.

13. The 5th Tank Group was redesignated as the 5th Armored Group on 1 December 1943. After the 784th Tank Battalion was detached and sent to Europe, the 5th Armored Group retained no organic units and had no reason for its existence. On 1 December 1944, the group was officially disbanded. "History of the 5th Armored Group"; pages 2–3; Records of the Adjutant General's Office, Record Group 407; E427; Box 16843; National Archives and Records Administration, College Park, Maryland.

14. Between 1942 and 1944, 22 U.S. Army divisions participated in training in the Tennessee maneuver area under the command of the Second Army. See: Woody McMillin, *In the Presence of Soldiers: The 2nd Army Maneuvers and Other World War II Activity in Tennessee* (Nashville, TN: Horton Heights Press, 2010).

15. Wilson, 38.

16. Ibid., 47–49.

17. Ibid., 51–53.

18. Ibid., 59–60.

19. Lawrence F. Becnel, "Historical Events of 758th Light Tank Battalion, 30 September-30 November 1944," 30 November 1944"; Records of the Adjutant General's Office, Record Group 407; E427; Box 16778; National Archives and Records Administration, College Park, Maryland.

20. Amazingly, the SS *John W. Brown* is one of only two remaining operational liberty ships from World War II. After completing thirteen transatlantic voyages during and immediately after the war, the ship was leased to New York City and served as part of the Metropolitan Vocational High School from 1946 to 1982. Thousands of students received their high school education aboard the ship, which prepared them for careers in the Merchant Marine, U.S. Navy, and U.S. Coast Guard. After extensive renovations, the ship was moved to Baltimore and currently serves as a floating, living museum.

21. Becnel, "Historical Events of 758th Light Tank Battalion, 30 September-30 November 1944."

22. Wilson, 76.

23. Ibid., 117.

24. Ibid., 76.

25. Ibid., 103.

26. Lawrence F. Becnel, "Report of Action Against the Enemy for the Month of April, 758th Light Tank Battalion"; 7 May 1945; Page 3; Records of the Adjutant General's Office, Record Group 407; E427; Box 16779; National Archives and Records Administration, College Park, Maryland.

27. Wilson, 133.
28. Mary L. Stubbs and Stanley R. Connor, *Armor-Cavalry*, Part I: *Regular Army and Army Reserve* (Washington, DC: Government Printing Office, 1969), 351–357.
29. "History of the 5th Armored Group"; Page 1; Records of the Adjutant General's Office, Record Group 407; E427; Box 16843; National Archives and Records Administration, College Park, Maryland.
30. There is an unverified rumor that the Black Panther Party, which became famous during the racial tensions of the 1960s and 1970s, took their name from the 761st Tank Battalion's nickname.
31. Kareem Abdul-Jabbar and Anthony Walton, *Brothers in Arms: The Epic Story of the 761st Tank Battalion, WWII's Forgotten Heroes* (New York: Broadway Books, 2004), 31.
32. Ibid., 32.
33. Ibid., 33.
34. Michael L. Lanning, *Court-Martial of Jackie Robinson: The Baseball Legend's Battle for Civil Rights during World War II* (Mechanicsburg, PA: Stackpole Books, 2020), 34–44.
35. Ibid., 47–48.
36. Ibid., 15.
37. Ibid., 52.
38. Ibid.
39. Ibid., 63–64.
40. Ibid., 53–54.
41. Ibid., 262.
42. Ibid., 88–89.
43. DiNicolo, 138–139.
44. Abdul-Jabbar and Walton, 71–78.
45. Ibid., 72.
46. Ibid., 78.
47. DiNicolo, 140–141.
48. Ibid., 142.
49. Abdul-Jabbar and Walton, 88–90.
50. DiNicolo, 224.
51. Ibid., 152–153.
52. Abdul-Jabbar and Walton, 126.
53. These tanks were variously reported as Panzer IVs, Panthers, or Tigers.
54. Abdul-Jabbar and Walton, 134.

55. During the Interwar Period, the 87th Infantry Division was an Organized Reserve unit from Louisiana, Mississippi, and Alabama. The Organized Reserve consisted largely of HQ detachments with nothing more than lists of the names of officers who were assigned to the unit during wartime. The division was not called to active duty until December 1942 when it was filled almost exclusively with draftees.

56. Joe Wilson, Jr., *784th Tank Battalion in World War II: History of an African American Armored Unit in Europe* (Jefferson, NC: McFarland, 2007), 47.

57. Abdul-Jabbar and Walton, 210.

58. DiNicolo, 248.

59. Ibid., 254.

60. James A. Sawicki, *Tank Battalions of the U.S. Army* (Dumfries, VA: Wyvern Publications, 1983), 335.

61. Abdul-Jabbar and Walton, 259–260.

62. Wilson, *784th Tank Battalion in World War II*, 22–23.

63. Ibid., 25–26.

64. Ibid., 37.

65. During the Interwar Period, the 104th Infantry Division was an Organized Reserve unit from Idaho, Montana, Utah, and Wyoming. The division was called to active duty in September 1942 and filled mostly with draftees. From October 1943 to the end of the war, the division was commanded by MG Terry de la Mesa Allen, Sr., a man generally considered one of the best division commanders of World War II and who had previously commanded the 1st Infantry Division in combat in North Africa, Sicily, and Italy.

66. Charles E. Miller, "After Action Report, 784th Tank Battalion"; 2 February 1945; Records of the Adjutant General's Office, Record Group 407; E427; Box 16792; National Archives and Records Administration, College Park, Maryland.

67. Wilson, *784th Tank Battalion in World War II*, 50.

68. CPL Earl Morgan, who died on 27 February 1945, was possibly the first member of the 784th Tank Battalion to be killed in action, but there is some confusion in the records as to whether a member of the battalion was killed in January. George C. Dalia, "Report After Action Against Enemy, 784th Tank Battalion"; 13 March 1945; Records of the Adjutant General's Office, Record Group 407; E427; Box 16792; National Archives and Records Administration, College Park, Maryland.

69. Dalia, "Report After Action Against Enemy, 784th Tank Battalion"; 13 March 1945.

70. George C. Dalia, "Report After Action Against Enemy, 784th Tank Battalion"; 5 April 1945; Records of the Adjutant General's Office, Record Group 407; E427; Box 16792; National Archives and Records Administration, College Park, Maryland.

71. Dalia, "Report After Action Against Enemy, 784th Tank Battalion"; 5 April 1945.

72. Ibid.

73. Ibid.

74. Ibid.

75. Ibid.

76. The *Volksturm* (People's Storm) was a last-ditch German military organization organized starting in October 1944. All males ages 16 to 60 not already in the German *Wehrmacht* were compelled to serve in the *Volksturm*. These units were organized by the Nazi party, rather than the German *Wehrmacht*, and consisted largely of men who were too old, too young, or otherwise unfit for military service. Poorly trained, poorly armed, and led by Nazi party officials rather than experienced soldiers, the *Volksturm* were generally militarily ineffective and resulted in the needless deaths of tens, if not hundreds, of thousands of German men.

77. Dalia, "Report After Action Against Enemy, 784th Tank Battalion"; 5 April 1945.

78. George C. Dalia, "Report After Action Against Enemy, 784th Tank Battalion"; 1 May 1945; Records of the Adjutant General's Office, Record Group 407; E427; Box 16792; National Archives and Records Administration, College Park, Maryland.

79. George C. Dalia, "Report After Action Against Enemy, 784th Tank Battalion"; 1 June 1945; Records of the Adjutant General's Office, Record Group 407; E427; Box 16792; National Archives and Records Administration, College Park, Maryland.

80. George C. Dalia, "Report After Action Against Enemy, 784th Tank Battalion"; 2 July 1945; Records of the Adjutant General's Office, Record Group 407; E427; Box 16792; National Archives and Records Administration, College Park, Maryland.

81. Wilson, *784th Tank Battalion in World War II*, 168.

82. Sawicki, 116–117.

Notes for Chapter 8

1. The exact name of the "branch" has been a continuing source of confusion, because it was never a true "branch" of the Army—just a temporary wartime organization. At times, the "branch" was referred to as the "Tank Destroyers" and, at other times, as the "Tank Destroyer force" (lower-case "f").

2. Christopher Gabel, *Seek, Strike, and Destroy: U.S. Army Tank Destroyer Doctrine in World War II* (Fort Leavenworth, Kansas: Combat Studies Institute Press, 1985), 10.

3. Shelby L. Stanton, *World War II Order of Battle* (New York: Galahad Books, 1984), 25.

4. Christopher Gabel, *U.S. Army GHQ Maneuvers of 1941* (Washington, DC: U.S. Army Center for Military History, 1992), 54.

5. Gabel, *Seek, Strike, and Destroy*, 15.

6. Ibid., 18, 28.

7. Stanton, 25, 326–331.

8. Gabel, *Seek, Strike, and Destroy*, 27.

9. The units were designated as: 614th, 646th, 649th, 659th, 669th, 679th, 795th, 827th, 828th, 829th, and 846th Tank Destroyer Battalions. Stanton, 334–338.

10. *Three Inch Fury: 614 Tank Destroyers WWII* (Germany: privately published, c.1945), 6–8.

11. *Three Inch Fury: 614 Tank Destroyers WWII*, 10.

12. *Three Inch Fury: 614 Tank Destroyers WWII*, 12.

13. Congressional Medal of Honor Society, accessed 9 March 2020, http://www.cmohs.org/recipient-detail/3016/thomas-charles-l.php.

14. General Orders Number 88; Headquarters, 103rd Infantry Division; 27 December 1944. Records of the Adjutant General's Office; Record Group 407; National Archives and Records Administration, College Park, Maryland.

15. Personal Account, Sergeant Dillard L. Booker. Records of the Adjutant General's Office; Record Group 407; National Archives and Records Administration, College Park, Maryland.

16. *Three Inch Fury: 614 Tank Destroyers WWII*, 13.

17. *Three Inch Fury: 614 Tank Destroyers WWII*, 13–14.

18. Ulysses Lee, *United States Army in World War II: Special Studies—Employment of Negro Troops* (Washington, DC: U.S. Army Center of Military History, 1966), 670.

19. *Three Inch Fury: 614 Tank Destroyers WWII*, 23.

20. Harry Yeide, *Tank Killers: A History of America's World War II Tank Destroyer Force* (Havertown, PA: Casemate, 2007), 232–233.

21. General Orders Number 59; Headquarters, 103rd Infantry Division; 15 February 1945. Records of the Adjutant General's Office; Record Group 407; National Archives and Records Administration, College Park, Maryland.

22. Lee, 672.

23. General Orders Number 100; Headquarters, 103rd Infantry Division; 6 April 1945. Records of the Adjutant General's Office; Record Group 407; National Archives and Records Administration, College Park, Maryland.

24. General Orders Number 142; Headquarters, 103rd Infantry Division; 23 May 1945. Records of the Adjutant General's Office; Record Group 407; National Archives and Records Administration, College Park, Maryland.

25. *Three Inch Fury: 614 Tank Destroyers WWII*, 33.

26. Stanton, 334.

27. Ibid., 336.

28. Route of Travel and Dates; Headquarters, 679th Tank Destroyer Battalion; Dwight D. Eisenhower Presidential Library, Abilene, Kansas.

29. Donald McGrayne, Report on Special Missions Fired by 697th Tank Destroyer Battalion. Records of the Adjutant General's Office; Record Group 407; National Archives and Records Administration, College Park, Maryland.

30. Stanton, 336.

31. History of the 827th Tank Destroyer Battalion. Records of the Adjutant General's Office; Record Group 407; National Archives and Records Administration, College Park, Maryland.

32. Lee, 487.

33. History of the 827th Tank Destroyer Battalion.

34. Stanton, 337.

35. Lee, 679.

36. Ibid., 679–680.

37. Ibid., 680–681.

38. Ibid., 681.

39. Unit history, 827th Tank Destroyer Battalion, 15 February 1945. Records of the Adjutant General's Office; Record Group 407; National Archives and Records Administration, College Park, Maryland.

40. CPT Louis Brescia and 1LT Bernard J. Winter were killed, while CPT Frank O. Caw, CPT Douglas H. Sullivan, 1LT Gerald R. Gamble, 1LT Lincoln C. McNeil, 1LT Harold E. Rosenbaum, 2LT Arthur L. Kelly, 2LT Grant Sourenian, and 2LT Orville K. Teske were wounded. Roster of officers, 827th Tank Destroyer Battalion, 31 January 1945. Records of the Adjutant General's Office; Record Group 407; National Archives and Records Administration, College Park, Maryland.

41. General Orders Number 11; Headquarters, 79th Infantry Division; 19 January 1945. Records of the Adjutant General's Office; Record Group 407; National Archives and Records Administration, College Park, Maryland.

42. Lee, 686.

43. Stanton, 337.

Notes for Chapter 9

1. Richard E. Miller, *Messman Chronicles: African Americans in the U.S. Navy, 1932–1943* (Annapolis, MD: US Naval Institute Press, 2004), 287–288.

2. Ibid., 310–311.

3. U.S. Department of the Navy, *Negro in the Navy in World War II* (Washington, DC: Navy Department, 1947), 8.

4. *Negro in the Navy in World War II*, 9.

5. Chief Petty Officers are the most senior NCOs in the Navy. They are roughly equivalent to a master sergeants and sergeants major in the Army.

6. Frank A. Blazich, Jr., "Building for a Nation and Equality: African American Seabees in World War II," accessed 13 April 2020, https://seabeemagazine.navylive.dodlive.mil/2014/03/06/building-for-a-nation-and-equality-African American-seabees-in-world-war-ii/.

7. Ibid.

8. Petty Officers were NCOs junior to CPOs. Petty Officer, 1st Class, was equivalent to an Army technical sergeant. Petty Officer, 2nd Class, was equivalent to an Army staff sergeant. Petty Officer, 3rd Class, was equivalent to an Army sergeant.

9. Blazich, "Building for a Nation and Equality."

10. Ibid.

11. Ronald K. Culp, *First Black United States Marines: The Men of Montford Point, 1942–1946* (Jefferson, NC: McFarland, 2007), 184.

12. Blazich, "Building for a Nation and Equality."
13. Mary P. Kelly, *Proudly We Served: The Men of the USS Mason* (Annapolis, MD: U.S. Naval Institute Press, 1995), 55.
14. Ibid., 56.
15. Ibid., 67.
16. Ibid., 91, 94.
17. Ibid., 99–100.
18. Ibid., 119–121.
19. Ibid., 153–154.
20. See: William Veigele, *PC Patrol Craft of World War II: A History of the Ships and their Crews* (Santa Barbara, CA: Astral, 2003).
21. Eric Purdon, *Black Company: The Story of Subchaser 1264* (Annapolis, MD: U.S. Naval Institute Press, 2000), 38.
22. Purdon, 41–43.
23. Veigele, 363.
24. Purdon, 127.
25. Ibid., 247.
26. The rationale for why the remaining three members of the initial group were not commissioned has never been sufficiently explained. Augustus Alves, Lewis Williams, and J. B. Pinkney stayed in the enlisted ranks for the remainder of their service. It has been suggested that the Navy considered them too radical in their racial outlook. See: Dan C. Goldberg, *Golden 13: How Black Men Won the Right to Wear Navy Gold* (Boston, MA: Beacon Press, 2020).
27. All were commissioned as limited duty officers, which did not limit their authority as officers, but rather restricted their career progression and generally meant they could never command a ship.
28. The ensigns were Jesse W. Arbor, Phillip G. Barnes, Samuel E. Barnes, Dalton L. Baugh, George C. Cooper, Reginald E. Goodwin, James E. Hair, Graham E. Martin, Dennis D. Nelson II, John W. Reagan, Frank E. Sublett, Jr., and William S. White. Charles B. Lear was appointed a warrant officer.
29. These officers were Lieutenant Junior Grade (LTJG) James R. Brown, Chaplain Corps; LTJG Thomas Parham, Jr., Chaplain Corps; Lieutenant Edward Hope, Civil Engineer Corps; LTJG Joseph Williams, Civil Engineer Corps; LTJG Ivan Fraser, Medical Corps; LTJG Cyril Jones, Medical Corps; LTJG Bernard Robinson, Medical Corps; LTJG Arthur Thompson, Medical Corps; LTJG Thomas Watkins, Jr., Medical Corps; LTJG Ulysses Wharton, Medical Corps; Ensign (ENS) Marron

Fort, Supply Corps; ENS Kenneth Robinson, Supply Corps; and ENS Giles Smith, Supply Corps. In addition, three African Americans were directly appointed as warrant officers: Louis Johnson, Boatswain; Sidney Smith, Machinist; and Willie Powell, Supply Corps. Dennis D. Nelson, *Integration of the Negro into the Navy, 1776–1947* (New York: Farrar, Straus, and Young, 1951), 229–230.

30. See: Paul Stillwell, ed., *Golden Thirteen: Recollections of the First Black Naval Officers* (Annapolis, MD: U.S. Naval Institute Press, 1993).

31. In addition to Gravely, twenty-eight other African Americans completed the V-12 program and were commissioned ensigns in the Navy during World War II. Nelson, 230–231.

32. See: Samuel L. Gravely, Jr., *Trailblazer: The U.S. Navy's First Black Admiral* (Annapolis, MD: Naval Institute Press, 2010).

33. Naval History and Heritage Command, "Port Chicago Naval Magazine Explosion, 17 July 1944," accessed 20 April 2020, https://www.history.navy.mil/content/history/nhhc/browse-by-topic/wars-conflicts-and-operations/world-war-ii/1944/port-chicago.html.

34. "Port Chicago Naval Magazine Explosion, 17 July 1944."

35. Robert L. Allen, *Port Chicago Mutiny* (New York: Warner Books, 1989), 75–88.

36. Ibid., 90–91.

37. Ibid., 127.

38. Ibid., 133–134.

39. Richard Goldstein, "Freddie Meeks, 83, Ex-Sailor Who Was Pardoned, Dies," *New York Times* (30 June 2003), accessed 21 April 2020, https://www.nytimes.com/2003/06/30/us/freddie-meeks-83-ex-sailor-who-was-pardoned-dies.html.

Notes for Chapter 10

1. U.S. Coast Guard Historian's Office, "African Americans in the U.S. Coast Guard: A Historical Chronology," accessed 6 April 2020, https://www.history.uscg.mil/Browse-by-Topic/Notable-People/Minorities/African Americans/African American-Chronology/.

2. Morris J. MacGregor, Jr., *Integration of the Armed Forces, 1940–1965* (Washington, DC: U.S. Army Center for Military History, 1989), 112.

3. The "ownership" of the Coast Guard has changed hands a few times. The service remained with the Department of the Treasury from its

origins until 1 April 1967 when it moved to the Department of Transportation. Then on 1 March 2003, the Coast Guard transferred to the Department of Homeland Security.

4. MacGregor, 99.

5. While this duty might seem a waste of manpower or an effort to create make-work for African Americans, there were more than one German attempts to land spies on American soil. See: Michael Dobbs, *Saboteurs: The Nazi Raid on America* (New York: Knopf, 2004).

6. MacGregor, 114.

7. Ibid., 116.

8. Ibid., 119.

9. Bernard C. Nalty and Morris J. MacGregor, *Blacks in the Military: Essential Documents* (Wilmington, DE: Scholarly Resources, 1981), 164.

10. Glenn A. Knoblock, *African American World War II Casualties and Decorations in the Navy, Coast Guard and Merchant Marine: A Comprehensive Record* (Jefferson, NC: McFarland, 2009), 402–403.

11. NavSource Online: Patrol Frigate Photo Archive, USS *Hoquiam* (PF 5), accessed 6 April 2020, http://www.navsource.org/archives/12/08005.htm.

12. MacGregor, 121.

13. Knoblock, 402.

14. Nalty and MacGregor, 165.

15. While Jenkins is generally credited as the first African American commissioned officer in Coast Guard history, he is technically only the first in the 20th century. During the 19th century, an African American man named Michael Healy served as an officer of the USRCS. However, Healy, the son of a white plantation owner and a black slave, was light skinned and self-identified as Irish, like his father, rather than African American like his mother. No one in the USRCS was aware of his African heritage and he might not have been able to earn a commission had it been known. Healy was highly respected in the USRCS and eventually achieved the rank of captain. See: Dennis L. Noble and Truman R. Strobridge, *Captain "Hell Roaring" Mike Healy: From American Slave to Arctic Hero* (Gainesville: University Press of Florida, 2017).

16. U.S. Coast Guard Historian's Office, "African Americans in the U.S. Coast Guard," accessed 6 April 2020, https://www.history.uscg.mil/Browse-by-Topic/Notable-People/Minorities/African Americans/.

17. William H. Thiesen, "Long Blue Line: Coast Guard Officers Jenkins and Russell—Trailblazers of Ethnic Diversity in the American Sea Services," accessed 22 June 2020, https://coastguard.dodlive.mil/2017/02/the-long-blue-line-coast-guard-officers-jenkins-and-russell/.

18. Again similar to the case with Jenkins, Samuels was only the first African American to command a Coast Guard vessel if you do not take into account Captain Michael Healy.

19. Truman Strobridge and Joseph Grecco, "Black Trailblazer Has Colorful Past," *Commandant's Bulletin*, Number 7-75 (14 February 1975), 11–12, accessed 6 April 2020, https://www.history.uscg.mil/Browse-by-Topic/Notable-People/Minorities/AfricanAmericans/AfricanAmerican-Chronology/Black-Trailblazer-has-Colorful-Past/.

20. MacGregor, 122.

21. Thiesen, "Long Blue Line: Coast Guard Officers Jenkins and Russell."

22. U.S. Coast Guard Historian's Office, "Notable People: Chief Journalist Alexander Palmer Haley, 1921–1992," accessed 26 June 2020, https://www.history.uscg.mil/Browse-by-Topic/Notable-People/All/Article/1857333/chief-journalist-alexander-palmer-haley/.

23. Naval History and Heritage Command, "USS *Murzim*," accessed 26 June 2020, https://www.history.Navy.mil/research/histories/ship-histories/danfs/m/murzim.html.

24. U.S. Coast Guard Historian's Office, "Notable People: Chief Journalist Alexander Palmer Haley, 1921–1992."

25. MacGregor, 122.

Notes for Chapter 11

1. Benjamin O. Davis, Jr., *Benjamin O. Davis, Jr., American: An Autobiography* (Washington, DC: Smithsonian Institution Press, 1991), 16–20.

2. John E. Barlow, ed., *Howitzer* (West Point, NY: U.S. Military Academy, 1936), 112.

3. Davis, 55–64.

4. Ibid., 65.

5. Ibid., 65–67.

6. Maurer Maurer, *Combat Squadrons of the Air Force in World War II* (Washington, DC: Office of Air Force History, 1982), 329.

7. Davis, 84.

8. On 28 February 1942, President Franklin D. Roosevelt signed Executive Order 9082 which established the Army Air Forces, Army Ground

Forces, and Services of Supply (later renamed Army Service Forces) to provide a modern organization structure for the U.S. Army.

9. Davis, 90.

10. Ultimately, in addition to Cassagnol, five other Haitians were trained as pilots at Tuskegee—Ludovic Audant, Philippe Célestin, Eberle J. Guilbaud, Nicolas Pelissier, and Alix Pasquet. Lynn M. Homan and Thomas Reilly, *Black Knights: The Story of the Tuskegee Airmen* (Gretna, LA: Pelican Publishing, 2006), 278.

11. See: Daniel Haulman, "Noel Parrish: A White Tuskegee Airman" (Maxwell AFB, AL: Air Force Historical Research Agency, 2017).

12. Since he was not dishonorably discharged, Colman was eligible for a pension at the rate of 37.5 percent of the active duty pay of a captain. In November 1954, Colman applied to the Air Force Board for Correction of Military Records and asked for promotion to lieutenant colonel on the retired list and granted the pension of a lieutenant colonel. The Board concluded he was ineligible for retirement at the grade of lieutenant colonel, but agreed to promote him to the rank of major. On 19 July 1961, Colman's appeal of the Air Force Board's decision reached the U.S. Court of Claims. The Court sided with the Air Force board. William T. Colman v. United States, 292 F.2d 283 (Ct. Cl. 1961), U.S. Court of Claims, 19 July 1961 (Rehearing Denied 4 October 1961).

13. Hall left active duty as a major and became a civilian employee of the U.S. Air Force, working at Tinker Air Force Base, Oklahoma, and later for the Federal Aviation Administration.

14. Davis, 100.

15. Daniel L. Haulman, *Tuskegee Airmen Chronology: A Detailed Timeline of the Red Tails and Other Black Pilots of World War II* (Montgomery, AL: NewSouth Books, 2017), 46.

16. His unfair assessment of the 99th Fighter Squadron was far from the last controversy of Momyer's career. He frequently clashed with superiors and was well known for almost completely shutting out the input of subordinates. He often developed a dislike for certain individuals for no apparent reason. Most famously, he expressed contempt for both Chuck Yeager and Robin Olds and tried to prevent both of their promotions to brigadier general. Momyer eventually attained the rank of "four star" or full general and became the commander of the Tactical Air Command for his final five years on active duty before retiring in 1973. Walter J. Boyne, "Momyer" *Air Force Magazine* 98:8 (August 2013), 64–65.

17. Alan M. Osur, *Blacks in the Army Air Forces During World War II: The Problem of Race Relations* (Washington, DC: Office of Air Force History, 1977), 48–49.

18. Ibid., 49.

19. Ibid., 50.

20. Davis, 105–106.

21. Osur, 51.

22. Roberts, one of the first five African American pilots in the U.S. Army, was nicknamed "Spanky" after the character in the "Our Gang" series of short films from the 1930s. He remained in the Air Force after the war, serving in the Korean and Vietnam Wars before retiring as a full colonel in 1968, accessed 12 October 2019, https://www.wvencyclopedia.org/articles/102.

23. Davis, 108.

24. Haulman, *Tuskegee Airmen Chronology,* 52.

25. Ibid., 49–50, 52–53.

26. Alan L. Gropman, *Air Force Integrates, 1945–1964* (Washington, DC: Office of Air Force History, 1985), 19.

27. Haulman, *Tuskegee Airmen Chronology*, 51.

28. While the P-47 was not the premier fighter of the United States during World War II, it was arguably the second best after the P-51. Equipped with a seemingly indestructible radial piston engine and eight .50 caliber Browning machine guns in the wings, the P-47 also had a large and comfortable armored cockpit. Over time the fighter was gradually recognized as a superior ground attack aircraft and added wing-mounted rockets to use against ground targets.

29. Davis, 118.

30. Ibid.

31. Daniel L. Haulman, "Twelve Greatest Air Battles of the Tuskegee Airmen" (Maxwell AFB, AL: Air Force Historical Research Agency, 2010), 3–5.

32. E. A. Munday, *Fifteenth Air Force Combat Markings, 1943–1945* (London, UK: Beaumont Publications, 1965) and email exchange with Dr. Daniel L. Haulman, 7 June 2019.

33. Haulman, *Tuskegee Airmen Chronology*, 85.

34. Ibid., 87–88.

35. Haulman, "Twelve Greatest Air Battles of the Tuskegee Airmen," 5–6.

36. Ibid., 6–8.

37. In 1947, Parrish was reassigned as a student to the Air Command and Staff College and then the next year to the Air War College. He wrote a thesis on the need for integration. In 1948, Parish moved to Washington, DC, and worked at Air Force Headquarters. In 1954, he was promoted to brigadier general and assigned North Atlantic Treaty Organization, but returned to the Pentagon in 1958. Parish was involved in controversy when he defended the Eisenhower Administration against the so-called missile gap accusations falsely leveled by Senator John F. Kennedy during the 1960 presidential campaign. As a result, he was reassigned to Air University at Maxwell Air Force Base in Alabama, where he spent the last few years of his career before retiring in 1964. In retirement, Parish earned master's and doctoral degrees in history from his alma mater Rice University and then taught military history at Trinity University in San Antonio, Texas. He died at Perry Point, Maryland, in 1987. See: Haulman, "Noel Parrish: A White Tuskegee Airman."

38. Haulman, *Tuskegee Airmen Chronology*, 127.

39. Daniel Haulman, "Tuskegee Airmen and the Never Lost a Bomber Myth" *Alabama Review* 64:1 (January 2011), 53–59.

40. Ibid., 30.

41. Ibid., 31.

42. Davis, 136–137.

43. Haulman, "Tuskegee Airmen and the Never Lost a Bomber Myth," 32–34.

44. Ibid., 60.

45. Haulman, "Twelve Greatest Air Battles of the Tuskegee Airmen," 11–12.

46. Daniel L. Haulman, "Legend of the African American Ace" (Maxwell AFB, AL: Air Force Historical Research Agency, 28 October 2010), 2.

47. Daniel L. Haulman, "112 Victories: Aerial Victory Credits of the Tuskegee Airmen" *American Aviation Historical Society Journal* (Fall 2008), 222–223.

48. Archer continued in the U.S. Air Force after its independence and retired as a lieutenant colonel in 1970.

49. Elsberry also continued in the Air Force and retired as a major.

50. Toppins died in 1946.

51. Haulman, "112 Victories: Aerial Victory Credits of the Tuskegee Airmen," 224.

52. Ibid., 223–224.

53. Haulman, "Twelve Greatest Air Battles of the Tuskegee Airmen", 13–14.

54. Haulman, *Tuskegee Airmen Chronology*, 127.

55. Ibid., 137–138.

56. Ibid., 138.

57. Gropman, 23.

58. J. Todd Moye, *Freedom Flyers: The Tuskegee Airmen of World War II* (Oxford University Press, 2010), 133, 135, 138.

59. Gropman, 25.

60. Ibid., 26.

61. Moye, *Freedom Flyers*, 141–142.

62. Despite the fact that a dishonorable discharge is largely seen as the equivalent of a felony conviction by civilian courts, Terry went on to have a very successful life after the Army. He graduated from law school and worked for the Los Angeles County prosecutor's office. In 1995, he was pardoned, refunded his $150, and received an honorable discharge. Haulman, *Tuskegee Airmen Chronology*, 170.

63. Gropman, 29.

64. Haulman, *Tuskegee Airmen Chronology*, 150.

65. Ibid., 152.

66. Daniel L. Haulman, "Tuskegee Airmen Chronology" (Maxwell AFB, AL: Air Force Historical Research Agency, 17 March 2016), 153–154.

Notes for Chapter 12

1. Ulysses Lee, *United States Army in World War II: Special Studies—Employment of Negro Troops* (Washington, DC: U.S. Army Center of Military History, 1966), 416.

2. Bell I. Wiley, *Training of Negro Troops*, Study No. 36 (Washington, DC: Historical Section, Army Ground Forces, 1946), 27.

3. Bernard C. Nalty and Morris J. MacGregor, *Blacks in the Military: Essential Documents* (Wilmington, DE: Scholarly Resources, 1981), 175.

4. Ibid., 175.

5. Ibid., 176–179.

6. Ibid., 179–182.

7. The other members of the word were MG Lewis A. Pick, BG Winslow C. Morse, and BG Alan D. Warnock. Pick, an engineer by training, served as the Chief Road Engineer in the China Burma India Theater during World War II, where he was largely responsible for

the successful construction of the Ledo Road, and later served as the U.S. Army's Chief of Engineers from 1949 to 1953, retiring as a lieutenant general. Morse, an air corps officer, commanded the Chinese American Composite Wing of the 14th Air Force during World War II and served in the Air Force until 1959. Warnock was the assistant division commander of the 5th Infantry Division during World War II. The choice of these four officers to be on the board appears to be completely random other than the fact that they represented the ASF, AAF, and AGF. None had any particular experience with or connection to African American soldiers to justify in any way any one of them being thought of as "experts."

8. Nalty and MacGregor, 194.
9. Ibid.
10. Ibid., 196–199.
11. Ibid., 199–201.
12. Ibid., 202.
13. Ibid., 203–206.
14. Daniel L. Haulman, *Tuskegee Airmen Chronology: A Detailed Timeline of the Red Tails and Other Black Pilots of World War II* (Montgomery, AL: NewSouth Books, 2017), 154–155.
15. Haulman, 159.
16. Ibid., 160.
17. Ibid., 163.
18. Nalty and MacGregor, 239.
19. See: Richard Gergel, *Unexampled Courage: The Blinding of Sgt. Isaac Woodard and the Awakening of President Harry S. Truman and Judge J. Waties Waring* (London, UK: Picador, 2019).
20. Truman K. Gibson, Jr., *Knocking Down Barriers: My Fight for Black America* (Evanston, IL: Northwestern University Press, 2005), 225.
21. The World War II draft ended on 31 March 1947, though no men were drafted in that year. Morris J. MacGregor, Jr., *Integration of the Armed Forces, 1940–1965* (Washington, DC: U.S. Army Center for Military History, 1989), 303.
22. MacGregor, 416
23. In 1945, African Americans made up 5.32 percent of the Navy. In 1946, the number went down to 5.07 percent. Followed by 4.82 percent in 1947, 4.91 percent in 1948, and 4.7 percent in 1949. Dennis D. Nelson, *Integration of the Negro into the Navy, 1776–1947* (New York: Farrar, Straus, and Young, 1951), 227.

24. Bernard C. Nalty, *Long Passage to Korea: Black Sailors and the Integration of the U.S. Navy* (Washington, DC: Naval Historical Center, 2003), 26–27.
25. The groups then recorded were White, Negro, American Indian, Filipino, Hawaiian, and Other.
26. See: Robert J. Schneller, Jr., *Breaking the Color Barrier: The U.S. Naval Academy's First Black Midshipmen and the Struggle for Racial Equality* (New York: New York University Press, 2005).
27. Haulman, 167.
28. MacGregor, 404.
29. Nalty and MacGregor, 309–310.
30. MacGregor, 458.
31. Nalty and MacGregor, 314.
32. Ibid., 318.
33. Ibid., 303.
34. MacGregor, 463.
35. COAST GUARD Compass, accessed 29 June 2020, https://coastguard. dodlive.mil/2017/05/the-long-blue-line-merle-smith-the-first-african-american-graduate-of-the-coast-guard-academy/.

Bibliography

Primary Sources

Manuscript Collections

Alfred M. Gray Marine Corps Research Center. U.S. Marine Corps Base, Quantico, VA.

National Archives and Records Administration. Archives II, College Park, MD.

U.S. Air Force Historical Research Agency. Bolling Air Force Base, Washington, DC.

U.S. Army Center of Military History. Fort Lesley J. McNair, Washington, DC.

U.S. Army Military History Institute. Carlisle Barracks, Carlisle, PA.

U.S. Marine Corps Historical Center. Washington Navy Yard, Washington, DC.

U.S. Naval Historical Center. Washington Navy Yard, Washington, DC.

Unpublished Primary Sources

Barringer, Albert L. "Combat Operations of the 370th Regimental Combat Team, 92nd Infantry Division." Fort Benning, GA: Infantry School, 1953.

Eddy, Robert N. "Operations of the 2nd Battalion (Reinforced), 25th Infantry (93rd Infantry Division) as a Part of a Pursuing Force on Bougainville, 2–4 April 1944 (North Solomons Campaign) (Personal Experience of a Regimental S-2)." Fort Benning, GA: Infantry School, 1950.

Hyssong, Glyde L. "Combat Experience of Negro Troop Units." Memo for Chief of Staff, Army Ground Forces, 9 March 1944.

Mack, Stephen B. "Policy for the Utilization of Negro Troops in the Armed Forces." Fort Leavenworth, KS: U.S. Army Command and General Staff College, 1946.

Parrish, Noel. *Segregation of Negroes in the Army Air Forces*. Master's Thesis, U.S. Air Force Air Command and Staff College, 1947.

"Opinions About Negro Infantry Platoons in White Companies of Seven Divisions." Washington, DC: HQ Army Service Forces, 3 July 1945.

Skinner, Carlton. "U.S.S. Sea Cloud, IX-99, Racial Integration for Naval Efficiency." 1949.

"Utilization of Negro Infantry Platoons in White Companies." HQ, ETO: Research Branch, Information and Education Division, June 1945.

Published Primary Sources

American Battlefield Monuments Commission. *American Armies and Battlefields in Europe: A History, Guide, and Reference Book.* Washington, DC: Government Printing Office, 1938.

Anderson, Trezzvant W. *Come Out Fighting: The Epic Tale of the 761st Tank Battalion, 1942–45.* Salzburg, Austria: Salzburger Druckerei und Verlag, 1945.

Baker, Vernon J. *Lasting Valor.* Columbus, MS: Genesis Press, 1997.

Berhow, Mark A., ed. *American Seacoast Defenses: A Reference Guide.* Bel Air, MD: CDSG Press, 1999.

Biggs, Bradley. *Triple Nickles: America's First All-Black Paratroop Unit.* Hamden, CT: Archon Books, 1986.

Blackford, Mansel G., ed. *Board the USS Mason: The World War II Diary of James A. Dunn.* Columbus, OH: Ohio State University Press, 1996.

Bland, Larry I., ed. *Papers of George Catlett Marshall.* Volume 2: "We Cannot Delay," July 1, 1939–December 6, 1941. Baltimore, MD: Johns Hopkins University Press, 1986.

———, ed. *Papers of George Catlett Marshall.* Volume 4: "Aggressive and Determined Leadership," June 1, 1943–December 31, 1944. Baltimore, MD: Johns Hopkins University Press, 1996.

———, ed. *Papers of George Catlett Marshall.* Volume 5: "Finest Soldier," January 1, 1945-January 7, 1947. Baltimore, MD: Johns Hopkins University Press, 2003.

Brokaw, Tom. *Greatest Generation.* New York: Random House, 1998.

———. *Greatest Generation Speaks: Letters and Reflections.* New York: Random House, 1999.

Brooke, Edward W. *Bridging the Divide: My Life.* New Brunswick, NJ: Rutgers University Press, 2007.

Byers, Jean. *Study of the Negro in Military Service.* Washington, DC: Department of Defense, 1950.

Chandler, Alfred D., Jr. *Papers of Dwight D. Eisenhower.* Volume IV: The War Years. Baltimore, MD: Johns Hopkins University, 1970.

Clay, Steven E. *U.S. Army Order of Battle, 1919–1941.* Four Volumes. Fort Leavenworth, KS: Combat Studies Institute Press, 2010.

Davis, Benjamin O., Jr. *Benjamin O. Davis, Jr.: American.* Washington, DC: Smithsonian Institution Press, 1991.

Dobak, William A. *Freedom by the Sword: The U.S. Colored Troops, 1862–1867.* Washington, DC: U.S. Army Center of Military History, 2011.

Fahy, Charles, et al. *Freedom to Serve: Equality of Treatment and Opportunity in the Armed Services: A Report by the President's Committee.* Washington, DC: Government Printing Office, 1950.

Gibson, Truman K., Jr. *Knocking Down Barriers: My Fight for Black America.* Evanston, IL: Northwestern University Press, 2005.

Gillie, Mildred H. *Forging the Thunderbolt: A History of the Development of the Armored Force.* Harrisburg PA: Military Service Publishing Company, 1947.

Gravely, Samuel L., Jr. *Reminiscences of Vice Admiral Samuel L. Gravely, Jr., U.S. Navy (Retired).* Annapolis, MD: Naval Institute Press, 2003.

Greenfield, Kent R., et al. *Organization of Ground Combat Troops.* Washington, DC: U.S. Army Center of Military History, 1947.

Gropman, Alan L. *Air Force Integrates, 1945–1964.* Washington, DC: Office of Air Force History, 1978.

Haulman, Daniel L. *Tuskegee Airmen Chronology: A Detailed Timeline of the Red Tails and Other Black Pilots of World War II.* Montgomery, AL: NewSouth Books, 2017.

Historical and Pictorial Review of the National Guard and Naval Militia of the State of Illinois. Baton Rouge, LA: Army and Navy Publishing, 1940.

Historical Committee, 92nd Infantry Division. *With the 92d Infantry Division, October 1942 June 1945.* Information-Education Section, Mediterranean Theater of Operations, 1945.

Kelly, Mary P. *Proudly We Served: The Men of the USS Mason.* Annapolis, MD: U.S. Naval Institute Press, 1995.

Lee, John W., Jr. *Reminiscences of Lieutenant Commander John W. Lee, Jr., U.S. Navy (Retired).* Annapolis, MD: Naval Institute Press, 1994.

Lee, Ulysses. *United States Army in World War II: Special Studies— Employment of Negro Troops.* Washington, DC: U.S. Army Center of Military History, 1966.

MacGregor, Morris J., Jr. *Integration of the Armed Forces, 1940–1965.* Washington, DC: U.S. Army Center for Military History, 1989.

Maurer, Maurer. *Air Force Combat Units of World War II.* Washington, DC: Office of Air Force History, 1983.

———. *Combat Squadrons of the Air Force, World War II.* Washington, DC: Office of Air Force History, 1982.

Nalty, Bernard C. *Right to Fight: African-American Marines in World War II.* Washington, DC: Marine Corps Historical Center, 1995.

Nalty, Bernard C., and Morris J. MacGregor. *Blacks in the Military: Essential Documents.* Wilmington, DE: Scholarly Resources, 1981.

Office of the Deputy Assistant Secretary of Defense for Civilian Personnel Policy and Equal Opportunity. *Black Americans in Defense of Our Nation.* Washington, DC: Government Printing Office, 1982.

Osur, Alan M. *Blacks in the Army Air Forces During World War II: The Problem of Race Relations.* Washington, DC: Office of Air Force History, 1977.

————. *Separate and Unequal: Race Relations in the Army Air Forces during World War II.* Washington, DC: Air Force History and Museums Program, 2000.

Owens, Emiel W. *Blood on German Snow: An African American Artilleryman in World War II and Beyond.* College Station, TX: Texas A&M University Press, 2006.

Palmer, Robert R., et al. *Procurement and Training of Ground Combat Troops.* Washington, DC: U.S. Army Center of Military History, 1948.

Purdon, Eric. *Black Company: The Story of Subchaser 1264.* Annapolis, MD: U.S. Naval Institute Press, 2000.

Rottman, Gordon L. *U.S. Marine Corps World War II Order of Battle: Ground and Air Units in the Pacific War, 1939–1945.* Westport, CT: Greenwood Press, 2002.

Sawicki, James A. *Cavalry Regiments of the U.S. Army.* Dumfries, VA: Wyvern Publications, 1985.

————. *Field Artillery Battalions of the U.S. Army.* Two Volumes. Dumfries, VA: Centaur Publications, 1977–78.

————. *Infantry Regiments of the U.S. Army.* Dumfries, VA: Wyvern Publications, 1981.

————. *Tank Battalions of the U.S. Army.* Dumfries, VA: Wyvern Publications, 1983.

Shaw, Henry I., Jr., and Ralph W. Donnelly. *Blacks in the Marine Corps.* Washington, DC: Marine Corps History and Museums Division, 1975.

Slonaker, John. *U.S. Army and the Negro.* Carlisle Barracks, PA: U.S. Army Military Research Collection, 1971.

Smith, Steven D., and James A. Ziegler, Eds. *Historic Context for the African-American Military Experience.* Champaign, IL: U.S. Army Construction Engineering Research Laboratories, 1998.

Stanton, Shelby L. *World War II Order of Battle.* New York: Galahad Books, 1984.

Stillwell, Paul, ed. *Golden Thirteen: Recollections of the First Black Naval Officers.* Annapolis, MD: U.S. Naval Institute Press, 1993.

Stubbs, Mary L., and Stanley R. Connor. *Armor-Cavalry*, Part I: *Regular Army and Army Reserve*. Washington, DC: U.S. Army Center of Military History, 1969.

Three Inch Fury: 614 Tank Destroyers WWII. Germany: privately published, c.1945.

Trice, Frasia D., and Thurlow B. Simons, Eds. *Thirty-Fourth U.S. Naval Construction Battalion*. San Francisco, CA: Schwabacher-Frey, 1946.

U.S. Army. *Pictorial History, Three Hundred Sixty-Sixth Infantry, 1941*. Fort Devens, MA: n.p., 1941.

U.S. Army. *Pictorial history, Forty-Sixth Field Artillery Brigade, 1942*. Camp Livingston, LA: n.p., 1942.

U.S. Army Service Forces. *Leadership and the Negro Soldier*. Army Service Forces Manual M5. Washington, DC: Government Printing Office, 1944.

U.S. Department of Defense. *Black Americans in Defense of Our Nation: A Pictorial Documentary of the Black American Males and Female Participation and Involvement in the Military Affairs of the United States of America*. Washington, DC: Government Printing Office, 1991.

U.S. Department of Defense. *Integration and the Negro Officer in the Armed Forces of the United States of America*. Washington, DC: Department of Defense, 1962.

U.S. Department of Defense. *Negro Officer in the Armed Forces of the United States of America*. Washington, DC: Department of Defense, 1960.

U.S. Department of the Navy. *Guide to Command of Negro Naval Personnel*. Washington, DC: Bureau of Naval Personnel, 1945.

U.S. Department of the Navy. *Negro in the Navy in World War II*. Washington, DC: Navy Department, 1947.

U.S. Department of War. *Command of Negro Troops*. Pamphlet No. 20-6. Washington, DC: Government Printing Office, 1944.

U.S. Department of War. *Utilization of Negro Manpower in the Postwar Army Policy*. Circular No. 124. Washington, DC: Government Printing Office, 1946.

U.S. Director of Selective Service. *Selective Service and Victory*. Washington, DC: Government Printing Office, 1948.

Webb, Howard E., ed. *Seabees Log of the Cruise: 80th USN Construction Battalion, 1943–1944*. Providence, RI: Blackford Engraving and Electrotype, 1944.

Wiley, Bell I. *Training of Negro Troops*. Study No. 36. Washington, DC: Historical Section, Army Ground Forces, 1946.

Wilson, John B. *Maneuver and Firepower: The Evolution of Divisions and Separate Brigades*. Washington, DC: U.S. Army Center of Military History, 1998.

———. *Armies, Corps, Divisions, and Separate Brigades*. Washington, DC: U.S. Army Center of Military History, 1999.

Secondary Sources

General Works

Alt, William E., and Betty L. Alt. *Black Soldiers, White Wars: Black Warriors from Antiquity to the Present*. Westport, CT: Praeger Publishers, 2002.

Astor, Gerald. *Right to Fight: A History of African-Americans in the Military*. Novato, CA: Presidio Press, 1998.

Bielakowski, Alexander M., ed. *Encyclopedia of Ethnic and Racial Minorities in the U.S. Military*. Two Volumes. Santa Barbara, CA: ABC-CLIO, 2013.

Binkin, Martin, and Mark J. Eitelberg. *Blacks in the Military*. Washington, DC: Brookings Institution, 1982.

Buckley, Gail L. *American Patriots: The Story of Blacks in the Military from the Revolution to Desert Storm*. New York: Random House, 2001.

Davis, Lenwood G., and George Hill. *Blacks in the American Armed Forces, 1776–1983: A Bibliography*. Westport, CT: Greenwood Press, 1985.

Dalfiume, Richard M. *Desegregation of the U.S. Armed Forces: Fighting on Two Fronts, 1939–1953*. Columbia, MO: University of Missouri Press, 1969.

Edgerton, Robert B. *Hidden Heroism: Black Soldiers in America's Wars*. Boulder, CO: Westview Press, 2001.

Ferrell, Robert H. *Unjustly Dishonored: An African American Division in World War I*. Columbia, MO: University of Missouri, 2011.

Field, Ron, and Alexander M. Bielakowski. *Buffalo Soldiers: African American Troops in the US Forces 1866–1945*. Oxford, UK: Osprey Publishing, 2008.

Gergel, Richard. *Unexampled Courage: The Blinding of Sgt. Isaac Woodard and the Awakening of President Harry S. Truman and Judge J. Waties Waring*. London, UK: Picador, 2019.

Goodwin, Doris K. *No Ordinary Time—Franklin and Eleanor Roosevelt: The Home Front in World War II*. New York: Simon and Schuster, 1995.

Greene, Robert E. *Black Defenders of America, 1775–1973: A Reference and Pictorial History*. Chicago, IL: Johnson Publishing, 1974.

Halberstam, David. *Coldest Winter: America and the Korean War*. New York: Hyperion, 2007.

Hanna, Charles W. *African American Recipients of the Medal of Honor: A Biographical Dictionary, Civil War Through Vietnam War*. Jefferson, NC: McFarland, 2002.

Hawkins, Walter L. *African American Generals and Flag Officers: Biographies of Over 120 Blacks in the United States Military*. Jefferson, NC: McFarland, 1993.

————. *Black American Military Leaders: A Biographical Dictionary*. Jefferson, NC: McFarland, 2007.

Hogg, Ian V. *Encyclopedia of Infantry Weapons of World War II*. London: Saturn Books, 1977.

Johnson, Charles. *African Americans and ROTC: Military, Naval and Aeroscience Programs at Historically Black Colleges, 1916 to 1973*. Jefferson, NC: McFarland, 2002.

————. *African American Soldiers in the National Guard: Recruitment and Deployment During Peacetime and War*. Westport, CT: Greenwood Press, 1992.

Johnson, John L. *Every Night and Every Morn: Portraits of Asian, Hispanic, Jewish, African-American, and Native-American Recipients of the Congressional Medal of Honor*. Winston-Salem, NC: Tristan Press, 2007.

Jordan, James F. "Triple Nickels: A Genesis for Change." U.S. Army War College Military Studies Program Paper, March 1990.

Krebs, Ronald R. *Fighting for Rights: Military Service and the Politics of Citizenship*. Ithaca, NY: Cornell University Press, 2006.

Lanning, Michael L. *African American Soldier: From Crispus Attucks to Colin Powell*. Secaucus, NJ: Carroll Publishing, 1997.

Latty, Yvonne, and Ron Tarver. *We Were There: Voices of African American Veterans, From World War II to the War in Iraq*. New York: Amistad, 2004.

McMillin, Woody. *In the Presence of Soldiers: The 2nd Army Maneuvers and Other World War II Activity in Tennessee*. Nashville, TN: Horton Heights Press, 2010.

Mershon, Sherie and Steven Schlossman. *Foxholes and Color Lines: Desegregating the U.S. Armed Forces*. Baltimore, MD: Johns Hopkins University Press, 1998.

Mahon, John K., and Romana Danysh. *Infantry, Part I: Regular Army*. Washington, DC: U.S. Army Center of Military History, 1972.

Nalty, Bernard C. *Strength for the Fight: A History of Black Americans in the Military*. New York: Free Press, 1986.

Patton, Gerald W. *War and Race: The Black Officer in the American Military, 1915–1941*. Westport, CT: Greenwood Press, 1981.

Putney, Martha S., ed. *Blacks in the United States Army: Portraits Through History*. Jefferson, NC: McFarland, 2003.

Reef, Catherine. *African Americans in the Military*. New York: Facts on File, 2004.

Salter, Krewasky A. *Combat Multipliers: African-American Soldiers in Four Wars*. Fort Leavenworth, KS: Combat Studies Institute Press, 2004.

———. *Story of Black Military Officers, 1861–1948*. New York: Routledge, 2014.

Sammons, Jeffrey T., and John H. Morrow, Jr. *Harlem's Rattlers and the Great War: The Undaunted 369th Regiment and the African American Quest for Equality*. Lawrence: University Press of Kansas, 2014

Stillman, Richard J. *Integration of the Negro in the U.S. Armed Forces*. New York: Praeger Publishers, 1968.

Sutherland, Jonathan. *African Americans at War: An Encyclopedia*. Santa Barbara, CA: ABC-Clio, 2003.

Weir, William. *Encyclopedia of African American Military History*. Amherst, NY: Prometheus Books, 2004.

Williams, Albert E. *Black Warriors: Unique Units and Individuals*. Haverford, PA: Infinity Publishing, 2003.

Wright, Kai. *Soldiers of Freedom: An Illustrated History of African Americans in the Armed Forces*. New York: Black Dog and Leventhal Publishers, 2002.

Pre–World War II

Barbeau, Arthur E., and Florette Henri. *Unknown Soldiers: African-American Troops in World War I*. New York: Da Capo Press, 1996.

Beattie, Taylor V. "Corporal Freddie Stowers: An Appointment with Eternity on Hill 188." *Army History: The Professional Bulletin of Army History*, No. 57 (Winter 2003): 14–20.

Christian, Garna L. *Black Soldiers in Jim Crow Texas, 1899–1917*. College Station, TX: Texas A&M University Press, 1995.

Cimprich, John. *Fort Pillow: A Civil War Massacre, and Public Memory*. Baton Rouge: Louisiana State University Press, 2005.

Egerton, Douglas R. *Death or Liberty: African Americans and Revolutionary America*. Oxford, UK: Oxford University Press, 2009.

Fowler, Arlen L. *Black Infantry in the West, 1869–1891*. Norman: University of Oklahoma Press, 1996.

Griffith, Robert K., Jr. *Men Wanted for the U.S. Army: America's Experience with an All-Volunteer Army Between the World Wars*. Westport, CT: Greenwood Press, 1982.

Haynes, Robert V. *Night of Violence: The Houston Riot of 1917*. Baton Rouge: Louisiana State University Press, 1976.

Hess, Earl J. *Into the Crater: The Mine Attack at Petersburg*. Columbia: University of South Carolina Press, 2010.

Leckie, William H. *Buffalo Soldiers: A Narrative of the Negro Cavalry in the West*. Norman: University of Oklahoma Press, 1967.

Mjagkij, Nina. *Loyalty in Time of Trial: The African American Experience During World War I*. New York: Rowman and Littlefield Publishers, 2011.

Noble, Dennis L., and Truman R. Strobridge. *Captain "Hell Roaring" Mike Healy: From American Slave to Arctic Hero*. Gainesville: University Press of Florida, 2009.

O'Toole, James M. *Passing for White: Race, Religion, and the Healy Family, 1820–1920*. Boston: University of Massachusetts Press, 2002.

———. "Racial Identity and the Case of Captain Michael Healy, USRCS." *Prologue* 29, no. 3 (Fall 1997): 190–201.

Roberts, Frank E. *American Foreign Legion: Black Soldiers of the 93rd in World War I*. Annapolis, MD: Naval Institute Press, 2004.

Robinson, Charles M. *Fall of a Black Army Officer: Racism and the Myth of Henry O. Flipper*. Norman: University of Oklahoma Press, 2008.

Sammons, Jeffrey T., and John H. Morrow, Jr. *Harlem's Rattlers and the Great War: The Undaunted 369th Regiment and the African American Quest for Equality*. Lawrence: University Press of Kansas, 2014.

Shellum, Brian G. *African American Officers in Liberia: A Pestiferous Rotation, 1910–1942*. Lincoln: Potomac Books, 2018.

———. *Black Cadet in a White Bastion: Charles Young at West Point*. Lincoln: University of Nebraska Press, 2006.

———. *Black Officer in a Buffalo Soldier Regiment: The Military Career of Charles Young*. Lincoln: University of Nebraska Press, 2010.

Short, Steven. "Scraping the Barrel: African American Troops and World War I." In *Scraping the Barrel: The Military Use of Substandard Manpower, 1860–1960*, Editor Sanders Marble. New York: Fordham University Press, 2012.

Weaver, John D. *Brownsville Raid: The Story of America's "Black Dreyfus Affair."* New York: W.W. Norton, 1970.

———. *Senator and the Sharecropper's Son: Exoneration of the Brownsville Soldiers*. College Station: Texas A&M University Press, 1997.

Williams, Chad L. *Torchbearers of Democracy: African American Soldiers in the World War I Era*. Chapel Hill: University of North Carolina Press, 2010.

Zucchino, David. *Wilmington's Lie: The Murderous Coup of 1898 and the Rise of White Supremacy*. New York: Atlantic Monthly Press, 2020.

General Works on World War II

Atkins, Johnnie J. *Army as a Profession of Choice for Black Americans in World War II: Assessing the Impact on Future Force Structure*. Carlisle, PA: U.S. Army War College Strategy Research Project, 2001.

Atkinson, Rick. *Day of Battle: The War in Sicily and Italy, 1943–1944*. New York: Henry Holt, 2007.

Bielakowski, Alexander M. *African American Troops in World War II*. Oxford, UK: Osprey Publishing, 2007.

Buchanan, A. Russell. *Black Americans in World War II*. Santa Barbara, CA: Clio Books, 1977.

Brandt, Nat. *Harlem at War: The Black Experience in WWII*. Syracuse, NY: Syracuse University Press, 1996.

Bruscino, Thomas A. *Nation Forged in War: How World War II Taught Americans to Get Along*. Knoxville: University of Tennessee Press, 2010.

Carter, Allene G., and Robert L. Allen. *Honoring Sergeant Carter: Redeeming a Black World War II Hero's Legacy*. New York: Amistad Press, 2003.

Converse, Elliott V., III, et al. *Exclusion of Black Soldiers from the Medal of Honor in World War II*. Jefferson, NC: McFarland, 1997.

Cutrer, Thomas W., and T. Michael Parrish. *Doris Miller, Pearl Harbor, and the Birth of the Civil Rights Movement*. College Station: Texas A&M University Press, 2018.

Davis, David B. "World War II and Memory." *Journal of American History* 77, no. 3 (September 1990): 580–587.

Dobbs, Michael. *Saboteurs: The Nazi Raid on America*. New York: Knopf, 2004.

Duffy, Peter. *Double Agent: The First Hero of World War II and How the FBI Outwitted and Destroyed a Nazi Spy Ring*. New York: Scribner, 2015.

Finkle, Lee. *Forum for Protest: The Black Press During World War II*. Cranbury, NJ: Fairleigh Dickinson University Press, 1975.

Gabel, Christopher R. *U.S. Army GHQ Maneuvers of 1941*. Washington, DC: U.S. Army Center for Military History, 1992.

Gawne, Jonathan. *Spearheading D-Day: American Special Units in Normandy*. Paris, France: Histoire and Collections, 2011.

Hill, Robert A., et al, Eds. *FBI's RACON: Racial Conditions in the United States During World War II*. Boston, MA: Northeastern University Pres, 1995.

Killingray, David. "Africans and African-Americans in Enemy Hands." In *Prisoners-of-War and Their Captors in World War II*, Editors Bob Moore and Kent Fedorowich. Washington, DC: Berg Publishers, 1996.

Kryder, Daniel. *Divided Arsenal: Race and the American State During World War II*. New York: Cambridge University Press, 2000.

Mandelbaum, David G. *Soldier Groups and Negro Soldiers*. Los Angeles: University of California Press, 1952.

McGuire, Phillip. *He, Too, Spoke for Democracy: Judge Hastie, World War II, and the Black Soldier*. Westport, CT: Greenwood Press, 1988.

Moore, Christopher. *Fighting for America: Black Soldiers - The Unsung Heroes of World War II*. New York: Ballantine Books, 2005.

Motley, Mary P., ed. *Invisible Soldier: The Experience of the Black Soldier in World War II*. Detroit, MI: Wayne State University Press, 1975.

Mullen, Robert W. *Blacks in America's Wars: The Shift in Attitudes from the Revolutionary War to Vietnam*. New York: Monad Press, 1973.

Munday, E. A. *Fifteenth Air Force Combat Markings, 1943–1945*. London, UK: Beaumont Publications, 1965.

Ottley, Roi, and Mark A. Huddle, ed. *Roi Ottley's World War II: The Lost Diary of an African American Journalist*. Lawrence: University Press of Kansas, 2011.

Reynolds, David. *Rich Relations: The American Occupation of Britain, 1942–1945*. New York: Random House, 1995.

Rosenthal, Nicolas G. "Racism, Activism, and Opportunity: African Americans in the Military and on the Home Front." In Timothy C. Dowling, ed. *Personal Perspectives: World War II*. Santa Barbara, CA: ABC-CLIO, 2005.

Sandler, Stanley. "Homefront Battlefront: Military Racial Disturbances in the Zone of the Interior, 1941–1945." *War and Society* (October 1993): 101–15.

Silvera, John D. *Negro in World War II*. New York: Arno Press, 1969.

Sklaroff, Lauren R. "Constructing G.I. Joe Louis: Cultural Solutions to the 'Negro Problem' During World War II." *Journal of American History* (December 2002): 958–83.

Smith, Graham. *When Jim Crow Met John Bull: Black American Soldiers in World War II Britain*. New York: St. Martin's Press, 1987.

Stouffer, Samuel A., et al. *American Soldier*. 2 Volumes. Princeton, NJ: Princeton University Press, 1949.

Takaki, Ronald. *Double Victory: A Multicultural History of America in World War II*. New York: Little, Brown, 2000.

Terkel, Studs. *"Good War": An Oral History of World War Two*. New York: Pantheon, 1984.

Walker, Wilbert L. *We Are Men: Memoirs of World War II and Korean War*. Chicago, IL: Adams, 1972.

Wynn, Neil A. *The African American Experience during World War II*. New York: Rowman and Littlefield, 2011.

U.S. Army

Abdul-Jabbar, Kareem, and Anthony Walton. *Brothers in Arms: The Epic Story of the 761st Tank Battalion, WWII's Forgotten Heroes*. New York: Broadway Books, 2004.

Arnold, Thomas S. *Buffalo Soldiers: The 92nd Infantry Division and Reinforcements in World War II, 1942–1945*. Manhattan, KS: Sunflower University Press, 1991.

Booker, Bryan D. *African Americans in the United States Army in World War II*. Jefferson, NC: McFarland, 2008.

Callaway, Redman. *White Captain, Black Troops: Stories of World War II*. Kansas City, MO: Lowell Press, 1993.

Clark, Mark W. *Calculated Risk*. New York: Harper, 1950.

Colley, David P. *Blood for Dignity: The Story of the First Integrated Combat Unit in the U.S. Army*. New York: St. Martin's Press, 2003.

Copeland, Jeffrey S. *Inman's War: A Soldier's Story of Life in a Colored Battalion in World War II*. St. Paul, MN: Paragon House, 2006.

Cunningham, Roger D. "2nd Cavalry Division." *On Point: The Journal of Army History* 15 (Winter 2010): 22–25.

DiNicolo, Gina M. *Black Panthers: The 761st Tank Battalion and Patton's Drive on Germany*. Alexandria, VA; St. John's Press, 2016.

Fletcher, Marvin E. *America's First Black General: Benjamin O. Davis, Sr., 1880–1970*. Lawrence: University Press of Kansas, 1989.

Gabel, Christopher R. *Seek, Strike, and Destroy: U.S. Army Tank Destroyer Doctrine in World War II*. Fort Leavenworth, KS: Combat Studies Institute Press, 1985.

George, Denise, and Robert Child. *Lost Eleven: The Forgotten Story of Black American Soldiers Brutally Massacred in World War II*. New York: Caliber, 2017.

Gibran, Daniel K. *92nd Infantry Division and the Italian Campaign in World War II*. Jefferson, NC: McFarland, 2001.

Gill, Lonnie. *Tank Destroyer Forces: WWII*. Paducah, KY: Turner Publishing, 1992.

Goodman, Paul. *Fragment of Victory in Italy: The 92nd Infantry Division in World War II*. Nashville, TN: Battery Press, 1993.

Hargrove, Hondon B. *Buffalo Soldiers in Italy: Black Americans in World War II*. Jefferson, NC: McFarland, 1985.

Hervieux, Linda. *Forgotten: The Untold Story of D-Day's Black Heroes, At Home and At War*. New York: Harper, 2015.

Hornsby, Henry H. *Trey of Sevens*. Dallas, TX: Mathis, Van Nort, 1946.

Jefferson, Robert F. *Fighting for Hope: African American Troops of the 93rd Infantry Division in World War II and Postwar America*. Baltimore, MD: Johns Hopkins University Press, 2008.

Johnston, Carolyn. *My Father's War: Fighting with the Buffalo Soldiers in World War II*. Tuscaloosa: University of Alabama Press, 2012.

Johnson, Gerald K. "Black Soldier in the Ardennes." *Soldiers* 36 (February 1981): 16–19.

Kesting, Robert W. "Conspiracy to Discredit the Black Buffalos: The 92nd Infantry in World War II." *Journal of Negro History* 72 (Winter-Spring 1987): 1–19.

Knapp, George E. *Buffalo Soldiers at Fort Leavenworth in the 1930s and Early 1940s*. Fort Leavenworth, KS: Combat Studies Institute Press, 1991.

Lankford, James R. "Battling Segregation and the Nazis: The Origins and Combat History of CCR Rifle Company, 14th Armored Division." *Army History* no. 63 (Winter 2007): 26–40.

———. "Gamecocks at War: The 614th Tank Destroyer Battalion." Unpublished article, 14th Armored Division Association.

Lanning, Michael L. *Court-Martial of Jackie Robinson: The Baseball Legend's Battle for Civil Rights during World War II*. Mechanicsburg, PA: Stackpole Books, 2020.

Lynch, Michael E. *Edward M. Almond and the U.S. Army: From the 92nd Infantry Division to the X Corps*. Lexington: University Press of Kentucky, 2019.

McGuire, Phillip, ed. *Taps for a Jim Crow Army: Letters from Black Soldiers in World War II*. Santa Barbara, CA: ABC-Clio, 1983.

Morehouse, Maggi M. *Fighting in the Jim Crow Army: Black Men and Women Remember World War II*. Lanham, MD: Rowman and Littlefield, 2000.

O'Donnell, Patrick K. *Beyond Valor: World War II's Ranger and Airborne Veterans Reveal the Heart of Combat.* New York: Free Press, 2001.

Palmer, Annette. "Politics of Race and War: Black American Soldiers in the Caribbean Theater During the Second World War." *Military Affairs* 47, no. 2 (April 1983): 59–62.

Parks, Robert J. "Development of Segregation in U.S. Army Hospitals, 1940–1942." *Military Affairs* 37:4 (December 1973): 145–50.

Robinson, Kevin L. "Triple Nickel: An Airborne Legacy." *Soldiers* 53 (February 1998): 18–19.

Russell, Harold E., Jr. *Company I, 366th Infantry.* Pittsburgh, PA: Rosedog Books, 2008.

Sasser, Charles W. *Patton's Panthers: The African-American 761st Tank Battalion in World War II.* New York: Pocket Books, 2004.

Shock, James R. *U.S. Army Barrage Balloon Program.* Bennington, VT: Merriam Press, 2006.

Stone, Tanya L. *Courage Has No Color: The True Story of the Triple Nickles—America's First Black Paratroopers.* Somerville, MA: Candlewick Press, 2013.

Truscott, Lucian K., Jr. *Command Missions: A Personal Story.* New York: Dutton, 1954.

Williams, David J. *Hit Hard.* New York: Bantam Books, 1983.

Wilson, Dale E. "Army's Segregated Tank Battalions in WWII." *Army History*, no. 32 (Fall 1994): 14–17.

———. "Recipe for Failure: Major General Edward M. Almond and Preparation for the U.S. 92nd Infantry Division for Combat in World War II." *Journal of Military History* 56, no. 3 (July 1992): 473–488.

Wilson, Joe, Jr. *758th Tank Battalion in World War II: The U.S. Army's First All African American Tank Unit.* Jefferson, NC: McFarland, 2018.

———. *761st "Black Panther" Tank Battalion in World War II: An Illustrated History of the First African-American Armored Unit to See Combat.* Jefferson, NC: McFarland, 1999.

———. *784th Tank Battalion in World War II: History of an African American Armored Unit in Europe.* Jefferson, NC: McFarland, 2007.

Winfree, Andrew N. *"Fire It": The African American Artilleryman in World War II (ETO)—A Chronology.* Victoria, Canada: Trafford, 2006.

Yeide, Harry. *Tank Killers: A History of America's World War II Tank Destroyer Force.* Havertown, PA: Casemate, 2007.

U.S. Army Air Force

Bracey, Earnest N. *Daniel "Chappie" James: The First African American Four Star General*. Jefferson, NC: McFarland, 2003.

Broadnax, Samuel L. *Blue Skies, Black Wings: African American Pioneers of Aviation*. Westport, CT: Praeger, 2007.

Brown, Harold H. *Keep Your Airspeed Up: The Story of a Tuskegee Airman*. Tuscaloosa: University of Alabama Press, 2017.

Bucholtz, Christopher. *332nd Fighter Group—Tuskegee Airmen*. Oxford, UK: Osprey Publishing, 2007.

Caver, Joseph, Jerome Ennels, and Daniel Haulman. *Tuskegee Airmen: An Illustrated History, 1939–1949*. Montgomery, AL: NewSouth Books, 2011.

Coggins, Patrick C. *Tuskegee Airman Fighter Pilot: A Story of an Original Tuskegee Pilot Lt. Col. Hiram E. Mann*. Victoria, BC, Canada: Trafford Publishing, 2008.

Dryden, Charles W. *A-Train: Memoirs of a Tuskegee Airman*. Tuscaloosa, AL: University of Alabama Press, 1997.

Francis, Charles E., and Adolph Caso. *Tuskegee Airmen: The Men Who Changed a Nation*. Boston, MA: Branden Publishing, 1997.

Handleman, Philip. *Soaring to Glory: A Tuskegee Airman's Firsthand Account of World War II*. Washington, DC: Regnery, 2019.

Hasdorff, James C. "Reflections on the Tuskegee Experiment: An Interview with Brig. Gen. Noel F. Parrish, USAF (Ret.)." *Aerospace Historian* 24 (Fall/September 1977): 173–80.

Haulman, Daniel L. *Eleven Myths About the Tuskegee Airmen*. Montgomery, AL: NewSouth Books, 2012.

Holway, John B. *Red Tails: An Oral History of the Tuskegee Airmen*. Mineola, NY: Dover Publications, 2012.

Homan, Lynn M., and Thomas Reilly. *Black Knights: The Story of the Tuskegee Airmen*. Gretna, LA: Pelican Publishing Company, 2001.

Jakeman, Robert J. *Divided Skies: Establishing Segregated Flight Training at Tuskegee, Alabama, 1934–1942*. Tuscaloosa: University of Alabama Press, 1992.

Jefferson, Alexander, and Lewis H. Carlson. *Red Tail Captured, Red Tail Free: Memoirs Of A Tuskegee Airman And POW*. New York: Fordham University Press, 2005.

McGee-Smith, Charlene E. *Tuskegee Airman: The Biography of Charles E. McGee—Air Force Fighter Combat Record Holder*. Boston, MA: Branden Publishing, 1999.

McGovern, James R. *Black Eagle: General Daniel 'Chappie' James, Jr.* Tuscaloosa: University of Alabama Press, 1985.

Moye, Todd J. *Freedom Flyers: The Tuskegee Airmen of World War II.* New York: Oxford University Press, 2010.

Norfleet, George. *Pilot's Journey: Memoirs of a Tuskegee Airman—Curtis Christopher Robinson.* Washington, DC: Robnor Publishing, 2005.

Paszek, Lawrence J. "Negroes and the Air Force, 1939–1949." *Military Affairs* 31, no. 1 (Spring 1967): 1–9.

Paszek, Lawrence J. "Separate, But Equal?: The Story of the 99th Fighter Squadron." *Aerospace Historian* 24 (Fall/September 1977): 135–45.

Phelps, J. Alfred. *Chappie: America's First Black Four-Star General—The Life and Times of Daniel James, Jr.* Novato, CA: Presidio Press, 1991.

Poole, Dorothy M. *Training the Best: Charles Herbert Flowers, Jr., Tuskegee Airman Flight Instructor.* Washington, DC: Robnor Publishing, 2007.

Purnell, Louis R. "Flight of the Bumblebee." *Air and Space* (October–November 1989): 32–40.

Sandler, Stanley. *Segregated Skies: All-Black Combat Squadrons of World War II.* Washington, DC: Smithsonian Institute Press, 1998.

Scott, Lawrence P., and William M. Womack, Sr. *Double V: The Civil Rights Struggle of the Tuskegee Airmen.* East Lansing: Michigan State University Press, 1994.

Stentiford, Barry M. *Tuskegee Airmen.* Santa Barbara, CA: Greenwood, 2012.

Warren, James C. *Freeman Field Mutiny.* San Rafael, CA: Donna Ewald Publishers, 1995.

U.S. Coast Guard

Johnson, Robert I. *Guardians of the Sea: History of the United States Coast Guard, 1915 to the Present.* Annapolis, MD: Naval Institute Press, 1987.

Thiesen, William H. "Pioneers of Ethnic Diversity in the American Sea Services." *Bulletin: U.S. Coast Guard Academy Association Alumni Association* 73, no. 5 (October 2011), 62–66.

Tidwell, Mike. "'Best Democracy I've Known,' It Existed Aboard a Millionaire's Yacht Converted for Service in World War II, An Experiment in Integrating the Military." *American Legacy* (Summer 2000): 30–40.

United States Coast Guard. *Seldom Told Tales: Sketches of Blacks in the Coast Guard.* Washington, DC: U.S. Coast Guard, 1978.

U.S. Marine Corps

Culp, Ronald K. *First Black United States Marines: The Men of Montford Point, 1942–1946*. Jefferson, NC: McFarland, 2007.

De Clouet, Fred. *First Black Marines: Vanguard of a Legacy*. Nashville, TN: James C. Winston Publishing, 1995.

Downey, Bill. *Uncle Sam Must Be Losing the War: Black Marines of the 51st*. San Francisco, CA: Strawberry Hill Press, 1982.

Fischer, Perry E., and Brooks E. Gray. *Blacks and Whites—Together Through Hell: U.S. Marines in World War II*. Turlock, CA: Millsmont Publishing, 1994.

McLaurin, Melton A. *Marines of Montford Point: America's First Black Marines*. University of North Carolina Press, 2007.

Ulbrich, David J. *Preparing for Victory: Thomas Holcomb and the Making of the Modern Marine Corps, 1936–1943*. Annapolis, MD: Naval Institute Press, 2011.

Willie, Clarence E. *African American Voices from Iwo Jima: Personal Accounts of the Battle*. Jefferson, NC: McFarland, 2010.

U.S. Navy

Allen, Robert L. *Port Chicago Mutiny*. New York: Warner Books, 1989.

Goldberg, Dan C. *Golden 13: How Black Men Won the Right to Wear Navy Gold*. Boston: Beacon Press, 2020.

Gravely, Samuel L, Jr. "Few Beers Ain't All Bad." Naval History 7, no. 1 (Spring 1993): 12–14.

———. *Trailblazer: The U.S. Navy's First Black Admiral*. Annapolis, MD: Naval Institute Press, 2010.

Harrod, Frederick S. "Integration in the Navy, 1941–1978." *Naval Institute Proceedings* (October 1979): 40–47.

Knoblock, Glenn A. *African American World War II Casualties and Decorations in the Navy, Coast Guard and Merchant Marine: A Comprehensive Record*. Jefferson, NC: McFarland, 2009.

———. *Black Submariners in the United States Navy, 1940–1975*. Jefferson, NC: McFarland, 2007.

Miller, Richard E. *Messman Chronicles: African-Americans in the U.S. Navy, 1932–1943*. Annapolis, MD: US Naval Institute Press, 2004.

Nalty, Bernard C. *Long Passage to Korea: Black Sailors and the Integration of the U.S. Navy*. Washington, DC: Naval Historical Center, 2003.

Nelson, Dennis D. *Integration of the Negro into the Navy, 1776–1947*. New York: Farrar, Straus, and Young, 1951.

Newton, Adolph W. *Better Than Good: A Black Sailor's War, 1943–1945*. Annapolis, MD: U.S. Naval Institute Press, 1999.

Schneider, James G. "'Negros Will Be Tested': FDR." *Naval History* 7, no. 1 (Spring 1993): 1115–1117.

Schneller, Robert J., Jr. *Blue and Gold and Black: Racial Integration of the U.S. Naval Academy*. College Station: Texas A&M University Press, 2008.

———. *Breaking the Color Barrier: The U.S. Naval Academy's First Black Midshipmen and the Struggle for Racial Equality*. NY: New York University Press, 2005.

———. "Oliver Holmes: A Place in Naval Aviation." *Naval Aviation News* (January/February 1998): 26–27.

Veigele, William. *PC Patrol Craft of World War II: A History of the Ships and their Crews*. Santa Barbara, CA: Astral, 2003.

Theses and Dissertations

Carhart, Thomas M. *African American West Pointers During the 19th Century*. Ph.D. Dissertation, Princeton University, 1998.

Ivy, Lenora A. *Study in Leadership: The 761st Tank Battalion and the 92nd Infantry Division*. M.M.A.S. Thesis, U.S. Army Command and General Staff College, 1995.

Murphy, John D. *Freeman Field Mutiny: A Study in Leadership*. Master's Thesis, U.S. Air Force Air Command and Staff College, 1997.

Squire, Willard S. *24th Infantry Regiment and the Racial Debate in the U.S. Army*. M.M.A.S. Thesis, U.S. Army Command and General Staff College, 1997.

Thomas, Joyce. *"Double V" Was for Victory: Black Soldiers, the Black Protest, and World War II*. Ph.D. Dissertation, Ohio State University, 1993.

Trice, Craig A. *Men That Served with Distinction "The 761st Tank Battalion."* M.M.A.S. Thesis, U.S. Army Command and General Staff College, 1997.

Woods, Louis L., II. *Messmen No More: African-American Sailors on the USS Mason in World War II*. Ph.D. Dissertation, Howard University, 2006.

Index

H

J

S